After the Revolution

After the Revolution

Youth, Democracy, and the Politics
of Disappointment in Serbia

Jessica Greenberg

Stanford University Press

Stanford, California

Stanford University Press
Stanford, California

© 2014 by the Board of Trustees of the Leland Stanford Junior University.
All rights reserved.

Printed in the United States of America on acid-free, archival-quality paper

Library of Congress Cataloging-in-Publication Data is available from the Library of Congress.

ISBN 978-0-8047-8900-4 (cloth : alk. paper)—
ISBN 978-0-8047-9115-1 (pbk. : alk. paper)
ISBN 978-0-8047-9117-5 (electronic)

Designed by Bruce Lundquist

Typeset by Newgen in 11/13.5 Adobe Garamond

Contents

Acknowledgments

AS WITH ANY INTELLECTUAL ENDEAVOR, this book is the result of years of conversation and collaboration with friends and colleagues. Research for this book was generously supported by the Council for European Studies and the Society for the Anthropology of Europe, a Fulbright Hays Dissertation Research Fellowship, and an International Research and Exchanges Board Research Fellowship. Additional research and writing was made possible by the American Council of Learned Societies. I'm also deeply grateful for my time as an Academy Scholar at the Harvard Academy for International and Area Studies. This fellowship provided not only time to write but also a wonderful community of scholars with whom to think. This book has benefited enormously from the guidance of Michelle Lipinski and Joa Suorez at Stanford University Press. I can't thank the two reviewers for Stanford University Press enough for their feedback. David Nugent's comments were particularly central to shaping the manuscript. The opinions expressed in these pages are my own, as, of course, are the shortcomings.

My thinking was, and continues to be, shaped by an incredible group of thinkers at the University of Chicago. Susan Gal was central not only to the development of this project but also to how I approach the ethics and values of scholarship. Jean Comaroff, Victor Friedman, Lisa Wedeen, and Elizabeth Povinelli provided patient guidance and much wisdom along the way. Rolph Trouillot was my first teacher at Chicago. His inspiration and provocations live in these pages.

This project would have been impossible without the support of a unique community of friends and peers in Chicago. I was lucky enough to think and write together with Andrea Muehlebach and Kelly Gillespie. They often knew what I wanted to say before (and better than) I did. More important, they made Chicago feel like home. Andrew Gilbert has been a pillar of intellectual support and friendship on both sides of the Atlantic. Anya Bernstein was always a ready partner in crime in matters of the mind. Alejandro Paz has offered years of good advice, enlightening conversation, and some pretty good jibes. The Anthropology of Europe Workshop provided a scholarly home for so many of us at the University of Chicago. The atmosphere was intellectually vibrant and always welcoming, for which credit goes to Dominic Boyer, Kriszti Fehervary, Andrew Graan, Gustav Peebles, Brian Schwegler, and Anwen Tormey, among others. Thanks also to Nada Petković-Djordjević for many years of support. Along the way my thinking was informed by lively debate with Mayanthi Fernando, Yarimar Bonilla, and Courtney Handman.

I have been fortunate to find a home among those who gather (however ambivalently) under the name of postsocialist studies. I have been inspired by the work and have benefited from the insights of Gerald Creed, Elizabeth Dunn, Kristen Ghodsee, Zsuzsa Gille, Bob Hayden, Julie Hemment, David Kideckel, Neringe Klumbyte, Alaina Lemon, Maya Nadkarni, Doug Rogers, Natalia Roudakova, Olga Sezneva, Katherine Verdery, and Alexei Yurchak. Nothing has made me happier than stumbling into a world of lively thinkers and all-around good people working in and on the former Yugoslavia, including Gretchen Bakke, Florian Bieber, Johanna Bockman, Keith Brown, Kim Coles, Pedja Cvetičanin, Ana Dević, Orli Fridman, Eric Gordy, Chip Gagnon, Elissa Helms, Azra Hromadžić, Stef Jansen, Larisa Kurtović, Sasha Milićević, Slobodan Naumović, Maple Razsa, Ivana Spasić, Paul Stubbs, and Marko Živković.

Many people have read and commented on versions of this manuscript, from inchoate conference papers to full-blown chapters. Michael Herzfeld, Daniel Goldstein, Hiro Miyazaki, Jeff Juris, Asad Ahmed, and Peter Wissoker were patient and generous enough to read the whole manuscript, for which I am eternally grateful. Others have provided invaluable feedback on portions of this book and related works, including Mark Goodale, Matthew Hull, Amahl Bishara, Betsy Levy-Paluck, Mark Hauser, and Elana Shever.

At Northwestern University, I found friends and mentors who made me a better scholar and teacher. Thanks go to my colleagues in the Department of Communication Studies, and especially to Dilip Gaonkar,

Angela Ray, and Janice Radway for their friendship and support. Jessica Winegar and Shalini Shankar gave me invaluable feedback on my writing. Lars Toender was a ready and willing partner in crime when it came to debating the finer points of political theory. More recently, I was fortunate enough to find myself part of a wonderful new community of anthropologists at the University of Illinois. Thanks to the Anthropology Department for welcoming me with open arms, and especially to Nancy Abelman, Matti Bunzl, and Andrew Orta.

I am indebted to the many friends and interlocutors in Serbia who allowed me into their lives, and without whom this work would have been impossible. They have been more than patient with my endless questions over the years, especially Jelena Šešlija, Saša Kovjanić, Alen Stanojević, Milorad Lazić, Dragana Dimitrijević, Jelena Kleut, Duško Spasojević, Goran Bogunović, Pedja Lažetić, Martina Vukasović, Srečko Šekeljić, Milica Savić, Nina Lazarević, Miloš Luković, Fuada Stanković, Mila Turajlić, Srbijanka Turajlić, and Maja Stojanović. I hope I have done some justice to your insight and efforts over the years.

This project began in 1998 with conversations I had with student activists when I worked with the STAR Project. I am so grateful for the support of Jill Benderly and Lael Stegall. They taught me so much about social change and feminist solidarity. They are both deeply missed.

Anne and Draško Jovović provided a home away from home, from the first moment Draško met me at the Belgrade airport waving a copy of the *International Herald Tribune* with my name jotted on top in pen. Rita and Joe Doussard provided support along the way, and I am particularly grateful for Rita's boundless energy.

Donald and Maxine Greenberg taught me to be curious about the world, passionate about ideas, and critical about politics, and to have a sense of humor about everything. Along the way my brother Josh Greenberg has always been with me in spirit. He never knew this strange part of my life as an anthropologist. No doubt he would have been both unduly proud, and a little worried, when I set off into the world.

This book is dedicated to Marc Doussard. There are simply no words to express the ways he has shaped how I see the world and how I write about it. I look forward to sharing our pleasure in thinking, talking, and laughing with Gabriel and Julian. Thanks to both of them for their patience and for the support they've given me in ways they can't yet fathom. Gabe will be particularly thrilled to see his name in print—again.

After the Revolution

After the Revolution

Introduction

MANY PEOPLE IN SERBIA speak of March 12, 2003—the date of
the assassination of Prime Minister Zoran Đinđić—as the day the spirit
of Serbia's democratic revolution died. Just two and a half years earlier, on
October 5, 2000, hundreds of thousands of people had poured into the
capital demanding the ouster of longtime strongman Slobodan Milošević.
October 5 came to be associated with many images: protesters storming
the parliament and state television buildings; the raised fist of the student
resistance movement Otpor; the lines of workers marching behind a bulldozer that had driven all the way from central Serbia (giving rise to the
term *bulldozer revolution*, or *bager revolucija*); the disarming, boyish smile
of Zoran Đinđić. A charismatic, staunchly pro-European politician and
former student protester, Đinđić was deeply linked to the youth movement largely credited with Milošević's downfall. His assassination—at
the hands of former members of state security who had ties to organized
crime—stood in marked contrast to the nonviolence of the October 5 protests. This contrast between the joyous crowds of the revolution and the
silent shock of the assassination became emblematic of Serbia's seemingly
failed democracy.

During the 1990s Slobodan Milošević had taken Serbia from the
largest republic in the internationally respected and cosmopolitan Socialist
Federal Republic of Yugoslavia to a pariah country plagued by nationalism, haunted by war crimes, and devastated by economic insecurity.[1] If
Milošević and other nationalist politicians represented violence and social
chaos, Đinđić, and the young people who rallied around him, came to

represent a hopeful new generation of educated, urbane citizens. But the disappointment of this generation was never clearer than on the day of the assassination. When I arrived that afternoon in 2003 at the main bus station in Belgrade, I was shocked to see so many people so utterly still and silent. Belgrade was a city of movement and energy, despite conditions of poverty and high unemployment. Cafés and streets were always packed, as people strolled or sat nursing a drink at the trendiest spots. The new upscale shops that lined the pedestrian thoroughfare in the city center were full of people browsing and dreaming, even if they couldn't afford to buy anything on their two-hundred-euro-a-month salaries. It was a city of contrasts—rich and poor, grand and decaying, cosmopolitan and revanchist—that buzzed with the desire for something better that lay just out of reach.

That afternoon the bus station was crowded as always, but the silence was palpable. Instead of the usual rushing to and fro, the pushing and jockeying for positions in line at the ticket counter, everyone seemed frozen in time. Unaware of the bloodshed that had transpired, I wandered over to a young woman to ask what was going on. She fixed me with a strange look before delivering the news. Zoran Đinđić was dead. Serbia had come to a standstill.

The image of Serbia at a standstill was resonant with language that Đinđić himself had used only a year earlier. In a now-famous 2002 speech, Đinđić posited a stark choice: Serbia could move forward toward Europe and democracy, or it could simply stop. "If Serbia comes to a standstill [*Ako Srbija stane*]," he cautioned, "this is my warning. . . . [W]e have a huge historical chance to do something big in this country. But we have to try hard to avoid risks and temptations. And it is not in any way a guaranteed thing [*i to nikakva nije garantovana stvar*] that we will accept democracy, that we will move towards economic reform and towards Europe. . . . [I]t is not guaranteed. It's a chance that could be wasted tomorrow."[2]

 This book is about that chance. It is about democracy not as a guaranteed outcome of a revolution but as a project always on the threshold of becoming. And it is about the experience of moving both forward and backward as student activists and former revolutionaries try to navigate a democratic present in the shadow of the past. The shift from the energy of the revolution to the quiet disappointment of Đinđić's assassination crystallizes the tentative experience of Serbia's democracy after October 5, 2000. If one takes the measure of Serbia's democracy as the relationship between revolutionary expectations and their fulfillment in the years after 2000, then Đinđić's death seems like the epitaph in a story of tragic failure. But this perspective would miss the ways in which democracy is always profoundly contradictory and flawed when measured against idealized moments and normative expectations. Such contradictions and disappointments are intrinsic to actually lived democracies, rather than their exceptions.

What I witnessed on March 12 at a crowded bus station bathed in the midday sun was the collective experience of a future not guaranteed. Many people I met referred to it in the months and years to come as they tried to make sense of what could and should have been. Later that evening, I joined hundreds of people in line in front of the headquarters of Đinđić's Democratic Party. We were waiting to sign the book of mourning mounted against an altar of flowers and candles that cast strange shadows in the night's thickening gloom. As we stood in line, a friend lamented that he could no longer imagine raising a family in Serbia. Another friend told me in the more sober vein of political analysis that Serbia's political system had come down to one man, as so often had happened in the country's history: "Now he is gone, and we will have to see if the institutions are strong enough to hold. I worry they won't be." A few nights later I met friends in a café. One of them looked at me as I walked up and simply said, "This country is . . ." and drew her finger across her throat. The imagery was violent, the sentiment not fully captured by words.

The Social Life of Disappointment

The 2003 assassination, and the years that followed, marked the end of a romance with democracy that began with student and opposition protests during the 1990s. The assassination and its coverage sparked a new, reflective genre of disappointment, particularly across mass media. Indeed, every year, October 5 becomes the occasion for narratives of disappointment and stocktaking. The fact of disappointment is so taken for granted that it is enough for a headline to simply declare, as the news site *B92* did last year, "Oktobar 5.—12 godina razočaranja," October 5—twelve years of disappointment.[3]

In the early years of the postrevolutionary period, the energy and movement of the protests had been something of an antidote to the sense that Milošević's Serbia was slipping backward in time.[4] This sense was best summed up by a professor of sociology who explained to me Serbia's role vis-à-vis other postsocialist transition countries: "In the nineties those countries were heading towards where Yugoslavia was in the seventies while Yugoslavia was heading towards where they were in the fifties." Milošević's overthrow was supposed to return Serbia to membership in the world community as a triumphant post–Cold War democracy. With Đinđić gone, the infighting that had plagued the post-2000 ruling coalition only worsened, which fueled the public's sense that the political system was broken. The assassination garnered international attention after the country's brief three-year honeymoon as an exemplar of peaceful democratic revolution. The shooting made clear that the Serbian state's ties to organized crime and the violent legacies of the past had not been broken. At the same time, unemployment continued to rise. Many felt trapped by poverty and isolation, exacerbated by harsh visa regimes for travel abroad. Serbian war criminals indicted for genocide and ethnic cleansing during the wars of Yugoslav succession continued to evade capture. Right-wing parties gained increasing support. Political and economic changes seemed to grind to a halt. Even before the assassination, it seemed impossible that Serbia would meet the conditions to begin accession to the European Union—a process many saw as Serbia's only hope for economic recovery.

The people I encountered during my field research between 2002 and 2004 struggled to build Serbia's democracy, despite these frustrations and setbacks. My research focused on those student activists who had gone from protesting Milošević to working within state institutions, and more specifically working on the reform of higher education within the state university system. As in other postauthoritarian and postrevolutionary contexts, activists struggled to engage with (rather than protest) the democratic state institutions that they had helped usher into being (Lukose 2009; Paley 2001; Alvarez 1997).[5] After 2000, student leaders, like other activists, translated political rhetoric and the symbolic vocabularies of mass protest into forms of engagement that made sense in the democratic context. Student groups moved from the streets to offices and meeting rooms; they crafted policy papers, donor reports, and promotional material in addition to placards and street theater; they focused on electoral procedures within their organizations; and they gained expert knowledge about complex matters of university reform.

University reform took on urgency because young people saw their own fates, and those of Serbia, as tied to processes of regional and

European integration. This process included adoption of the European Union's higher education reforms. No longer a site of state power to be resisted, the university provided an institutional framework that produced subjects capable of building viable democratic futures for themselves and the nation. But even as they tried to engage the new realities of democratic politics, student activists also tried to live up to older expectations for how students ought to behave as political and moral actors. The collision of expectations was frustrating both to students and other citizens. Given the popular narrative of the youth-led revolution as the moment when democracy arrived, it made sense for people to focus on former revolutionaries when expressing their frustration with the new democratic state. Ordinary citizens, and even activists themselves, pointed to the chasm between the excitement and hope of the democratic revolution and the messy and painful realities of building a democratic state and society. If the state was rife with corruption and factionalism, the figures associated with the revolution must have betrayed their ideals. At the same time, student leaders who remained active found that university reform was far less exciting than bringing down a dictator. At every turn, students were measured (and measured themselves) by revolutionary qualities they no longer seemed to possess and democratic ideals they no longer seemed to embody.

Student organizations were both a microcosm for the experiment with democracy and a publically available site for policing the parameters of political and activist engagement. The formal shift from an authoritarian state to a formal democracy opened up opportunities for new kinds of citizen practice overnight.[6] But making sense of these new arenas of politics was a complex process. Long-standing associations with politics as corrupt and morally suspect made it hard for new democratic actors to justify their engagement as in the service of a common good. The problem of articulating a common political agenda was exacerbated by the divisiveness of post-2000 Serbian public discourse and politics. The coalition of opposition parties, citizens' organizations, and ordinary people that joined forces to overthrow Milošević was politically and ideologically diverse. Once the unifying goal had been achieved, fractiousness followed, particularly in the context of competitive elections.

In addition, the process of state democratization was highly contentious. Essential questions of democracy were debated through seemingly mundane disagreements over administrative policies, such as state decentralization or budgetary policy. Although most groups at the university agreed on the necessity of university reform, student activists within and across organizations disagreed on the means for achieving that goal. They fiercely debated what democracy meant in practice. Some of these arguments broke down along ideological lines and reflected highly charged debates within Serbian politics at the time: Kosovo's bid for independence, newly visible social movements advocating gay and lesbian rights, the capture and extradition of war criminals to the United Nations' International Criminal Tribunal for the Former Yugoslavia (ICTY) at The Hague. Conflicts among student activists over issues like EU-driven curriculum reform or the proper way to run student elections seemed less immediately charged. But these deceptively mundane questions closely echoed larger public debates in Serbia about the role of Serbian tradition in the wake of nationalist violence, the proper distribution of political power in a democratic state, and the legacy of socialism that shaped state institutions, like the university. Even a narrow focus on university reform meant taking a stand on the often unsaid but always present issues of the day.

Activists and others often had contradictory expectations of what politics ought to look like and the ways in which it ought to be enacted. These contradictions forced students, like other political actors, to experiment with socially authoritative forms of postrevolutionary action in a shifting ideological and social terrain. The story of these student organizations tells us about how democracy is made and experienced both in terms of and against the expectations of political transformation. The social life of such expectations shapes political horizons and democratic action after a revolution.

Postpessimism and the Politics of the Present

My interest in democracy activists and student organizing in Serbia stems from several years of volunteer and nongovernmental organization (NGO) work in the region, beginning in 1996. In speaking with students and other young activists during the Milošević regime, I was often struck by the way they narrated both deep frustration and a pragmatic urge to change the situation around them. This commitment to action in the face of frustration was best summed up by the name of a youth activist group that I met with in Belgrade in 1998 while on a research trip for an international NGO that I worked for at the time. The group had taken the name the Postpessimists.[7] The name struck me as unique in a context of deep cynicism about the possibility for social and political change. The Postpessimists arranged arts and cultural exchanges across the former Yugoslavia. They fostered networks among young people by highlighting their commonality as youth or artists. In so doing, they tried to sidestep categories of ethnic and national belonging that defined and constrained dominant social imaginaries at the time.[8] The students I spoke with were savvy analysts and operators in the complicated world of NGOs and donor politics, even as they were earnest and sincere in the conversations I had with them about their hopes for social change. The *post* in Postpessimists was anything but a Pollyannaish trust in the future. Rather, the Postpessimists seemed to move beyond the binary of cynicism versus hope. Instead, they opted for some kind of practical action in the interstices of the two.

When I began my initial field research in 2001, I was curious as to how this late 1990s generation of youth activists and student organizations would move from struggling against a state to working for and within state institutions. And I wondered how the contradictory experiences of hope and frustration would shape democratic ideals and practices with the formal arrival of political democracy. Young men and women in Serbia were beginning to confront the fact that democracy did not solve the painful realities of social conflict and impoverishment overnight. Some retreated into their own private lives. Others, in smaller numbers than before, began to focus on education reform and university student organizing. Everywhere people had to develop new vocabularies for making sense of a rapidly transforming society.

As scholars of social movements have demonstrated, authoritative frames for social action can change quickly with the arrival of formal democracy (Junge 2012; Harper 2006; Paley 2008). Social actors must frame interventions in socially resonant and historically meaningful ways while simultaneously trying to change the terms of politics.[9] Politics thus entails articulating and practicing new horizons and possibilities in and against existing discursive frames and practices (Dave 2012; Scott 2004). This dynamic of creativity and foreclosure is critical for understanding the challenges of postrevolutionary activism and why people practicing democracy may be "frustrated with the categories available to them" (Paley 2008, 7).

The work of making the inconceivable possible in a postrevolutionary context is particularly challenging for those figures who come to be most associated with the revolution itself. As in other "post" contexts, those most

:d with collective resistance to the state in Serbia became a site for the boundaries of the political (Chakrabarty 2007; Siegel 1998). As ethnographies of student protest have shown, the narrative frames and institutional forms central to mass mobilization become both creative resources and potential traps for student activists over the long term (Calhoun 1997; Burawoy 1976).[10] Indeed, in Serbia after 2000 student activists were haunted by the same discursive frames that they had used to generate support and to direct meaning making during their period of unruly activism. Under Milošević, students had drawn on socially resonant histories of youth politics, traditions of civil society and protest in formerly socialist Eastern Europe, as well as local and international interpretations of democracy and citizen entitlements. As these frames circulated and were picked up by later protesters and media the meaning of individual protest events was more easily laminated onto recognizable frames of authoritative political action and civic organization. Student unruliness had been iconic of democracy before 2000, but after the revolution protest and dissent were often framed as disruptive in the context of the democracy they had helped to achieve.

In this book, I develop the frame of a politics of disappointment to analyze how student activists manage the contradictions of democratic practice as they play out in real time. Disappointment emerged as people compared the expectations of revolution to the realities of democracy in an impoverished country marked by the legacies of state violence and repression. It also emerged as people contended with the murkiness and contingency of political agency under such conditions. A "politics of disappointment" is evident in students' flexible negotiation of changing meanings of youth politics in such a context. It is defined by student activists' awareness of the contingency of action, as well as knowledge that their activism would inevitably be disappointing to others. Student activists were both objects of disappointment, given long-standing ideological investment in youth revolutionary politics, and well poised to confront the contingencies of activism as they moved between street protest and institutionally based democratic engagement and reform.

Disappointment was thus a condition of living in contradiction, of persisting in the interstitial spaces of expectation and regret. In mapping the field in which democratic practice unfolded, I seek to show the conditions under which the coherence of practice is impossible, and yet action takes place nonetheless. Here I take disappointment seriously as the ethos of many new (and not so new) democracies. Disappointment is neither an absence—of hope or possibility—nor the aftereffect of "real" politics having taken place in another time or place. It is a complex political and affective form in its own right.[11] An attention to the politics of disappointment is not intended to heroicize student groups as fighting the odds at all costs. Rather, it is to draw the lesson that democracy happens even in the face of disappointments. Why don't more students show up for rallies? Why do "grown-ups" constantly make promises they cannot keep? Why do students persist in being "political" when they should get back to their studies? Why do violent nationalisms persist? How can the hope and excitement of revolution fade so quickly? These questions appear antithetical to democracy, but they are in fact the essence of it. People construct a sense of postrevolutionary agency not by avoiding the messy answers to these questions but by navigating them, sometimes skillfully, and sometimes with disappointing and undesired results.

Revolution and Youth

A politics of disappointment in contemporary Serbia unfolds in the context of modernist understandings of political transformation. "Revolution talk" was a genre through which people made sense of and critiqued post-2000 political life in Serbia.[12] When people mobilized the idea of revolution, they also invoked the ideas of a desirable form of total political transformation and the utopian reorganization of society. Yet when taken as an ideal for measuring political progress, revolution inscribes messy and complicated social practices in a temporality of rupture and progress (Graeber 2004; Donham 1999; Koselleck 2004; Berman 1988).[13] These narratives of modernist political transformation map the world along a trajectory of political social progress, creating what Donald Donham (1999, xv) has called "people's sense of living vis-à-vis."[14] Thus, as a model of political transformation, revolution lends itself to precisely the comparative logics and idealized expectations that produce disappointed forms of politics. The idea of revolution sets up an (impossible) expectation in which "one totalizing system [could] be replaced by a completely different one" (Graeber 2004, 44). When political transformation is tied to valorized notions like modernity, European civilization, and democracy, these temporal frames become important ways that people judge themselves (and are judged) as modern political subjects on a world stage (Ferguson 1999; Trouillot 1995).

As a narrative framework through which people conceptualize the world and order social relations, revolution is a way of organizing time, narrating history, and understanding agentive action. In other words, the temporalities and expectations built into the idea of revolution can shape how those engaged in political transformation understand their own (and others') successes and failures. At the same time, the idea of a revolutionary politics is inseparable from the social categories through which politics is authorized and made meaningful. Like tropes of nostalgia so common to the postsocialist context or discourses of sacrifice and redemption at the heart of contemporary liberal imaginaries, projections of idealized futures are best understood as processes of making and interpreting life in the present (Todorova and Gille 2012; Povinelli 2002, 2009; Boyer 2006; Nadkarni 2007; Berdahl 2001).[15] The ideal of transformation becomes a socially meaningful and lived metric for comparing before and after, success and failure, democracy and its discontents.

At the same time that revolution lends itself to a particular utopian imaginary, one cannot have a revolution without revolutionaries. It is for this reason that youth is such a productive lens for analyzing ideologies of political transformation, particularly in the postsocialist context. The idea of youth as a future-oriented vanguard has long fit hand in glove with modernist ideals of revolution as a moment of total social transformation (Passerini 1997). Across the globe, youth participation has become central to globally circulating models of political empowerment and social change (Greenberg 2012; Kwon 2013). Rather than take the link between youth and social change for granted, I join many scholars in using ideologies of youth and generation as a critical lens for analyzing the specificities of social and political practice (Stubbs 2012; Lee 2011; Shankar 2008; Cole and Durham 2007; Honwana and De Boeck 2005; Pampols and Porzio 2005; Sharp 2002). Such expectations about generational politics affect how all citizens authorize democratic action in the aftermath of mass mobilization and youth protest (Lukose 2009; Manning 2007; Varzi 2006; Anderson 1972).

Key to this literature is an examination of the particular links between conceptions of youth agency and political modernity (Bucholtz 2002). As Deborah Durham (2008) has argued, both policy interventions and scholarly literatures on youth political participation tend to reproduce twentieth-century Western understandings of youth agency as made possible by extrication from the social ties and obligation of early childhood. Yet as she demonstrates in the case of youth groups in Botswana, this perspective misses locally meaningful forms of personhood that link matu-ration, social power, and status to embeddedness in relations of reciprocity and obligation that are grounded in expanding kinship networks. Thus, what at first blush look like reinscriptions of generational hierarchies, or even apathy, are in fact socially powerful ways of signaling and enacting youth agency.

Although Durham's account is an important one for understanding the critical blind spots of romanticist accounts of youth, it perhaps offers too partial a picture of twentieth-century modernist understandings of the relationship between youth and political agency. While twentieth-century developmentalist state projects entailed the production of modern, secu-lar citizens freed from domination by "traditional" social relations, they also frequently reinscribed social embeddedness through state-mediated institutions and practices. These publically mediated forms of obligation bound citizens to one another over time through highly affective rituals, registers of talk, and bureaucratic practices. That such practices were highly gendered, particularly in the socialist context, is no surprise. The project of state-socialist "alternative" modernity entailed no less than the reworking of social reproduction as a site of public intervention (Haney 2002; Gal and Kligman 2000; Rofel 1999). Yet scholars have devoted less time to ana-lyzing age and generational belonging as key frameworks for understand-ing new citizenship regimes and political practices for all citizens in the postsocialist context (Fournier 2012; Hemment 2012; Hromadžić 2011).

Indeed, even within the context of the modernizing Western European social-welfare state coming of age as a *citizen* entailed embed-dedness in state-mediated networks of intergenerational solidarity. The nation-state as both a home and a political-economic project grounded in a Durkheimian model of organic solidarity relies on temporal imagi-naries (Peebles 2011; Holmes 2000). This has perhaps become clearer as the dismantling of European social welfare has proceeded by reworking specifically *generational* relations of ethics and care under conditions of neoliberalism (Muehlebach 2012).

The centrality of generationally configured citizenship opens up important comparative possibilities for understanding the mutual imbri-cation of youth, politics, and social reproduction within modernist state projects. For example, in her ethnography of nostalgia for the early mod-ern, secular Turkish state, Esra Özyürek (2006) demonstrates how impor-tant metaphors of kinship and generational identifications were to Turkey's modernist state project. Lisa Rofel (1999) has argued that the project of generational difference was essential to alternative socialist modernities in China. Jessica Winegar (2006) has shown how state resources in socialist and postsocialist Egypt were negotiated through competing claims to modernist "authenticity" that took place in generational terms. Thinking about socialist modernity comparatively, through the lens of generation, allows us to better understand why the particular disappointments of the post–Cold War and post-Fordist context so often take the form of experiences and rhetorics of generational betrayal, nostalgia, and discourses of "failed" or dangerous youth (Comaroff and Comaroff 2005). It also helps us understand why youth movements associated with political vanguardism and social renewal are so frequently sites of disappointment. Indeed, it is no coincidence that disappointment in the generation most iconic to youth revolution and political renewal—the students of 1968—intensified with the dismantling of the social and economic conditions that brought them into being as politically active subjects (McAdam 1988).

The New Model of Post–Cold War Youth Revolution

If the Cold War world was a site of experimentation for radical politics, the fall of official state socialism was a crucial spark for the reconceptualization of democracy in the post–Cold War period.[16] Formerly communist Eastern Europe became a central site for the redefinition of revolution. Where socialism had long been tied to revolutionary politics through the postwar and postcolonial conflicts that swept communist regimes to power, the exit from socialism tied transformative politics to liberal (and later neoliberal) democratic imaginaries.[17]

In the wake of the collapse of state socialism, policy makers, scholars, politicians, and activists scrambled to make sense of what had finally brought down the Berlin Wall. Accompanying this process was a scholarly and political redefinition of mass protest as a particularly civic endeavor, severed from socialist origins and distinguished from uncivic, nationalist forms of populist protest (Kalb 2009). More radically destabilizing discourses of worker control, social solidarity, and workers' rights, like those in Poland in the early 1980s, quickly blended with more liberal formulations of civic rights and civil society promulgated by students, dissidents, and other activists throughout the region (Ost 1990). In the early 1980s citizens began to challenge the socialist state through protest; strikes; and nonviolent, citizen-based mass organizing. Protesters drew on both socialist genres of critique and humor, music, and theater to create spaces of ludic performance and resistance (Kenney 2002). Socialist states' use of force against protesters placed violence on the side of the state against the people. Such performances shifted the meaning and signs of revolutionary politics away from those long dominated by the revolutionary socialist state, thereby redefining the meaning of revolution as a civic endeavor.

At the same time, scholars and civic activists struggled to make sense of the political formations that emerged after the fall of European state socialism. The combination of working-class, and formerly socialist, solidarities with emerging nationalist and xenophobic agendas is a phenomenon that has occurred across the formerly state-socialist European states (Bracewell 2000; see also Holmes 2000). In part, rather than deal with these complex and disturbing imbrications, scholars often moved to discredit the form that protest took: the mass, populist protest (Tismaneanu 2000; Mudde 2000). The problem of the crowd—affective, unmediated, violent, without clear will or controlled intentionality—came to substitute for analysis of the increasingly ambiguous relationship between economic and civil rights in the age of Eastern European liberalism. Everyone from local media to scholars juxtaposed the unruly (and often youthful) crowd to an idealized civic crowd for whom democratic practice was rational, contained, and transparent (see Manning 2007). As I show throughout this book, the meaning of crowds on the street was thus an emerging site of contestation over what democracy could and should look like. These distinctions are important to understanding how the notion of civic or electoral revolution contains fundamentally classed assumptions that continue to shape the legacies of dissident civil society movements in the formerly socialist world.

Such ideas ironically wedded socialist understandings of the revolutionary society to triumphalist models of postsocialist transition as a process that would wipe away a communist past and build democracy on a tabula rasa.[18] Taken together, the fear of the crowd and the idea of a liberal configuration of state and society aligned with liberal, democratic, and free-market logics promulgated within Western critiques of state socialism in the Cold War period. The triumphalism of 1989 laid the groundwork for new ways of thinking about transformative politics as tied to, rather than antithetical to, liberal and market-based configurations of popular sovereignty and democratic participation.[19] What came out of this productive relationship between indigenous activists and foreign policy makers and funders was a distillation of the lessons of 1989: a model in and through which nonviolent democratic revolution was tied to civic-minded youth movements.

The early 1990s saw the explosion of the promotion of "civil society" and the rise of democratization as a basis for US intervention after the Cold War (Hemment 2007; Brown 2006; Guilhot 2005; Dunn and Hann 1996). Toward the end of the decade, and in the face of recalcitrant authoritarianisms, such as those in Slovakia, Serbia, Belarus, Georgia, Kyrgyzstan, and later Ukraine, international policy experts, democratization workers, and academics mobilized the notion of civil society as a mode of soft intervention that would reproduce the nonviolent overthrow of European state socialism (Carothers 2004). As US academics and policy makers trained and funded student and opposition groups for civic revolution, they also reinvented revolution as a liberalizing reconfiguration of state, economy, and society that could be achieved through elections.[20]

In Serbia, student organizations and opposition politicians had already been actively protesting against Milošević for some years. But by the late 1990s, the US Agency for International Development began funding and training activists with Otpor in their attempts to challenge the regime. In the years that followed, Serbia became one of a handful of models of "color revolutions" that would form the basis for a new benchmark of democratization policy and scholarship (Greenberg 2012; Rosenberg 2011; Bunce and Wolchik 2006, Kuzio 2006). The Serbian revolution became the exemplar of a nonviolent, civic revolution founded on liberal democratic commitments, a focus on elections and other forms of democratic proceduralism, and youth-led antiauthoritarian mass protest. As Slobodan Naumović (2006) has argued, Otpor was a complicated and deeply contradictory organization: creative and pragmatic, hierarchically and horizontally organized, and rooted in long-standing Serbian (and Yugoslav) protest traditions and internationally supported approaches to democratic revolution. I see these contradictions not as a "Faustian bargain" (Naumović 2006), or as an imposition of democracy from the outside. Rather, Serbian student activists cocreated and popularized forms of political organizing, and they were in some ways shadowed by their own success.

Ironically, Serbian student activists were measured by expectations they had helped to popularize as part of a model of youth and civic revolution that was taken up in different sites beyond Eastern Students were able to draw on youth as a socially resonant category, but this also limited the ways in which they could authorize political action as political subjects outside that category. Within East European communist states, youth was a discursive and representational genre through which people negotiated their relationship to the state and through which entitlements were mediated and categories of belonging were defined (Taylor 2006; Yurchak 2006). The category of socialist youth provided critical cultural and political materials that communist officials and media elites used to represent the state's revolutionary project (Kürti 2002; Gorsuch 2000). Along with workers, youth and students were among the limited categories of people that the Yugoslav communist state allowed to form associations and organize (Vladisavljević 2008; Carter 1982; Pervan 1978). Yugoslav leader Josip Broz Tito depended on ritual representations of youthful regeneration in generating popular support (Bringa 2004). Youth had also served as a socially resonant category of citizenship that derived political significance through their link to revolutionary practice and vanguardism. Official state rhetoric and student activists justified extraparty political action through culturally resonant images and associations with altruistic youth, regeneration of community, and socialist modernity.[21]

The prominence of youth and student organizing in popular local and international imaginaries generated widely circulating narratives that ordered the experience of social change. Student activists in Serbia built on Yugoslav histories of protest and organization, sometimes consulting with professors who had been involved in earlier periods of protest. They were hooked into local and international NGO and activist networks and borrowed from the playbooks of dissidents that had been critical to the overthrow of communist regimes in other parts of Eastern Europe. For example, by refusing to endorse any particular opposition party and distancing themselves from "formal" politics, student protesters positioned themselves as altruistic representatives of the people, as other generations had before them.[22] In addition, youth activists grafted older associations with youth politics onto new protest tactics borrowed from democratic activists in socialist Europe leading up to 1989 (Kenney 2002). The use of music, concerts, and logos made activism and protest "cool" (Collin 2004). Highlighting play and creativity during street protests was also a way to distinguish the student movement from a regime that often relied on mass protests of rural and older citizens to demonstrate public support.

The competing visions of citizenship embodied in these protests produced a politics of age, in which nationalism, war, and Milošević were aligned with older rural populations, and democracy, urbanism, and international-ism were aligned with youth.[23] These tactics, which included political per-formance—street theater, humorous banners and chants, dancing, and live music—strengthened public perceptions that youth politics meant energy, fresh perspectives, and creativity.

In addition, activists also staged public, nonviolent confrontations with authorities. The often violent response of police produced a sense that protesters were vulnerable and innocent, thereby promoting a sense of responsibility among adults toward the welfare of protesters and, by extension, the movement (Binnendijk and Marović 2006). Youth activ-ists thus played on the idea of youth in two deeply resonant, if somewhat contradictory ways. They promoted themselves as a youth revolution-ary vanguard: ideal citizens who could actively forge a democratic future through their energy and commitment to their cause. And they mobilized images of innocence and vulnerability, highlighting the responsibility of citizens (as parents) to protect future generations from the violence of the state.[24]

Changing international policy priorities and local political condi-tions mediated how students in Serbia understood themselves in relation to a global mass-mediated space. Students had to contend not only with the local meanings and expectations generated by their past political en-gagement. They also had to contend with the new meanings that accrued to those actions as different actors moved them out of Serbia and back in through specific policy interventions, international funding regimes, and mass-mediated representations. In the emerging post–Cold War con-text, policy makers, media pundits, and democracy activists openly judged newly emerging democracies on timelines of social and political progress that reinscribed modernist temporalities of political progress. Serbian po-litical actors were aware of these regional and international expectations for what postrevolutionary democracy ought to look like, even as they contended with local meanings and practices. As in other newly demo-cratic contexts, the arrival of formal democracy did not erase existing power dynamics, forms of inequality, state-citizen relations, practices of collective action, or understandings of the political (Alvarez 1997; Coronil 1997; Nugent 2002; Comaroff and Comaroff 1999; Markoff 1999). These traces become part of the complex field of action in which "post" political practice unfolds in often contradictory and disappointing ways.

Democracy on a Local and Global Stage

Juggling competing expectations and practices of "the political" thus became an essential exercise in democracy work after 2000. The complexity of this task first became clear to me when I met with Vlada, the international officer from Serbia's (and Yugoslavia's) oldest student organization, Student Alliance (Savez Studenata).[25] It was a sunny afternoon in Belgrade in 2003. We sat outside, at a loud and busy café, crowded with well-dressed young people sipping afternoon coffee. The scene could have taken place in any European capital. And yet when I turned on my recorder, Vlada leaned in to make an appeal from the margins of Europe, his voice traveling from the periphery out to an imagined global audience. He leaned into the microphone and spoke in English, loud enough to be heard above the din of the outdoor café: "Please there are some normal people. And they are enough educated, and enough wide, broad in their minds. Invest here please or we are gonna die." At that point his voice trailed off. Despite his quiet intensity, the theatrics of his statement revealed an element of humor. Laughing, I asked why he would say something so depressing. "Because it's like that here," he replied matter-of-factly. Then he laughed, short and quick, and immediately launched into formal interview mode. In an instant he had moved from black humor and theatrics, to resignation, to once again being "on," in his official role as student representative, international officer, and expert.

Vlada's opening comment was striking for the way in which he called forth an international public produced and mediated by the imagined trajectory of a recorded voice. The plea targeted me, as an American. But his appropriation of my voice recorder as a site of appeal invoked an imagined audience that had the power to judge and influence local contexts. No stranger to the genres of appeal honed with international donor agencies, reporters, or even visiting anthropologists, Vlada imagined his world as one in which local interactions were mediated by global audiences. His half-joking desperation crystallized the complicated ways in which the experience of Serbian citizenship continued to be marked by a desire for international recognition.[26]

At the same time, the local was also deeply written into the exchange, often through the same gestures and inflections that called forth a spectating international community. His humor, his matter-of-fact pessimism, his authoritative position as an expert within an organization—all echoed countless public performances of democratic action, from meetings to press conferences to protests. In these contexts student audiences negotiated multiple audiences for whom the performance of democracy might be signaled by different and even conflicting modes of communication.

Such quick shifts in footing signaled by a move from vulnerable appeal to authoritative confidence were the warp and woof of how students managed to engage in a messy and discursively unstable world (Goffman 1979). But these deft shifts in communication also fed a widespread sense across different audiences that students were doing something wrong. Students were inconsistent, overly pushy, not pushy enough, too professional, too immature, too syndicalist, too directive, or not representative. They were unable to live up to the expectations of revolutionary action in large part because the work of defining democratic practice entailed sometimes-fractious disagreement that opened them up to accusations about whether they were "authentically" democratic or not.

As student leaders like Vlada took up particular understandings of democracy, they had to navigate a social field increasingly defined by the seeming circulation of political models, practices, and publics (Wedeen 2008; Chakrabarty 2007; Gaonkar 2007; Brown 2006; Gal 2006; Gutmann 2002; Paley 2002). Hierarchies of political value and knowledge were translated across borders through a democratization industry that calculated, assessed, and ranked "newly democratic states"—and the political maturity of their citizens—according to normative criteria, from elections to participation and free markets (Guilhot 2005; Coles 2007; Leve 2001; see especially Hull 2010). For many newly emerging democracies and postconflict countries, local political movements take place in a field of mediated spectatorship in which people juggle locally relevant forms of action and the reverberations of this action across multiple mass-mediated publics (Graan 2010; Bishara 2008). This is especially true for those places identified as possible models for democratization or as cautionary tales from which internationally circulating rankings, "lessons learned," and strategic objectives can be culled and redeployed in other newly democratic contexts. Serbia is a unique case in that it brings together both the cautionary tale of virulent nationalism and the model of civic democratic revolution, leading to an often-pervasive sense among Serbian citizens of "being watched."

Structure of This Book and Defining the Field

This book is based on eighteen months of fieldwork between 2002–04 as well as periods of short-term field research in 2001 and between 2005–11. During this time I worked with student and youth activists, professors, university administrators, members of NGOs, ministry officials, and university students. Each chapter follows students as they encounter and respond to the disappointments of democratic activism and politics. I chart histories of "expectation-generating" categories of youth and revolution and actually lived student organizational practice. Each chapter details how students try to anticipate and build these expectations into their approaches to activism, as well as how such "pragmatic politics" often result in unanticipated consequences.

Chapter 1 examines the relationship of youth, politics, and time in contemporary Serbia, as well as the central role of youth politics in socialist Yugoslavia. I argue that both disappointment and students' "pragmatic politics of the present" are responses to utopian, future-oriented politics that many young people associate with the failures and betrayals of their parents' generation. In Chapter 2, I examine the changing political meanings of urban space and protest after the mass citizen protests that toppled Slobodan Milošević in October 2000. With the withdrawal of visible forms of state power from public space, the democratic legitimacy of protest no longer rested in large numbers of citizens taking to the streets against an authoritarian state. Instead, student activists tried to reframe protest after 2000 in terms of the rights of particular kinds of valued citizens. In turn, their efforts were often greeted with disdain, as smaller protests were unfavorably compared to past actions. Chapter 3 examines the move from the streets to the halls of the university, as students took up efforts at university reform within the context of European Union higher education initiatives such as the Bologna Process. Contrary to notions that reform efforts are distinct from revolutionary forms of politics, I argue that students employed tactics from both in their efforts to democratize the university. Chapters 4 and 5 take up the everyday semiotic textures and practices of student reform efforts. Chapter 4 examines the rise of expertise talk as a form of student activism, and Chapter 5 explores how students managed perceptions of their activism in the context of widespread beliefs in Serbia that politics was corrupting and dirty. Both chapters explore how students attempted to discursively manage tensions between expectations for altruistic youth politics and the everyday realities of political engagement and limits of democratic representation.

The ethnographic material here is drawn from work with three student organizations across three different university cities: the capital, Belgrade; the northern town of Novi Sad; and Niš, in the south of Serbia.[27] I attended organizational meetings, press conferences, student-sponsored forums and conferences on university reform, and public events. I observed election campaigns and media strategy sessions, as well as meetings at the Ministry of Education and faculty and administrative councils. I also attended freshman (*brucoši*) mixer parties, hung out with students in the cafés and clubs they frequented, and sat on buses that crisscrossed the country as students traveled from one meeting or event to another.

In particular, I worked with three organizations. Student Union (Studentska Unija) was founded in the early 1990s as an early response to the Milošević regime. The group promoted itself as the oldest independent student organization in the country. Student Union's leadership was galvanized in the protests of 1996 and 1997, and it continued to play a central role alongside Otpor in the events leading up to October 5. Student Alliance played a very different role in the 1990s. As the only official student organization under socialism, Student Alliance was directly tied to the state during the 1990s and was frequently instrumentalized by the regime. After 2000, Student Alliance's leadership quickly left the organization, and it was taken over by students who had been active in the student resistance movement Otpor. Finally, Student Association (Studentska Asocijacija) was founded in Niš by members of Otpor after October 5, 2000. The founders wanted the group to strike a balance between Student Union and Student Alliance, bridging a focus on expertise and policy with serving local student constituents.

Each group took up issues of university reform, democratic participation in the university, and improving the lives of students. As I detail in later chapters, each group had a very different approach to these issues, as well as competing ideas about the "most democratic" way to structure organizations; represent students; and interface with faculty, ministers, and other activist groups. It will become clear from the kinds of data that I draw on throughout this book that my own ethnographic practices were in part dictated by the differences in these groups. Each produced and circulated knowledge about itself, but the groups often assumed very different audiences and made use of institutional and public space in varying ways. The kinds of events that organizations planned, their decision-making processes, and their use of media and documents made participant observation easier in some cases than in others.[28]

In analyzing the meanings of youth politics and their impact on contemporary democratic practices in Serbia, I focus on institutional practices and categories, discursive frameworks and everyday talk about both democracy and revolution. Throughout this book, I show the ways in which expectations and lived democratic practice—all in a context of feeling "watched"—came into powerful and generative contradiction. These democratic ideals existed in dialectical tension with long-standing social relations, institutional forms, and cultural practices. Such political practice is fundamentally hybrid, shot through with multiple meanings and histories. Politics or democracy as abstract concepts necessarily take textual, narrative, and embodied forms that are subject to framing and reframing as they circulate. A politics of disappointment emerges when messy realities move within the same discursive field as normative ideals and expectations. When revolution and democracy don't live up to their promises, people produce forms of "secular theodicy," or ways of making sense of and negotiating the space between ideal and everyday lived experience (Herzfeld 1992). In studying these forms, and their conditions of possibility, I show how postrevolutionary democracy is made both through and despite such disappointments.

Taken together, however, the three student groups were embedded in a broader field of student activism at the university, and they were often tied to one another in direct and indirect ways. As rival organizations they watched one another, gossiped, hotly debated which group was better and why (e.g., more representative, less elite, more democratic). Oftentimes, they engaged in intense battles over resources, like office space and student votes in elections. They developed networks of allies and created publics through the circulation of magazines, newspapers, and other media. Sometimes student activists from different groups presented a united front, and sometimes they bickered in front of minister representatives and professors. Some adults with whom they negotiated had clear views on which groups they preferred. But many others simply lumped them all together as "student organizations," despite the group members' efforts to distinguish themselves. All groups, however, operated under the long shadow of the socialist legacies of student organizing, the Milošević period, and October 5. In their struggles with one another, and with larger publics, they attempted to authorize their participation and engagement both in terms of and despite these histories.

1

Against the Future
Youth and the Politics of Disappointment in Serbia

IN FEBRUARY 2003, I sat down for an interview with Zoran, part of the leadership of Student Alliance (Savez Studenata) at the Faculty of Technical Sciences (Fakultet Tehničkih Nauka) in Novi Sad, Serbia. Armed with my list of questions about student organizations, I set my recorder out on a sticky table in the cavernous, gray-lit student cafeteria. Zoran, like other activists, was quick to inform me about the everyday problems of students—the length of study, which could be upward of ten years for a bachelor's degree; the outdated system of pedagogy; terrible conditions in student dorms and cafeterias; the rising cost of education; and rampant corruption within the university.[1] Like other representatives of student organizations, he believed that reform efforts ought to help students with these practical problems and make the university a more democratic place. Zoran detailed what seemed (to me) the byzantine system of student representatives across the university. As I scrambled to get it all down, I commented on how complicated the structure was. He laughed and told me, "That's democracy."

Zoran was only partly joking. Like many other members of student groups with whom I spoke, he saw the mundane, sometimes technical, aspects of student organizing as central to democracy after the 2000 democratic revolution. After years of war and international isolation, the nitty-gritty details of reform and student representation were necessary to bring order to a system in chaos and to root out the corruption that was so endemic during the Milošević period. Many felt that democracy would be impossible without such administrative and procedural *techne* to ensure order (Coles 2007).

These practical activities stood in marked contrast to the more visible and rebellious forms of social activism during the Milošević period. For many onlookers, the changing zeitgeist among student activists was a sign that the grand visions of the revolution were gone. But as this particular exchange with Zoran shows, the stakes of these seemingly banal administrative tasks were quite different for members of student organizations. The practices were a way of orienting oneself toward political possibilities in the present rather than in relation to a vague utopian future. Although student organizations were often deeply invested in ideas of democracy or Europe, these idealizations existed side by side with pragmatic approaches to Serbia's disappointing postsocialist and postrevolutionary reality.

Toward the end of our conversation, Zoran and I began to discuss the extremely difficult prospects for employment in Serbia. His future job prospects in a country with unemployment at higher than 30 percent were uncertain.[2] The situation seemed bleak, and in a move to deal with my own discomfort with the difficulties he faced, I reached for a familiar sentiment. I had often heard people use the phrase *biće bolje*, or "it will be better," when bringing closure to tales of hardships in Serbia. It was even the title of a song by the popular band Kanda, Kodža, i Nebojša, whose lyrics provided rallying cries and common cultural reference points for countless young people in the dark days of Milošević. Having been schooled over the course of many conversations in this almost reflexive gesture toward a better possible future, I told Zoran that it seemed like things were going to get better. Zoran, who had been polite in the face of my endless questions, grew suddenly impatient. *Biće bolje* is exactly the problem, he said. People told themselves that for ten years under Milošević. They waited, and it didn't get better.

Zoran had given me a sober accounting of the challenges he and other students faced day in and day out at the university. In response, I had given him a well-worn platitude. What's more, it was a platitude that stood for those people who had gotten everyone into trouble in the first place: those who had stood by doing nothing and hoping things would simply change. "It will be better" represented a false hope in a future that never came. It was a justification of inaction among those who had let Milošević rule for more than a decade. Walter Benjamin's (1968) fierce and beautiful essay on the angel of history describes the angel gazing into the past while being swept forward into the future by the inevitable rush of time. Those who uttered, "It will be better," were the angels of the future, staring toward a utopian horizon while standing utterly, and pointlessly, in place. Zoran and many student leaders in the post-2000 period had had enough with utopia, whether socialist, nationalist, or revolutionary.

What struck me about my exchange with Zoran was his deep frustration with the present and his unwillingness to cede the possibility for change to some as-yet-undetermined future. Indeed, his refusal of "it will be better" was a rejection of an idealized futurity that resonated with the present-oriented pragmatism of many reform-minded university student activists. Like the Postpessimists in the introduction, his was a determination that reflected neither blind faith nor cynicism. Frustration signaled not necessarily the end of political engagement but instead the site for its realization. This approach to the realities of everyday life in Serbia stood in sharp contrast to other popular narrative frameworks of victimhood, tragedy, hopelessness, nostalgia, and cynicism.[3] Even as they often reproduced those tropes, young activists struggled to move beyond these commonplace ways of representing Serbia and their own life trajectories.[4]

Zoran's impassioned rejection of an idealized futurity is an impetus to rethink the relationship among youth, politics, and utopia at the beginning of the twenty-first century. Why is a particularly democratic politics figured through the rejection of futurity, the very temporal imaginary around which youth political participation was configured under socialism? This turn toward the present signals a refusal of a long-standing modernist link between youth and futurity. It is no surprise that this refusal emerges from the rubble of twentieth-century visions architected around future-oriented progress (Koselleck 2004). Several theorists of new social movements have analyzed the hopeful but markedly antiutopian politics of contemporary youth activism (Juris 2008, 2012; Razsa and Kurnik 2012; Graeber 2007). Such activist practices refuse the telos of modernist revolutionary politics (and their state-centered vision; Holloway 2002). However, the case of student activists in Serbia demonstrates not the hopeful refusal of the state but a disappointed youth politics architected in the shadow of modernist expectations.

If visions of youth politics were central to modernist revolutionary imaginaries of the twentieth century (Wohl 1979), then it is perhaps not surprising that disappointment in the failure of those projects would also be configured in and around youth. In the socialist and revolutionary context, youth politics was oriented toward an idealized—and thus impossible—utopian future. The democratic era has ushered in a new pragmatic politics of the present in which the contradictions of democratic representation become terrain for political action. Here, disappointment in a utopian future that never came to pass is the condition of possibility for a reassessment of the limits and possibilities of youth agency in the present.

Histories of Youth, Politics, and Futurity in Yugoslavia

The image of youth as a site of social and political (re)generation and futurity suffused state discourse and popular media under European state socialism (Kürti 2002). Young people across socialist contexts were emblematic of revolutionary promise. Such links were often embodied through highly staged public rituals (Taylor 2006). In Yugoslavia, the special role of young people was codified through legal and institutional regimes that recognized secondary and university students as unique and important political subjects in their own right (Carter 1982). Youth were granted the ability to self-organize, alongside other important social groups, such as workers. At the same time, countrywide celebrations of Youth Day (*Dan Mladosti*) and the institution of Tito's pioneers (*pioniri*) enforced the popular link between Tito as a leader and father figure and "his" youth (Bringa 2004). Indeed, after the 1948 split from the Soviet Union, the "ideology of the happy child" was used to differentiate Yugoslav self-managing socialism as freer and as less bureaucratic than surrounding communist countries still in the Soviet sphere of influence (Erdei 2006, 170). Representations of a creative, joyful socialist childhood—figured through the Pioneers—were mobilized in the battle against the "the dangers of bureaucracy" in Yugoslav society and other socialist contexts (Erdei 2006, 170).

In addition, young people were also materially and ideologically integrated into postwar building efforts, most visibly through the extensive system of youth worker brigades and work actions (*radne akcije*). Drafted to rebuild postwar Yugoslavia and to meet the need for rapid construction and modernization of infrastructure, the brigades were also central to public representations of a modern Yugoslavia built on socialist revolution and brotherhood and unity (*bratstvo i jedinstvo*).

These revolutionary tropes of transformation and progress took on embodied forms through which socialist configurations of time and space could be realized in practice. In his book *Time and Revolution*, Stephen Hanson (1997) argues that socialist temporalities were built around the tension between two contrasting notions of time: charismatic and rational. Socialist conceptions of time were charismatic insofar as they envisioned a revolutionary transformation that would found a new social order. This required charismatic leaders who "reordered the normal course of time" and history (Hanson 1997, 12). At the same time, socialist forms of modernity encompassed developmentalist conceptions of time rooted in specific material and historical conditions. People were subject to the exigencies of history, even as the revolution superseded those conditions. Hanson argues that the contradictions of Marx's utopian and historical frameworks were reconciled in institutions and forms of labor that were historically bound, yet transcended and tamed modernist calculations of time.

These insights into the paradoxical nature of time in Marxian revolutionary ideologies are important for understanding why the category "youth" was so productive in the socialist context. "Youth" was a social and political category that fused the social reproduction of the socialist nation with the progressive logics of the revolutionary society. It thus incorporated two temporal dimensions: progress and transcendence through cyclical renewal. Material labor produced social(ist) subjects as embodied examples of the triumph of labor over time. Youth brigadiers literally created the revolutionary society through their physical labor. At the same time, these particularly embodied socialist subjects could be newly regenerated with the passage of modern time, as generations of youthful subjects moved on and others took their place. Like the socialist revolution itself, progress was enabled by the renewed triumph of particular individuals over material conditions and of generational epochs over the future itself.

These dynamics are particularly evident in the 1968 student protests in Belgrade, part of the broader wave of student protests in Europe but unique in Yugoslavia for their scope and impact. The protests deeply shaped the experience and representations of youth politics in the Yugoslav context for years to come. Tito's response to the protests illustrates how notions of regeneration and progress, transcendence and teleology, were so productive for configuring the legitimacy of Yugoslavia's state-socialist project.

Student protesters initially focused on material conditions at the university and high rates of unemployment among youth. But the military's violent response to students sparked a far-reaching critique of Tito's regime that was centered on the failures of self-managing socialism (Pervan 1978, 15–39; Popov 1978; Carter 1982, 207–18; Rusinow 1977, 232–39). Rather than crack down on the students and discredit their criticism and demands, Tito co-opted their demands for increased democratization within socialism as evidence for the rightness of the principles underlying the system, thus preserving his, and the party's, role as ideological guide (Pervan 1978, 16). By doing so, Tito was able to stage a renewal, through the idiom of the youth protesters, of the socialist revolution itself. At the same time, party officials and state media drew lines in the sand between acceptable and unacceptable forms of critique by distinguishing good (altruistic and vanguardist students) and bad (self-interested, fifth-columnist) young people (Pervan 1978, 25).[5] Such students fit well into a trope of "the people" and "enemies" that defined socialist discourse of collective belonging (Verdery 1996, 93).

Tito's co-optation of the 1968 Belgrade protests demonstrates the centrality of youth tropes to the regeneration of his own political authority. With each passing generation of youth brigadiers, pioneers, and students, Tito maintained a structured and institutionalized connection to those who embodied revolutionary spirit par excellence. At the same time, defining a split between good and bad forms of youth protest and activism enabled the regime to make clear the limits of critical political discourse and to manage citizens' expectations of the state. Such distinctions helped set the stage for what a "good" youth politics might look like: altruistic; innocent of the desire for personal political gain; and representative of young people, and by extension, the social collective, more broadly. The idea that youth were a source of political renewal and a much-needed resource in need of protection would prove advantageous for subsequent generations of activists but also would come to be their burden.[6]

Ultimately, youth solved the problem of revolutionary time as both transcendent and teleological by combining the founding of a new social order with temporalities of progress. The category "youth" tied successive generations of young people to the development of the socialist state. As Katherine Verdery has argued, state-socialist practices organized people's relationship to time by "seizing it" through a variety of practices, such as having to wait in endless lines. Verdery (1996, 40) refers to this seizure of time as "etatization." Focusing on the category "youth" reveals that the etatization of time included not only daily practices such as "ritual waiting" but also the capture of futurity itself (Verdery 1996).[7] The revolution could transcend time through the constant renewal of its youthful character; in this way, people defied the limits of the inexorable historical passage of history. By doing so, the socialist state harnessed time in the service of a transformative communist future, thereby reconciling the contradictions of a permanent revolution.

Generational Citizenship and Betrayal

Examining shifts in generationally marked practices and the intersubjectivities they called into being helps us understand why young activists like Zoran no longer invested hope in unspecified futures. Indeed, the rejection of a utopian future (of *biće bolje*) for action in the present was an implicit critique of generational temporalities of renewal at the heart of Yugoslav socialism. This rejection was at the heart of a politics of disappointment—a rejection of modernist, utopian progress—and its expectations for the generational and future-oriented renewal of politics.

In many ways, the experiences of Alek, a young postman in Niš, was exemplary of how a once-ordered social compact among generations was upended in the postsocialist context. In his early thirties, when I met him, Alek was just old enough to have experienced the aspirations of socialist Yugoslavia, the violence of its disintegration, and the disappointed realities of its democratization. He was extremely bright and held a university degree in chemistry. But the only steady employment he could find was as a postman, a job he despised. Alek had the cosmopolitan aspirations of internationalist Yugoslavia and the revanchist and parochial leanings exemplary of the country's disintegration. He was a passionate student of French and could always be found at the newly opened French cultural center in Niš. Even as he dreamed of walking the streets of Paris, he harbored intense anger at "the West." Because he viewed me as a representative of the United States, the nation he held responsible for Serbia's bombing and humiliation, Alek persisted in calling me *dušman*, a Turkish word that designates a mortal enemy. And yet he counted me a friend. And in a contradiction that was hardest for me to reconcile, he seemed to harbor no personal animosity toward his fellow former Yugoslavs—his dearest friend was originally from Sarajevo, of mixed Bosnian Muslim and Serbian heritage. Yet Alek had at least once voted for the Serbian Radicals, a virulently nationalist and xenophobic party, out of anger and frustration with the lack of change in post-2000 Serbia. In many ways, Alek was a true child of the former Yugoslavia: he dreamed of Paris and hated the West, finished university and wound up a postman, had little passion for nationalist rhetoric, and yet voted for a party that had promulgated war and violence.

Alek's story also reveals how the never-fully-realized hopes of many young Serbs—and the political costs of their disappointment—were narrated in terms of changing relations among generations. This was clear to me from a particular anecdote that made the rounds among Alek's tight-knit group of friends, many of whom were also struggling with the mismatch between their personal ambitions and their economic and social realities. Alek would often regale his friends with stories of his adventures as a postman. One oft-cited anecdote was always told and retold among the group with a combination of bitterness and joy—a rhetorical style meant to reflect an inner state of melancholic pleasure that Lacan would call jouissance and that these friends would recognize in the Bosnian notion of *sevdah*, a lyrical genre of loss and pathos.[8]

As a postman, Alek was tasked with delivering the often late, and always meager, state benefit checks to pensioners in Niš. On the days when the checks might be expected (or were past due), Alek was compelled to vary his route through his particularly hilly *rejon* (district). Otherwise, he would be tracked down and mobbed by a horde of desperate old people who were stalking the streets in anticipation of his arrival. As a mutual friend recounted, the "game" went as follows. Alek would always "go for the grease" (*mrsnoća*, his best-tipping customers) first and then hop in his car to avoid "ambush." The pensioners would chase him up the hill "like a pack of wolves." Years later, the same friend recalled wondering how it was that those leading the attack "were the ones you would expect to just drop dead any minute in the street, only a second before spotting him."

In the telling, Alek was described as a hapless trickster, hounded by the old and the desperate. He kept one step ahead by grace of his quick wit and his younger, fleeter feet (not to mention his car). The story had a number of twists. The most obvious irony was that Alek's friends all referred to him by his affectionate nickname "Old Man" for his curmudgeonly ways. The fact that he came to be the representative of youth in comparison to the horde of old pensioners was thus especially funny.

But on a deeper level, Alek's role in the story was tragicomic: a young, educated man intent on traveling the world was instead doomed to a restless and circulatory journey through the streets of Niš. He moved across space but never forward in time. His peripatetic movement across the city was propelled by the endless temporal loop (month to month, check to check) connecting the crisis-ridden Serbian state to the people who most relied on it. At the same time, the desperate pensioners were caught in the past of a system that had promised to care for them in their old age and a present that left them unmoored. They were doomed to chase an uncertain future symbolized by a weary young man who fled before them.

Alek's story reveals how a changing postsocialist Serbian state—and regimes of social support and entitlements—comes to be mediated through interactions among differently positioned citizens. Alek and the pensioners experienced the changing nature of their citizenship vis-à-vis antagonistic, and yet dependent, relations. In this case, that relationship was structured around generational difference inscribed through different temporal and spatial—that is, chronotopic—practices (Bakhtin 1981; Dick 2010; Lemon 2009; Graan 2013). Kesha Fikes (2009, xiv) has argued that one must approach the practices and meanings of citizenship not only by analyzing the categories of belonging defined by state institutions but also through the enactments that "teach citizens how to be citizens" in their interactions with one another. Here, the pensioners' relationship to the state is redirected through their relationship to the young postman, who weaves and dodges to avoid them, propelled by a state with no money on one side and the desperation of an abandoned population on the other.

The humor and pathos of Alek's plight throws into relief his own dissatisfied labor practices, his unsatisfying present, and his potentially (since he, too, relies on the coffers of the state) insecure future. It also demonstrates how young people's individual life trajectories are increasingly affected by changing global economic conditions that reinscribe geopolitical hierarchies of progress and modernity.[9] Indeed, given the rise of precariousness, particularly among youth in European peripheries, young people's experience of time and progress stands to change drastically (Mole 2011; Standing 2011). As in the tale of Odysseus, youth narratives may be wedded to nonlinear chronotopes that upend temporal certainties of late modernity: "passing time" (Jeffrey 2010); "doing nothing" (Graan 2012); "mixing" (Hromadžić 2011); and in Alek's case, constant fleeing.

If intergenerational relations were a site for enacting politics in socialist Yugoslavia, then it is not surprising that people used those frameworks to try to make sense of their relationship to upheavals in state, economy, and society beginning in the 1990s. As in Alek's tale, sh the space-time of citizenship were frequently mediated through talk about changing relationships between generations. For young activists, the stakes of this betrayal were high. Indeed, many young people argued that they could not trust their parents' generation to secure them a decent future because their parents' irresponsibility was what had gotten Yugoslavia into trouble in the first place. Many university students I spoke with had given up on trusting that adults could be relied on at all, so closely were they identified with the turbulence, violence, and unpredictability of then-recent history. Indeed, the theme of generational betrayal came up frequently over the course of my fieldwork. Young people argued that they could not trust their parents' generation because it was their irresponsibility that squandered the legacy to which their children had been entitled: a modern, prosperous, and stable Yugoslavia. Ivan, a student activist in his twenties, explained much of Serbia's recent history in these terms. As a member of the Social Democratic Youth, the youth wing of the progressive Social Democratic Union, Ivan had not given up on political life in Serbia. But his anger with his parents' generation was still raw less than a year after the revolution, when we spoke. It was their pampered generation that had ruined Yugoslavia because dissatisfaction with their quality of life drove Tito to take on increasing debt. This legacy of debt and economic crisis, he argued, set the stage for people like Milošević to step in and claim to represent change through a nationalist idiom.

Ivan's points were not too far from some critical explanations of the origins of Yugoslavia's dissolution, particularly the role of mounting debt and economic crisis (Woodward 1995). But his version of recent history was also exemplary of the way that generation had become a way to figure politics as a site of collective betrayal rather than solidarity. Members of the generation of 1968 whom I spoke with often saw their participation in student activism as a new and rejuvenating political moment in Yugoslavia (often favorably comparing their actions to contemporary youth politics). Ivan presented their coming of age as the beginning of the end of Yugoslavia.

Such narratives of generational betrayal were not exclusive to young people. A member of the Ministry of Education told me with regret, "The younger generation does not trust us, and they are right not to." She felt very strongly that the decisions and mistakes of her generation, particularly in the 1990s, were her children's burden to bear. When I mentioned the very real sense of pain and guilt at this generational failure to a young student activist who knew the ministry official well, she told me she had heard that from her before. At first she thought it was merely "pretty words," but she had come to believe that the minster's sense of guilt and her critique of the protesters of the 1968 generation was deeply felt. The student's initial sense of distrust at the merely "pretty words" from her mentor was itself indicative of the ways in which intergenerational tensions structured people's everyday and often intimate relationships.

Political Futures and Democratic Presents

Generational tensions thus became the terrain on which changing forms of postsocialist citizenship were enacted. Young people's pragmatism was underpinned by the sense that they were the ones who would have to change Serbia. Moving forward entailed a rejection of their parents' idealism and the social crisis it had wrought. The future did not lie with the older generation that had gotten them into trouble in the first place. Where their parents' generation had been spoiled, they would work hard. Where Tito's Yugoslavia had been some kind of dream or fantasy, they lived in a more sober reality, one ironically of their parents' making.[10] As one student activist told me during a long rant about the uselessness of pensioners, the society they (older people) had created (*društvo koje su oni stvorili*) was doomed to failure because it was grounded in mistaken ideologies. In lieu of the artifice of a society forged with revolutionary ideology, students articulated their politics within a pragmatic present that was inevitably incomplete, partial, contradictory, and disappointing. Although such pragmatism was no less an ideology than that of the "revolutionary society" that this student was referencing, it did entail a different orientation toward present-focused action. Rejecting the fantasies that structured their own parents' hopes and dreams became a way to navigate the disappointments that were the legacies of an older generation's failures. Pragmatism was a call to action that rejected the future-oriented idealism of the socialist modernist project and its investment in the future. It was also a reaction to the lack of action (and perhaps complicity) represented by an older generation's response to Milošević's Serbia: "it will be better."

Pragmatism and idealism were distributed generationally, and thus formed the basis for a pragmatic and present-focused youth activism. This was evident in an encounter with Milena, a student activist from Novi Sad. Milena had caught my attention for her unsparing lack of roma and her commitment to student activism. A petite woman with a heart-shaped face and jet-black dyed hair, she toughened up her natural prettiness and warmth with a no-nonsense attitude that often made her seem unapproachable. Given her usually cool demeanor, I was particularly taken back by the anger and vulnerability she expressed one day when we were talking about prospects for work in Serbia. Over drinks, she recounted a story about an interaction with her father in which she scolded him for his unrealistic views about how the world should work. The anecdote made clear how her own pragmatic activism was tied to her and her family's intimate encounters with disappointment.

Milena, her boyfriend, and I were sitting at an Irish pub in Novi Sad one warm afternoon. We had just come from the Europe Day events (*Dan Evrope*), sponsored by Student Union, in which Milena and her boyfriend, both students, were very active. As a student of economics interested in public relations and marketing, Milena was well aware of the employment situation in Serbia. We discussed different conditions for work in different places, comparing the longer working hours in the United States and Japan to people's expectations about the workday in Serbia. Although Milena's parents were both employed as schoolteachers, they were still forced to supplement their meager salaries by giving private lessons. She said her mom was more like her—adaptable to any situation and able to work the hours without complaining. But her father was much more upset about the situation. She recounted a recent fight in which her father had insisted that his longer working hours "weren't human." Milena was visibly frustrated as she recounted to us her response to him: "Fine, they're not human, but you don't have choice. This is the way things are changing, and there's nothing you can do about it, and you are going to have work that way from now on."

Milena's harsh response to her father's inability to deal with his condition is a telling example of the reversals of generational responsibility that characterized the period. Milena played the role of parent, educating her father about the ways of the world, dealing with his complaints, and scolding him as a parent might a whining child. That this tension would come out around labor practices is not surprising in a postsocialist context, in which relationships to work are a central site for renegotiating personhood (Dunn 2004; Kideckel 2008).

One could interpret Milena's frustration with her father as a kind of apathetic acceptance. And yet Milena was a committed student and an active participant in student organizing. She herself had worked hard to get out of the small suburb in which she was raised, a place she hated because, as she told me, "Intelligence is not a value [there]." The profile of apathy did not sit with the person I knew. She was hungry for interesting, lucrative work; the chance to travel and experience life abroad; and the opportunity to be a city girl, like many of her more privileged peers at the university. At the same time, she was savvy about Serbia's position in the world and often cynical about the possibilities for change. In a striking moment, amid the talk of both the limits and the possibilities for work, Milena sighed in frustration and anger, and she told me that she didn't want to be hired only because she was cheap labor. As I wrote in my field notes, I was struck at the time by the gap between Milena's analysis of the situation—after all, we had been talking at length about new inequalities in the context of the global reorganization of capital and labor—and her anger that she might get caught in that structural trap.

As I talked with two students who saw themselves on the losing side of the economic equation, I also watched them struggle to negotiate their own position between hope and disappointment. As was her father, Milena was disappointed and frustrated with the situation in Serbia. But her fatalism—indeed, her disciplining of her own father about that fatalism—went hand in hand with her ability to play the possibilities available to her. I began to see how student activism as a present-focused commitment to small-level change could emerge as a survival strategy in the context of disappointment. Indeed, student activism in Serbia was not only about bringing about a promised future but also about negotiating the tensions of the present moment. A politics of disappointment was thus also a kind of "affective activism"—a survival strategy for young people in the face of precariousness, social isolation, and uncertainty (Allison 2009). Student organizations became a place to perform a new kind of self: educated, expert, cosmopolitan, savvy, and realistic, as well as hopeful and disappointed.

Disappointment as a Postsocialist Political Modality

At the same time that student activists and young people felt betrayed by their parent's generation, many in Serbia were disappointed in them. In part, this disappointment was tied to the shape and form of the youth-led anti-Milošević movement, which generated implicit expectations not only for the specific goal of his overthrow but also for the purification of politics itself. When people complained that student groups after 2000 were no longer unified, overly professional, and nonrepresentative, they were in part comparing their experience of post-2000 groups to a highly mediated representation of student organizations. The clarity of antistate resistance had given way to the compromises of rule and, in the minds of many, the betrayal of earlier ideals. Who better to stand in for the failure of revolutionary expectations than the figures most iconic with those expectations?

These expectations stood at sharp odds to the pragmatic, and at times technocratic, work of university student groups after 2000. Many saw the turn toward university reform as mundane in juxtaposition to earlier calls for democracy and electoral freedom. Protests over issues such as the easing of exam requirements and tuition fees appeared self-serving. The emphasis on expertise seemed antithetical to the image of altruistic young people fighting, protesting, and singing in the streets. The infighting that resulted from student groups engaging in competitive elections seemed antithetical to a movement that once claimed to speak for all young people.

Serbia after 2000 was by no means the first, and will not be the last, society to configure disappointment around a group of young protesters. Other storied generations of protesters and revolutionaries have become yardsticks for judging the subsequent actions of either future generations or the protest generation itself. As Meta Mendel-Reyes has shown in her analysis of the 1960s as a metaphor in the US context, that decade still has a profound impact for framing what politics "ought" to look like today on the basis of narratives of what politics looked like then (Mendel-Reyes 1995; see also Gitlin 1993). Indeed, the more recent case of student protesters being harassed and "kettled" by police in the United Kingdom demonstrates that the phenomenon of criminalizing student activists is alive and well (Power 2012; Hancox 2011). Narratives of student altruism and betrayal are inextricably bound to the histories of specific youth and revolutionary movements elevated to the level of myth, metaphor, and cautionary tale.

For example, as a founding member of the student resistance movement Otpor, Mihajlo was central to the production of the mythology of youth revolution in Serbia. His own move from revolutionary to politician was emblematic of the way that people expressed disappointment in the revolution and its aftermath. Given this, it was particularly apt that he was the first who suggested disappointment to me as the ethos of postrevolutionary Serbia. As we sat in his office on a hot summer day, less than a year after the revolution of October 5, 2000, he explained to me that people were let down by the lack of change after October 6. By October 10, he said, people woke up in the same room as always and felt disappointed. Mihajlo had skillfully navigated this postrevolutionary disappointment by finding new ways to engage in social activism. Indeed, he was not alone in moving from the student movement to a professional career in politics; many high-profile former student activists did the same. From Mihajlo's perspective, this specialization of politics was necessary for Serbia to become a "normal" country, and it entailed creating a space between politics and people's everyday lives. Such sentiments were common among student activists after 2000, many of whom were tired of the risks and constant politicization of everyday life under Milošević.

Yet Mihajlo's own trajectory was part of a familiar narrative of disappointment in youth activists after 2000. In 2003, two years after Mihajlo and I spoke, Otpor had become a political party, but it did terribly at the polls. The party ultimately disbanded in the shadow of accusations of financial mismanagement and embezzlement. As the group devolved into infighting and scandals, and launched a new nationalist platform, it suffered from comparison to the carefully crafted image that had made it so successful during the late 1990s. There is no better illustration of the group's declining public image than a 2003 editorial cartoon by the beloved political cartoonist Corax (Predrag Koraksić). It depicted the iconic Otpor fist lazily slouching in a chair and channel surfing. A direct critique of Otpor's transformation from energetic youthfulness to lazy complacency, the cartoon distilled people's disappointment in the figures who had been most emblematic of the democratic revolution.

More generally, laments about moral breakdown among young people were the stuff of everyday talk, movies, newspaper articles, and academic research.[11] Professors and teaching assistants complained about the lack of initiative among university students. Secondary school teachers, themselves barely out of university, complained about lack of respect and the rampant cheating and corruption they witnessed. While adults were decrying the moral turpitude of young men and women who had grown up under the Milošević regime, those same young people, then in their late twenties and thirties, had similar complaints about young people born in the 1990s. So thoroughly did this narrative of decline saturate talk a post-2000 student activism that even the students with whom I conducted my research—in other words, those who were targets of precisely those critiques—reproduced it in later years. Talking over coffee one day in the late 2000s with two former university student activists, I was shocked to hear them call the new leadership of their former organization a bunch of "student yuppies" and "technocrats." It was ironic considering that this earlier generation of activists had generated the very procedures and policy culture that they were lamenting. That these usually sophisticated analysts of the political scene were disappointed in some of the same ways others had been disappointed in them was also a testament to how difficult it is to change the terms of political engagement.

If students suffered from comparison to their own earlier practices, the democratic context also generated new sets of expectations that stood in sharp contrast to the unruliness of revolutionary action. Yet consistency was difficult given the competing expectations and demands that could populate even a single conversation. Indeed, one exchange I had with a high-ranking official from the University of Belgrade revealed the dizzying number of expectations of students that might jostle and compete over the course of a single interaction. When we met in his office at the Rectorate Building at the University of Belgrade, the professor argued that students should represent a unified student voice, "innocent" of political interest, career goals, and concern with power and resources; have control and in-fluence over other students and force professors to consider their interests; have less influence than they did in the 1990s; be professional and easy to deal with; and be knowledgeable and well-organized experts. The problem was not simply that students didn't live up to a single ideal picture of ac-tivism in the 1990s; it was that these ideals existed side by side with new sets of concerns and demands that made it impossible to authoritatively inhabit one consistent way of being socially and politically engaged.

The point of drawing out discussion of this exchange is not to iden-tify any one person for having multiple, contradictory expectations for how students ought to behave. Rather, the exchange is exemplary of the kinds of competing demands and roles that student activists had to nego-tiate. Meeting one expectation necessarily meant falling short of another. Indeed, so prevalent was this kind of contradictory discursive web that student activists learned to anticipate, critique, and manage their image even as part of the most seemingly routine activities. Anticipating the ways in which they would be disappointing to observers became a condition of possibility for postrevolutionary action.

A Politics of Disappointment

This dual tension of being disappointed and disappointing to others produced a particular approach to student activism that I call a politics of disappointment, in which the contradictions and contingencies of democratic practice became a terrain for a new kind of democratic agency. Despite the deeply normative commitments that student activists in Serbia had toward procedural and liberal forms of democracy, their experience of democratic politics as imperfect and contingent produced a pragmatism that allowed for a break with the temporal logics of modernist and utopian political horizons—a rejection of the futurity experienced as a rejection of intergenerational solidarity. This restless and dissatisfied pragmatism meant embracing a present suffused with the disappointments of impossible revolutions and unrealizable futures. Disappointment became a necessary feature of, rather than an exception to, democratic practice. Students drew on their own frustrations with democracy and their experiences as disappointments to others to frame and stage a present-focused politics that was necessarily contradictory and inconsistent.

Serbian student activists were not alone in struggling with democratic politics as a contradictory field of normative expectations, ethical commitments, and social meanings. Scholars have pointed to the increasing global salience of normative, Western, democratic frameworks, even as they argue that those frameworks are historically specific and idiosyncratic (Nugent 2008). At the same time, scholars have demonstrated the proliferation of multiple kinds of democracies (Paley 2008) that defy easy categorization. This multiplicity throws the very meaning of democracy into question within and across any particular social-political field. The absolutism of normative democracy on the one hand and its contingent manifestation on the other hand can give way to both experimentation and disappointment. In other words, although democracy may have particular ideologies of progress and futurity—what Elizabeth Povinelli (2002, 33) calls "the future perfect," in her critical analysis of late liberalism—the practice of democracy is shot through with contradictions and compromises in the present.

How, then, did the anticipation of disappointment and the contingency of political practice shape a range of activist practices focused on present-oriented negotiation rather than future-oriented idealism? For one, a politics of disappointment was grounded in awareness and embrace of adaptability. More than just a coping logic, this approach to activism was about understanding how imperfection—indeed, all that is disappointing—was a necessary part of the terrain of activism. Negotiating contradictory roles and demands thus became one key strategy in the politics of disappointment.

This strategy was evident in a Student Union (Studentska Unija) training in Novi Sad one May afternoon in 2003. The training was part of Student Union's broader effort to support local Student Union activists and to coordinate activities and expertise across universities, or what they called the National Training Team (NTT). The trainings were meant to address two seemingly contradictory images of the organization. Student Union was trying to promote the reputation of the group as representative of a broad base of students through local participation and increased membership. However, it was also trying to promote its image as an exclusive group of skilled experts. The training was thus an attempt to negotiate the kinds of contradictory roles and expectations that groups were juggling in the post-2000 period.

The session was facilitated by two NTT trainers who had been with Student Union for a while and were considered experts within the organization. While the training content was centered on university reform, the trainers also spent a good deal of time educating students on how to deal with perceptions about student organizations. Part of this process was the exercise "defining our environment" (*definisanje okruženja*). One of the facilitators wrote "SUS" (Student Union of Serbia) in the middle of a blank sheet on a flip chart and asked participants to call out different actors and institutions that affected them. The list was long and included students in general, other student organizations, the university, the state and provincial government, and other nongovernmental organizations. The exercise was supposed to help participants assess the kinds of expectations (and inevitable disappointments) that students would face when planning campaigns. For example, the partially reproduced chart in Table 1 shows a list of what different actors thought about themselves, what they thought about Student Union activists, and what Student Union activists thought of them—a kind of strategic Rashomon-effect exercise.

TABLE 1. Partial reproduction of "Defining Our Context"

	Think about themselves	What Student Union thinks about them	What they think about Student Union
Students	Powerless, without rights	Uninformed, uninterested, we [Student Union] need them and they need us, passive, impudent and disrespectful (*bezobrazni*), selective in their interests	We don't work for them, sect (*sekta*), political, closed society (*zatvoreno društvo*), misuse position (*zloupotrebljavaju svoju poziciju*)
Administration	Democratic and/or bureaucratic, perfect, working in the interests of faculty and students	Important to us, conservative, corrupt, interested in helping only good students (discriminating), uncommunicative, ignorant	Closed, not transparent, a threat, supported by political parties, defends the interest of bad students, are bad students, children of politicians, radicals, youthful and impatient
Rival student group on campus (here referring particularly to Student Association)	Well organized, the one and only (*jedini i pravi*), useful, cooperative, innovative, powerful, works in interests of students, uncorrupted	Personal interests, monopolist, corrupt, don't work for students, criminals, political, kiss-asses (*poltroni*), use student organizing to make their studies easy, undemocratic, misusers (*oni koji zloupotrebljavaju*), fictive membership, intolerant, arrogant	Funded by foreigners, personal interests, corrupt, monopolist, misusers, don't work for student interests, arrogant, don't have support of students, political, threat (to rival student groups)

At the end of the exercise, the chart was covered with a range of contradictory roles, assumptions, and ideas. Not surprisingly, the roles were often marked by intergenerational tensions (students were seen as irresponsible and stuck-up kids or overly powerful for their age; adults were portrayed as alternately irresponsible and incompetent or arrogant and all-powerful).

Overall, though, it was clear from the exercise that it would be impossible to inhabit all the roles or anticipate all the critiques within any one strategic frame or campaign. The NTT trainers were aware of ways in which perceptions—both about their own organization and assumptions student activists had about other actors—shaped possibilities for how to plan and discursively manage interventions. The new skill set of student activists thus had to include the management of such perceptions.

The list of conflicting perspectives was not merely theoretical. It was a pedagogical exercise to teach students to analyze the field of social relations in which they were embedded. Students had to embody and perform their "studentness" in order to make their claims and demands persuasive. In doing this, student activists couldn't simply ignore the perceptions of others. Managing their image was a central part of establishing themselves as particularly democratic actors. Being self-interested, disingenuous, or overly bureaucratic didn't (only) make student activists irritating to others. It served as evidence that student groups weren't really representative of student interests more generally.

Such representation was a key catchphrase in newly democratic Serbia, and the professors and administrators with whom students dealt often wondered whether students were really representative of their constituents' interests. Students also hotly debated this issue within and across organizations. Yet it wasn't always clear how students could convince others that they were representative, especially because the very meaning of democratic representation was up for grabs. Should they be protesting on the street? Conducting elections? Speaking for all young people or only for students? Convincing others that they were representative required students to make authoritative discursive links between specific representational practices and competing understandings of democracy that were in circulation in Serbia at the time. Student activists thus had to constantly renegotiate how "a people comes into being in particularly situations labeled democracy" (Paley 2008, 10). As Julia Paley (2008, 10) has noted, this is not a static process; rather, "the act of constituting a people happens within political action and public rhetoric on an ongoing basis." Activist interactions with a multitude of interlocutors meant juggling contradictory roles in a context in which the meaning of representation was up for grabs on an ongoing basis.

Indeed, students in the NTT training session were called on to practice role-playing to help them develop strategies to deal with accusations that they were not representative. And, as in the exercise to define their environment, role-playing also taught students to deal with contradictory expectations. For example, at one point over the course of the training session that weekend, participants were asked to play out a scenario in which two students were negotiating with a university dean (*dekan*) and vice president (*prorektor*). The students' goal was to get permission to implement a new course in the middle of the year, taught by a graduate assistant with an innovative pedagogical approach. Two students played the administrators, and two played student activists initiating the appeal. The role-play exercise was a chance to see how students took on the language of power and authority, and how they understood their own position vis-à-vis figures in the administration. The role-play lasted only a few minutes, but the extent to which the actor playing the vice president sounded like administrators I had interviewed was uncanny. Taking on the authority and gravitas of an upper-level administrator, the role-playing student insisted on two criteria that the appealing students must meet. First, the students appealing for the course would have to come back in two weeks, after having conducted a survey that demonstrated they had 70 percent or more student support for the initiative. Second, the "vice president" said that their appeal was misguided anyway, because a faculty statute forbade the introduction of a new course in the middle of the year. Using the dual rhetoric of student representation and the legalistic language of statutes, the role-player pinned the student representatives into a corner.

Throughout the performance, the audience of student trainees laughed and squirmed at the dead-on arguments of the administrators, nodding enthusiastically at the familiar story playing out in front of them. I, too, recognized the discursive strategies from real-time negotiations among students, faculty, and administrators. Students were caught between dual demands that they authentically represent an idealized voice of the student body (ironically represented through a technical instrument like a survey) and that they work according to legalistic mechanisms such as university statutes.

The students' performance within the context of the training was playful and exaggerated. But it also revealed how students experienced, voiced, and embodied the complexities of trying to successfully perform their democratic capacities and persuade audiences that they deserved particular entitlements and rights. In large part, the critiques that students anticipated in this performance rested on whether the student representatives actually represented the interests and voice of all students. This is not surprising given the extent to which democratic practices so often rest on producing evidence of being representative of "the people."

In a context in which mass student protests were made to stand in for "the people," new practices of representation and new sites of negotiation (e.g., two student representatives negotiating with a dean in his office) were highly suspect. The training exercise revealed the difficulties that might ensue when people mobilized different expectations of how students should behave democratically. The participants and audience were playing out the difficulties that students faced in speaking across the very real power gap that existed between themselves and administrators, even as they tried to formulate a new language to make their claims heard.

The fact of negotiating their proper role and image for multiple audiences meant that students often had to be on their toes and ready to respond to contradictory pressures in ongoing, real-time interactions. In other words, rather than seeking assimilation to a perfect, future-oriented norm of how student activists ought to behave, students grounded their actions in the real time of negotiation.

Such an approach was built into the way students planned campaigns, appealed to different audiences, and tried to mobilize different populations. As the foregoing example shows, student activists tried to pay attention to the ways in which all everyday interactions were bound to be disappointing to someone. Trainers used specific pedagogical exercises to teach other activists how to anticipate and manage such disappointments as part of a broader terrain of democratic action. While they tried their best to manage expectations, they were also aware that the process had limits. In turn, they produced a politics of disappointment, rather than a politics against disappointment.

Pragmatism Revisited

It was the embrace of the necessarily open-endedness of meaning and action that made a democratic politics of disappointment particularly pragmatic. Such open-endedness calls to mind George Herbert Mead's (2002, 75) observation that the social character of the universe includes "the situation in which the novel event is in both the old order and the new which its advent heralds. Sociality is the capacity of being several things at once." This coexistence of irreconcilable and multitudinous presents—here, the multiple roles and perspectives that informed student activism—was the antithesis of a teleological revolutionary logic.

This hopeful pragmatism was best articulated by a student activist who I admired for her passion but also for her crystal-clear strategic thinking. Danica had been involved in Otpor since her high school days and in Student Union since 2000. She had held important leadership roles in the organization, and I had known her since the start of my research in 2001. But when we sat down for an interview in 2004, it was the first time I asked her to reflect on how student activism had changed over the years. Danica was a central figure in redefining Student Union as an organization dedicated to university reform. Nonetheless, she saw this as continuity with her earlier commitments to student and human rights and democratization of Serbia. Although she was critical about some aspects of the group, she did not express regrets about the trajectory that student organizing had taken since 2000. Indeed, she saw the shifts in the focus of student organizing as necessary not only to the organizations' survival but also to their flourishing as democratic organizations.

Danica mobilized some familiar narratives about youth. She spoke of the loss of energy and commitment to mass demonstrations, and she described this shift through the language of generational differences. For example, Danica cited one of the biggest changes between the 1990s and post-2000 as a general loss of motivation among students, noting that the new generation of activists had lost the "spirit of mass demonstration and protest and everything."

And yet rather than framing this lack of motivation as an end point to the story of student activism, Danica took it as a kind of beginning—not without regret—as part of a larger narrative of how student groups rise to new challenges. Despite the lack of motivation among students, she was not worried about the future of student organizations. She told me: "A lot of things can happen. Even shit can happen in organizations, but [they] won't cease to exist. Definitely, because now it's too big, there's too many people involved. You can close Student Union of Serbia and university unions and try to ban the work . . . but some of them will still [continue their work]. . . . I think it's too late [to] stop it."

Danica's narrative makes room for change, but not through the idiom of transformation. Rather, it is a matter of adaptation, negotiation, and compromise. For example, in describing the differences between Student Union and Otpor, she noted:

Student Union managed to find another goal, because similar to Otpor, Student Union . . . had a goal to [bring down] Milošević and end his regime and have a democratic country, [a] European-oriented country. But Student Union managed . . . to really have some smaller-scope activities . . . not only connected with Milošević but also with teaching stuff at the universities, matters of process, small campaigns on faculties, . . . so we managed very successfully, you know, to change and modify [our] goal. . . . That's what made [the] difference between Otpor and Student Union. . . . Student Union managed to change . . . and Otpor never did.

Whatever the limitations or merits of this approach, Danica does not describe successful student activism through the frames of youth innocence and revolutionary vanguards. She made possible, at least in the course of our conversation, a new way of conceptualizing student action around incremental strategic goals and planning, precisely those features of student organizations that are so often met with skepticism and criticism. At the same time, she saw these emerging techniques of organization as having some continuity with earlier commitments, concerns, and practices forged in the 1990s. Indeed, Danica argued, it is precisely this more complicated and nuanced history of student organizing that enabled the survival of activism in the post-2000 present. Danica compares Student Union's energy and its anti-Milošević commitment, as well as its early commitment to human rights and students' rights issues, to Otpor's inability to shift toward other kinds of organizing.

In part, this attitude stems from Danica's own mixed feelings about her experiences in the 1990s and her relief to have moved on to other kinds of protest. If Danica had fond memories of the period, she was also somewhat skeptical about her own experience of nostalgia. When I asked her if she missed the days of protest, as she had once told me, she responded ambivalently at first:

I don't know. . . . At that time, it was kind of like . . . [we were] on the first front lines. . . . I have this nostalgia. Everything was so simple. You had Milošević, and his crew, and they were guilty of *everything*. Being poor, being isolated, and having too much to study. Not having books. They were guilty of everything. And it was easier. It was simply easier.

While Danica's comments may seem nostalgic, her conversational tone was ironic. She both longed for the moment when she deeply felt that everything was easy, simple, and obvious. At the same time, she realized how unrealistic those expectations had been. Drawing both on her experience of protests and on her understanding of the risks and difficulties they entailed, Danica was able to develop some critical distance from her earlier experiences, even as she acknowledged their legacy in her own life (she, like other members of Student Union, still "felt the spirit" of mass demonstrations). In her emphasis on practical strategies, she described a "very organized, diplomatic, student organization" that was able to negotiate, lobby, organize campaigns, and achieve public influence without mass protest. In part, students were fed up with mass demonstrations and saw other more effective ways of engaging publics and state authorities. But the focus on other kinds of engagements also had roots in the experiences of risk taking in the 1990s. As Danica noted, post-2000 Serbia was a different environment from what it had been in the 1990s, and student groups need to take that into account:

It's understandable from my point, you know. And once people stop being so passionate in a way . . . [T]here were a lot of people [willing to] to get killed in the streets if it was necessary to bring Milošević down. You know, people . . . now are thinking, What are my duties? What are my responsibilities? What is my mandate? Which is good in a way.

Here the "loss of passion" narrative is a beginning rather than an end point, as well as an adaptation to changing circumstances. But Danica also put these experiences into context, highlighting the affective and political commitments of students in the 1990s, as well as the intensity and danger of the protest experience.

It was at precisely the moment when I would have expected disappointment that Danica produced an alternate way to understand political engagement as a living, growing process. Her model was not without its own vision of a future-oriented end point—in this case, oriented toward a notion of Europe. But it was not a vision of politics that tied specific actions to necessary teleological horizons of progress. Rather, it was an acknowledgment of the starts and stops. This was not only a personal philosophy but also an approach to organizational leadership and specific forms of activism, as many of the examples in the following chapters show.

My conversation with Danica ended with her unexpected vision for what student organizations were all about. When I asked, "What do you feel the role of student organizations should be?" Danica began by talking about the role of students as equal participants in institutions. Yet as she reflected, Danica did not offer a specific political vision per se. Instead, she imagined a new kind of sociality brought about by student organizations. This was unusual for her, at least in our conversations, given her incredible strategic sophistication about the organization. It was thus a surprise to hear her talk about student organizations as a form of sociality and as a way of creating affective connections and solidarities. She answered:

They have found their role. . . . I think that we really are the engine of changes in reform; you can clearly see it. But on the other hand, I think it's very good that student organizations keep gathering students on whatever basis. I hope that one day we will have a lot of student groups that will deal with fishing and . . . stuff like that. . . . Because, you know, you're an anthropologist. You know it best, this basic feeling of people to join and work on their ideas together. So that will always be the role of student organizations, no matter how different they are. They gather people who have same ideas and who want to change similar things.

Danica's vision is notable for its lack of teleology. Rather, as her comments here have shown, she presented student organizations in the post-Milošević era within the framework of the present—not without goals, but nonetheless oriented toward relations of solidarity in the moment of coming together. The work of student politics has shifted temporalities; it is still perhaps oriented toward a future, but one that is more uncertain because its goals could only be worked out in open-ended and contingent ways. Student organizations in the end became a place to produce affective connections, a "basic feeling." There is something about Danica's vision of sociality that is fundamentally tied to the experience of negotiating manifold and conflicting roles, as students did in the 1990s and after 2000. It is a form of sociality, again in Mead's (2002, 75) words, that is "the capacity of being several things at once." Danica's comments demonstrate how some student activists try to think against and beyond the space of youth politics as it had been configured in Yugoslav and Serbian history. For them, the future-oriented temporality of change that had defined the Yugoslav socialist revolutionary project and the idea of revolution more generally actually worked against political agency. A politics of disappointment was thus a rhetorical strategy but also an approach to navigating and representing the meaning of student activists' actions.[12] Indeed, a politics of disappointment is the ability to negotiate being several things at once. The character of a present-focused politics of disappointment is perhaps the opposite of revolutionary time.

How, then, does one get out of the trap of failed youth revolution and the cycles of generational betrayal? How does a generation move forward when it feels abandoned by an older generation stuck in the past? And how did this pragmatism, this combination of hope and disappointment, translate into agendas for student organizing? If the practices of student activists are any clue, this process requires taking a certain kind of critical distance in order to sidestep the expectations and disappointments that I have discussed through the chapter. Of course, critical distance is enabled by assumptions and frameworks that are no less historically situated and ideologically charged. For example, as I discuss throughout this book, many students turned to ideas like responsibility, expertise, procedure, and reform as an alternative way to frame their political interventions. I subject these tropes to critical analysis in later chapters.[13] For now, I want to consider the productive aspects of these ways of imagining politics. They open up ways of understanding democratic engagement different from the future-oriented teleology of youth revolutionary action. Expertise, professionalism, and institutionalization were narrative and practical strategies through which student activists reconfigured a political field of action outside the logics of failed expectations and totalizing revolutionary transformation.

The combination of sober assessment and action in the present—along with the frustration it inspired in observers—prompted me to rethink narratives of disappointment in Serbia after 2000 not as endings but as possible beginnings for political engagement. If disappointment emerges from the gap between expectations of political and social transformation and the complexities of social change over time, then a politics of disappointment is a form of engagement that incorporates the contradictions, uncertainties, and impossibilities of social change into the very model of action itself. Disappointment, like Hirokazu Miyazaki's (2004) "method of hope," is a particular stance toward the present that opens up a space for future action, without committing that present to the burden of necessity. Such an affective politics of disappointment is not grounded in an internal (and thus unknowable) psychic state. Rather, it is a kind of historicity, a socially mediated stance on action, agency, and political possibility that rejects the ideal of the future (or the past) for the compromises of the present.

2

Embodying Citizenship
The Changing Politics of Protest

ON FEBRUARY 11, 2003—roughly three years after the democratic revolution of 2000—around fifty student protesters gathered at the main intersection in front of the University of Novi Sad. It was a bitterly cold day, and the wind coming off the Danube kicked up clouds of snow that had settled on campus. I headed over to meet with the protest organizers in their drafty Student Union office, which was tucked away in a campus courtyard between a concrete soccer field and a tavern. They had already set up a table, speakers, and DJ equipment at one of the main entrances to the university, just across from the intersection where the protest and press conference would be held. I joined a small team armed with flyers and set out for the site. The flyers listed the names of several sponsoring organizations that called students to a "quality protest" (*kvalitetni protest*). The flyer went on to say:

Why are credit and stipends late?

Why does the student center not have money to feed students?

Why are professors paid from student tuition?

LET'S IMPROVE THE STANDARD OF LIFE AT THE UNIVERSITY

Below this, the flyer listed the time and place of the event. The protest, organized by Student Union of Novi Sad, was meant to draw attention to the fact the provincial-level education ministry had failed to provide funds for professors' salaries and students' stipends and credit. With the Serbian state- and provincial-level governments in ever-increasing fiscal trouble, payments to the university were frequently in arrears. Leaders of

Student Union had identified this as an important advocacy issue. The protest would both draw attention to students' immediate needs and highlight the state's responsibilities to the university and its "student citizens" (*gradani studenti*).

Passersby took the flyers we were handing out, but few stopped to learn more or stay for the event. At about 1:20, the protesters convened a press conference to present student demands. By then it was clear that that the majority of the attendees were members of Student Union or other co-organizing groups. There were fewer than a hundred people in attendance, standing in groups, bundled against the snow and cold. At two o'clock the organizers announced the beginning of the protest, and people filed slowly and uncertainly into the street. Protesters blocked only part of the street, and impatient drivers slowed to navigate their way through the group. For student activists who were always hyperattentive to planning and detail, I was surprised at the small smattering of signs, the lack of noise and chanting, and the anemic attempts to rally support from passersby. Although one of the organizers told me she was hoping to provoke a response among those driving by, the halfhearted blockade did not seem designed for an immediate audience. Indeed, other organizers told me that the media was the intended audience for the protest. In contrast to earlier student protests in the 1990s in which the goal was to gather bodies to claim public space, this event was meant to claim space in the pages of newspapers.

The student activists who organized the quality protest had come of age in a period of frequent street actions. But the difference between the "quality protest" and tales I had heard of past events—with their masses of young people in the street, noise, and energy—was striking. Students had long used protests as embodied performances of specific kinds of citizenship. In a context in which an authoritarian state had tight control over public space, unruly bodies on the street were a clear mark of resistance to the regime. They were also a hard-to-ignore counterargument to the Milošević regime's claim to represent the interests of the Serbian people. The shift in the relationship among citizens, state, and protest practices necessitated the kinds of pragmatic approaches to democratic activism that I laid out in Chapter 1. In the shadow of the expectations students had helped produce for mass democratic protest, activists had to try to forge new ways to publically enact democratic rights. These newer protest forms were often disappointing to student organizers and observers. At the same time, student groups were reluctant to abandon protest as a strategy altogether. Activists experimented with ways to establish themselves as democratically representative without a mass of participants.

But in the newly democratic context, it wasn't entirely clear to whom protest was addressed. Nor was it clear what (or whom) small groups of protesters were supposed to represent. Given new spaces for the enactment of democracy—from the voting booth to the pages of newspapers—the meaning of street protest seemed destined to change. After 2000, students and others began experimenting with what democratic representation could and should look like. These experiments produced protests that were indicative of a changing relationship of public space, state-citizen relations, and mass politics. The "quality protest" was an attempt to fit protest practices into a new democratic and neoliberalizing context and in opposition to a long history of Serbian populism. It was part of a larger ongoing experiment to reconfigure the meaning of activism in relationship to an idealized past and an open-ended present.

Protest and Representation

As Serbia's largest independent student organization, Student Union activists had been experimenting with the nature, form, and practices of democratic representation since the mid-1990s. As did Otpor, Student Union became a national student movement after the 1996–97 protests, although it had an earlier presence in individual university departments across the four major universities in Serbia. Many of the older members of the group had come of age as members of Otpor and in participating in mass protests, including those in 2000.

By 2003, the group had a complex system of representation. In my encounters with a range of members of student groups, I heard countless discussions about how to make their groups representative, how to conduct elections, and how the structure and function of organizations could best reflect the needs of the student body these groups were supposed to represent. Student Union held local-level elections, as well as elections for a national executive board (*izvršni odbor*) and an oversight board (*nadzorni odbor*), all of which met at a semiannual congress (*skupština*). Being "democratically representative" was also one of the requirements for admission to the European Association of Student Unions, the largest association of student organizations in Europe. Student Union leadership prided itself on having met the criteria for membership.

It was thus striking that students so deeply committed to democratic practice and being representative saw a "quality" protest, with its exclusionary implications, as an ideal form of democratic participation. I found it curious that students had come to understand their relationship to state institutions as newly channeled through nodes of mass mediated publicity, whereas only a few years before, mass public protest in the streets was the preferred mode of appeal and resistance to an authoritarian state. The shift from mass protest to protests of specific kinds of citizens signaled the rise of new repertoires of representation. The anti-Milošević movement had brought very different groups of people together across the social, political, and generational spectrum for one common goal: the overthrow of Milošević. October 2000 ushered in new arenas and practices for representing the interests and needs of citizens. In the new democratic context, formal electoral institutions channeled citizen will, and the state became accessible through formal institutional appeal. What could it mean, for example, to demonstrate against elected officials that protesters were overwhelmingly responsible for electing to public office?[1]

The quality protest was part of a set of larger shifts and debates in Serbia about where politics could and should take place, who should be involved, and at what levels of inclusion. It also emerged with the rise of a multiparty political system in which electoral processes played on ideological and social distinctions. Despite the range of diverse political and ideological commitments in socialist Yugoslavia, the existence of a one-party state did not leave much room for such distinctions to be publically enacted or expressed through the formal political system. With the rise of the multiparty system, political affiliation offered a way to talk about and represent social differences. These included class, education, and urban and rural belonging. Social difference was also signaled through one's stance on a range of issues, from the extradition of indicted war criminals to The Hague to civil liberties and Serbia's possible accession to the European Union.

It should thus not be a surprise that mass protest also gave way to new vocabularies of differentiated citizenship. In the 1990s students tried to take back public spaces controlled by state forces and institutions and to counter the regime's claims that it democratically represented the will of Serbian citizens. Mass protests in the streets hinged on who was going to control public space—"the state" or "the people"—and in turn, whether Milošević's rule really represented popular will. After 2000, students grappled with the problem of where protest should take place in a democracy and how they should position themselves as deserving of entitlements, even as the state was pulling back from public institutions. The object of struggle was not whether the state would be a representative democracy, as in the 1990s, but which kinds of citizens would be represented. The significance of protest shifted from a performance of "the people," in which masses of bodies on the street were an icon of mass citizen will, to an argument about why certain citizens (and not others) should receive entitlements and political representation in the context of state withdrawal and fiscal crisis. The questions students and others faced were, how, where, and for whom should such performances of citizenship take place?

Bodies in Public Space

The quality protest was emblematic of changing, but not wholly novel, ways in which state-citizen relations were enacted in public space. There is a long-standing link between citizenship and public space in Yugoslavia. This history sets the stage for understanding why students might frame an exclusionary form of protest as a mode of democratic participation and representation after 2000.

Protest practices drew on spatialized forms of state power and political resistance in Yugoslavia. By "spatialized forms" I mean the material impact of state policies on the built environment. This includes such things as the use of architecture both to symbolize modernist ideology and to reorganize social relations, decisions to fund (or defund) public institutions and services that affected how people moved through the city, housing policies that changed the physical landscape of urban areas and affected intimate familial relations, and the decentralization of administrative authority through localized forms of town and city governance (Ferguson and Gupta 2002; Holston 1989). By "spatialization" I also mean how people understood state power through their embodied experience of moving through the spaces these practices produced.

Several aspects of Yugoslav state policy and practice established urban space as a site through which state-citizen relations were defined and contested. As in other socialist contexts, urban versus rural belonging took on intense ideological and social significance in defining a particularly socialist modernity (Fehervary 2011). The rapid urbanization of postwar socialist Yugoslavia was accompanied by a civilizing narrative that posited rural areas as backward and traditional and cities as the site of utopian and modernist futures.[2] While some nationalist writers and thinkers celebrated folk and countryside and decried the moral degeneration of urban (socialist or bourgeois) contexts, the notion of the modern, socialist, and revolutionary citizen was decidedly urban (Yeoman 2006; Dragović-Soso 2002). Political ideology and social class were thus inscribed through geographical metaphors that mapped "who" people were to particular places (Bakić-Hayden and Hayden 1992; see also Green 2005; Razsa and Lindstrom 2004). Promulgated at the level of official state ideology and policy, these categories also circulated powerfully in everyday, material ways (Spasić 2006; Jansen 2005; Van de Port 1998; Simić 1973).

The relationship between socialist state power and the institutional configuration of urban space took many forms. In the immediate postwar era, the state's central role in urban policy and planning was to "translate national economic goals into spatial terms at the local level" (Hirt 2009, 296). In later periods, the Yugoslav state's unique system of worker self-management spatialized the relationship of labor, social entitlements, and political power through a system of localized and decentralized municipalities or communes (*opštine*). Town and city administrative management thus reflected the ideological goals and administrative practicalities of decentralized state power (Woodward 1995; Carter 1982). State-socialist policies also affected postwar settlement through urban planning policy and housing development (Vujošević and Nedović-Budić 2006; Blagojević 2009, 278; Hirt 2009), as well as the extraction of resources from the countryside to support urban growth (Allcock 2000, 75). Urban architecture was a key site for the visual representation of particularly Yugoslav socialist ideals and the materialization of Yugoslavia's geopolitical position and ideological commitments (Bitter, Derksen, and Weber 2009).[3]

State power and urban space were intimately bound through administrative organization, ideologies of modernization, and socialist citizenship. Such policies transformed urban space into a theater for communicating and enacting socialist ideological and political commitments, both to citizens and to a larger global public. However, such spatially mediated communicative practices did not go uncontested. At several points in Yugoslavia's history, urban space became a battleground for defining "authentic" Yugoslav or socialist citizenship. Given that state-socialist policies often focused on material conditions, it is no surprise that critiques ?-socialist politics were framed as responses to the deterioration of those conditions. Such responses included student protests about the quality of student housing and general living conditions, particularly during the 1968 student protests in Belgrade (see Chapter 1). Insofar as signs of progress and modernity were often figured in material terms, it was through a critique of material form itself that students articulated their demands. These questions of living standards eventually paved the way for the protesting students to articulate more abstract concerns with the future of democratic participation in self-managing socialism.

The year 1968 set a significant precedent for the importance (and limitations) of mass student protest as a response to perceived gaps between state ideologies and everyday realities. Histories of protest and Yugoslav state and military responses established urban space as a theater for citizen resistance and ultimately as a site for the consolidation of state power over protesters. The protests also established scripts for protest, including blocking off or marching through streets and the takeover of key institutions associated with state power, such as the university. Albanian student protesters would take up these lessons in 1980 at the University of Priština, Kosovo, as would later protesters in the 1980s who were part of a movement known as the antibureaucratic revolution (Vladisavljević 2008).[4]

Protests in socialist Yugoslavia were thus responses to specific forms of "urban citizenship" (Zhang 2002, 313). Dominant socialist ideologies of revolution and modernization were configured through social and moral categories mapped onto place. In addition, material entitlements were mediated through spatial relations, whether the architectural landscape or concrete policies affecting the distribution of housing or investments in urban infrastructure. Urban spaces became sites of contestation because they were central to people's experience of the ways in which citizenship was embodied and state power was enacted.

Geographies of State Power During the Milošević Regime

If the city was a site of socialist promise, it quickly turned into a space of fear during the 1990s. Given Milošević's use of urban space to control or stifle potential dissent and destroy everyday forms of sociability (Gordy 1999), state repression itself became spatialized. Militarization, deterioration of urban space, and the rise of an elite mafia and criminal class with ties to the state reshaped how ordinary citizens moved through their cities. If earlier periods of protest were articulated in terms of self-managing socialism, then anti-Milošević protesters positioned themselves directly against the regime. Urban space had become a battleground.

Given the ties among socialism, internationalism, and urban elites, antiurban sentiment was central to emerging nationalist ideologies among politicians and intellectuals that repudiated the socialist past of the 1980s and 1990s (Gordy 1999, 12; Dragović-Soso 2002). This was particularly useful for Milošević, whose support was weakest among urban, educated Serbs (Gagnon 2004). In addition to his own staging of mass protests, Milošević targeted possible sites of urban resistance in an attempt to maintain the authority of his regime. Beginning in the late 1980s, Milošević staged a number of highly publicized "mass happenings," co-opting the earlier protests of the so-called antibureaucratic revolution through top-down strategies and rightest, nationalist discourse that pitted ethnically defined citizens against one another. These were highly staged and ritualized events in which Milošević whipped crowds of older (often rural) supporters into a frenzy with provocative nationalist rhetoric. In tapping into traditions of mass protest, he reversed a valorization of urban space in favor of rural sites and populations that served his ideological needs.

The 1990s saw additional forms of state power materialized in urban space, including increased control over media, police surveillance, and sometimes violent crackdowns on protesters. The built environment, especially in Belgrade, changed significantly in this period. The state's presence in urban space was signaled by the decay of the city itself, as valuable resources for public transportation and city infrastructure dwindled. At the same time, illegal construction, once a strategy for more marginal populations in the socialist era, became common among an emerging wealthy elite, which benefited directly from cronyism between state and private interests (Vujović and Petrović 2007, 363). If housing policy was central to urban development and the materialization of the socialist state's political commitments, then the chaotic, unregulated spurt of housing construction during the 1990s pointed to a very different relationship between state power and urban space. The urban landscape during the 1990s was most visibly marked by massive, unregulated, and frequently illegal construction, in large part to meet a crisis-level shortage in available and affordable housing (Vujović and Petrović 2007, 363). Although housing was initially privatized in 1992, cuts in public-sector funding for housing maintenance and production "meant that the existing stock began to visibly deteriorate and the number of dwellings built per year dramatically declined, leading to near-crisis conditions in large cities like Belgrade" (Hirt 2009, 298).

At the same time, a new elite took advantage of poor regulation of public space and infrastructure to build massive new homes in exclusive neighborhoods, often on public space and disregarding basic building codes (Hirt 2009, 298). These styles have been referred to as "turbo-architecture" (Hirt 2009) and "mafia baroque" (Hirt 2008b, 803), both of which link "turbo-folk" music; the values of the newly wealthy, pro-Milošević class; and criminalization of society to Belgrade's changing urban landscape. If housing and other material forms once represented a promise to all citizens, then the rise of spatially realized inequalities in urban centers signaled a new kind of privileged citizenship (Hirt 2008a). In addition, long-standing residents of Belgrade saw these "peasant" elites as dominating the cultural landscape. The kind of music played in bars, the presence of luxury cars on the streets in a time of rising poverty, and the presence of young women dressed provocatively in the style of turbo-folk (a pop-folk style associated with Serbian nationalism) became markers of how the social and political landscape of the city was changing. The city became a battleground for which kinds of citizens (with which kinds of values) had "the right to urban space—the right to 'be there' in the city" (Zhang 2002, 316).

In addition, the regime challenged citizens' relationship to urban space in more everyday ways. The sociologist Eric Gordy (1999, 2) has argued that Serbia in the 1990s was defined by a battle of "state against society," which was produced through "conflicts between the regime and citizens wanting to expand political space, broaden cultural space, or simply live ordinary lives." In examining why Milošević was able to hold on to power despite a string of military defeats, international isolation, and tremendous decline in the standard of living, Gordy (1999, 7) argues that the regime operated through "the destruction of alternatives" and the "production of habituation, resignation, and apathy." Critical to this process was the regime's direct and indirect attack on the everyday practices by which people navigated their world.

This was particularly true during the period of hyperinflation in 1992–93. Activities such as grocery shopping, cooking, and bathing were compromised by general scarcity, massive power shortages, and a currency that lost value hourly. The emotional turmoil and fear that characterized this period for many urban, educated Serbs also meant a withdrawal from public engagement. Gordy (1999, 103) notes that many people felt that, "short of leaving the country, their best option was to withdraw into private life and pleasure and to act as though the alternatives not available to them in the public sphere could somehow be compensated for by free enjoyment in the private sphere."[5]

Even the regime's extensive control over media took on geography, especially in cities where alternatives were available. Radio Television Serbia was the only television channel available across the country, and it was difficult to find alternative newspapers outside of urban areas. However, some alternative sources were available in cities, especially Belgrade (Cohen 2001). The search for alternative sources of information required knowledge, both of the social networks and of the political geography of a city (where, for instance, could one actually buy an antiregime paper (Gordy 1999, 97)? Networks of "alternative voices," including antiwar activists, feminist groups, and student groups provided ways to navigate the city socially as well as politically (Fridman 2006).

This consolidation of power through formal institutions made challenging Milošević's hold on power both difficult and dangerous. His tight rein on organs of state—from special ops police to the courts and the parliament—meant that official institutions were unavailable as sites of appeal. Milošević's policies of supporting paramilitary organizations, often with ties to mafia elites and war profiteers, meant that the Serbian state not only tolerated but also enabled illegal practices like smuggling and extrastate violence.[6] With corrupt political institutions and an arbitrary system of justice, relations of power were murky and contributed to the sense that power was everywhere and nowhere at once.

According to the anthropologist Marko Živković (2001, 235), the arbitrary nature of state power produced a situation in which people found it difficult to "cognitively map" everyday life in the 1990s, thereby producing "poetic opacity" and bewilderment (see also Živković 1998). Živković's metaphor of opacity and the experience of hidden powers controlling and directing people's everyday lives are critical to understanding the emergence of mass street protest as a key political form in the 1990s. Street protests made clear what was opaque and rendered critique of the regime visible through movement across the very spaces in which mysterious powers seemed to operate. The criminalization of the state, an arbitrary justice system, and state-controlled media left citizens with no other place to   · ·ly appeal state policy. State power was understood, framed, and   n terms of movement and stasis in the city (see Jansen 2001).

Taking over public space could counter the effects of regime policies that produced geographies of constraint, fear, and uncertainty.

Mass protest thus emerged as a response to forms of power that included silencing, stasis, and opacity. It also emerged as a response to the ways in which citizens were forced (directly or indirectly) to move through urban space. In response, bodies in motion on the streets were loud, visible, and evidently quantifiable. The anthropologist Daniel Goldstein (2004, 19) argued in his work on protest in Bolivia that in the face of exclusion from state institutions, citizenship may take on a spectacular form: such "spectacular performance is interesting not merely because it is performed in public, but because spectacular events enable groups of people to establish themselves *as* a public, to define themselves as part of the public, or a as a special kind of public in a particular society." Similarly, in Serbia protest spectacles countered Milošević's monopoly on formal institutions and the effect those institutions had on people's daily lives. They also created a public that loudly and visibly challenged the regime's claim to speak for "the people."[7]

Protesters in the early 1990s tried to counter Milošević's claims to represent Serbia by framing a mass of bodies in the streets as a more authentic form of representation. These actions made sense in a context in which citizens understood the state to be materially present in urban space. Protests throughout the 1990s centered on key areas in Belgrade, including the central Republic Square (Trg Republike) and the area in front of the Philosophy Faculty at the University of Belgrade, also in the center of town. Rigged elections and parliamentary proceedings were countered with alternative forums for representation, such as student parliaments. For example, during the 1991 protests, students formed the Terazije Parliament, named for the part of city center in which they gathered. The student parliament served as both an actual and a symbolic counter to Milošević's control over formal political processes outside of explicitly regime-controlled spaces. By 2000, the strategy had become more explicit, and institutions of the state had literally come under attack. On October 5, 2000, protesters charged the parliament building and set fire to the building of Radio Television Serbia. The logic of alternative institutional space gave way to the destruction of the institutions most identified with Milošević's tight hold over the city and the state.

Another response to spatialized state power was the framing of mass bodies on the street as the true source of democracy in Serbia. This was

ʹ important in the 1996–97 protests that emerged in response to fraud on the part of the regime. The protests were characterized numbers of citizens walking, dancing, performing street theater, and playing music in public space. Protesters were highly visible and impossible to ignore as they moved through city streets and squares. Using signs and chants, protesters claimed that they were taking back their cities from a regime that had ignored the electoral will of the people. Stef Jansen (2001) has argued that the 1996–97 protests turned Belgrade into a "terrain of resistance" through the symbolic and material capture and reconfiguration of urban space. Student protesters used multiple forms of discursive and embodied communication—loud noise and music, walking in city streets, smells, signs, modes of dress—to target multiple audiences and to capture real and virtual spaces. The ways in which protesters resignified the spaces that they occupied served as a spatially mediated argument against the regime and for a particular vision of citizenship.

Bodies on the street also challenged the regime's political discourse by pitting a textually mediated message against the authenticity of embodied protest. The anthropologist Ivan Čolović (2002, 298) has argued that in 1996 and 1997, "the citizen who protests as a responsible and skeptical individual is also suspicious of communication through slogans, because it is a form of communication aimed at suggestiveness, at 'beguiling,' and is therefore characteristic of the language of political demagogy and advertising." Čolović (2002, 298) cites a number of signs that indicated refusal to play the game of political rhetoric, such as "It doesn't matter what it says here, what matters is what it's for," and "Have you come here to protest or to stare at the placard?" Such signs highlight the space between the empty signifier of political speech and the reality of protesting citizens on the street: a creative play with language to subvert the power of speech itself. The signs argued that bodies meant more, and signified more transparently, than words. Words were corruptible, able to be manipulated, and subject to reframing in ways that bodies on streets were not.

Of course, the specificities of the bodies also mattered in ensuring that embodied signification was truer than texts or words. Embodied protest as opposed to disembodied state discourse in the media was central to the logic and meaning of resistance. Many have argued that the period 1996–97 was more directly "civic" in character because of the makeup of protesters, and the focus on elections (Lazić 1999). The civic nature of the protests was as much about embodied performance as it was about the specific ideological commitments and proelection rhetoric of protesters. Protesters were largely urban, drawn from the ranks of educated, professional families (the would-be middle-class) and students.

The anti-Milošević student movement Otpor (which means "resistance") that emerged from the 1996–97 protests was particularly deft at expanding the base of those represented in and through embodied protest. A key element in the group's strategy was to reach beyond Belgrade to produce a sense of a nonelite, national movement. Otpor developed a widespread, networked organizational form in which it could mobilize activists across the country, thus taking back public spaces across Serbia. The use of graffiti, slogans, and symbols spray-painted on city streets and the walls of municipal offices left traces of the organization and helped to define both urban and rural spaces as Otpor territory. Such practices also helped to link small towns and rural spaces to the city, thereby undercutting regime attempts to drive wedges between different populations. This simple, effective use of space helped create a sense that Otpor was everywhere and nowhere— and therefore that it represented everyone. Otpor effectively challenged the regime's claims to represent citizens by countering centralized state power with a headless student movement, visibly present across the country and grounded in local communities. Otpor mobilized young people and created networks of activists who targeted their own neighborhoods and emphasized their local community ties. These young activists were both representatives of a broad-based movement and grounded in their communities.

As opposed to earlier protests, the 2000 revolution included a variety of differently embodied forms of citizenship. In addition to youthful energy, rock-and-roll music, and the cosmopolitan forms of dress of younger protesters, opposition members of the protest coalition included larger numbers of people from outside the major urban areas. Union activists and agricultural workers, rural and urban citizens, joined the protests, unifying a more diverse population through one single message: Milošević must go. The presence of nonurban, nonelite, and formally not "civic" protesters gave October 5, 2000, the character of a mass revolutionary event in which the people were embodied against the state in a theater of public resistance.

Protest Post–October 5

One June day less than a year after the revolution, I wandered over to Belgrade's Republic Square. I could hear the protesters before I saw them—a large crowd had gathered to protest Milošević's imminent extradition to the International Criminal Tribunal for the Former Yugoslavia at The Hague. Seeing an older crowd of Milošević supporters made the event feel like a throwback to the early years of the "mass happenings." But as the protesters began their long march to Dedinje, the suburb where Milošević was under house arrest, they pulled out whistles and began to blow at the top of their lungs. I had run into two young journalists and former student activists who were covering the event for a small, independent website. They pointed out the irony in the use of the whistles, a common feature of antiregime protests and a symbol of Otpor. It seemed that even Milošević supporters bore the legacy of the recent student movement.

If some symbols of protest lingered, the meaning of public protest was nonetheless changing in Serbia's new democracy. For one, there were no conditions that resulted in mass protest after October 5, 2000. Instead, specific kinds of citizens took to the streets, representing narrower sets of interests and voices: workers went on strike for better wages; small groups of feminist activists held vigils demanding accountability for Serbian war crimes; sports fans took to the streets, at times inciting violent riots that bled into xenophobia. While very different ideologically, none of these groups claimed to speak for the citizenry as a whole, and all of them struggled to make particular features of social belonging the relevant criteria for membership in a legitimate Serbian public.

Indeed, that same summer, I witnessed a potent sign of the emerging conflict over which citizens would control public space. After a decade of repressive nationalism, intensive homophobia and misogyny in official political discourse and media, gay and lesbian youth organized Belgrade's first gay pride parade. The protest ended in violence when waves of young men swept the central square and attacked protesters while police largely stood by. In addition to demonstrating the continued presence of nationalist forces, the protest was significant in another way: it signaled that identity-based groups were beginning to express themselves as citizens entitled to the recognition of difference (Greenberg 2006c).

The gay pride parade is the most evident example. But in the period following October 2000, taking to the streets became an act of claims making and an expression of discontent among distinct types of citizens: unemployed workers, frustrated students, human rights activists, and furious and xenophobic young men. The kinds of identities that could be collectively expressed in public protest were up for grabs as different groups fought for dwindling state resources and public recognition. It was becoming clear that Serbian state institutions—from the police to state social services—could not or would not protect or support all citizens.[8]

At the same time that protest practices shifted, so, too, did the spatialization of state power. Post-Milošević urban Serbia was being greatly reshaped by new economic and investment strategies, the pressures of a financially strapped state that was defunding public services, unregulated and often nontransparent privatization, rapid commercialization and deindustrialization, and massive corruption (Hirt 2009; Vujović and Petrović 2007; Vujošević and Nedović-Budić 2006). As in other contexts, the rapid commercialization of public space went hand in hand with the pullback of fiscally strapped state institutions that no longer addressed inequality through citizen entitlements and safety-net policies (Zhang 2002; Caldeira 2001). Policy makers, city officials, and investors saw Belgrade, as a postsocialist city, as "a terrain that need[ed] to be conquered, with demarcation lines now set by multinational capital. . . . [N]ew borders are put in place, e.g.[,] glitzy development versus dilapidation, gentrification versus depravation, depoliticization versus peripheralization, and desecularization versus public space" (Blagojević 2009, 133). The post-2000 Serbian city was also marked by new forms of spatialized inequality that pit citizens against one another, including elite housing blocks, gated communities, blocks of ethnically marginalized populations, and slums (Erić 2009, 147; Hirt 2008a, 2009). If the city was no longer the site for the production of socialist collectivity, where and how might one make public appeals to the state? If urban space was no longer considered wholly captured by an authoritarian state, where (and whom) should one resist?[9] The battle over who had the "right to the city" was no longer fought in terms of antiregime and proregime forces. It was a question of which citizens could use urban space and how, and how the state might mediate those rights (Mitchell 2003).

During this period, students continued to protest, mostly for lower tuition, educational reform, better material conditions, and changes to exam schedules and curricula. The question of whether to protest was a fraught one for student leaders. Many had come of age protesting with Otpor before and during the 2000 revolution. Memories of the excitement, thrill, and danger of October 5 were still fresh. And yet with a new focus on legal and institutional reform and ties to European student organizations, student leaders were pushing for a role in official decision-making processes. Many students were disillusioned with protest and relieved to have other channels for student activism.

For example, Marina, a member of Student Alliance (Savez Studenata) in Belgrade was fed up with the unruliness and unpredictability of protest. Student Alliance was less centrally organized than Student Union, and those I spoke to in the group often distinguished themselves by emphasizing their focus on the immediate and local needs of students within different departments. They tended to do better than Student Union in local elections, and they often combined rhetorics of reform with more immediate services like organizing student trips, discount cards, and dealing on a case-by-case basis with student complaints against faculty. At the same time, this often meant that different Student Alliance representatives were caught up in the kinds of issues that still provoked small, yearly student protest, such as tuition hikes and exam schedules.

With a sigh of exasperation, Marina narrated the yearly cycle: the university failed to set tuition policy until the last minute and then a handful of students, unhappy with rising costs, held protests. Marina told me, "It feels like we are in the *pijaca* [an open-air market where people might haggle over prices]." She told me she was not satisfied with bargaining: "We want to know in advance what tuition will cost. We don't want a reason to have to protest. We want to do something constructive, not to go on the streets and yell." She was concerned that protests were leading to bad habits among students: "We don't want all of that," she insisted. "There should be order on all levels. . . . We want to know the rules and that they will be the same in October [at the beginning of the school year]."

In the face of Serbia's many problems, Marina didn't "want to create protests but to create something constructive." She saw protests as part of a past chaotic order, an unregulated space—like open-air markets—in which formal rules did not apply and bargaining is the norm. Marina's comments are resonant with geographer Don Mitchell's (2003, 130) argument that "the central contradiction at the heart of public space is that it demands a certain disorder and unpredictability to function *as* a democratic public space, and yet democratic theory posits that a certain order and rationality are vital to the success of democratic discourse." For Marina, Serbia's development as a democracy meant that the bad habits and unruly behavior of protests should no longer be necessary. With institutions available as spaces for student advocacy, Marina saw less need, and more danger, in using public space.

At the same time, it was unclear who protests even represented, other than the groups narrowly defined by the issues at hand. It was also unclear which audiences they hailed. Groups like Otpor had been able to mobilize large sections of the population in protests against a specific regime. In turn, students became metonymic with citizen protests more generally. With the galvanizing force of the regime gone, students no longer stood for all citizens. Those who protested after the revolution were often seen as selfish, not serious, and particularistic. Protests over bread-and-butter issues, like tuition and exam periods, seemed petty compared to the revolutionary battles of the 1990s. Popular perceptions of student "innocence" were changing. One professor and former anti-Milošević activist at the University of Belgrade summed it up perfectly:

Life was very strange in these parts during the nineties. . . . And [there] was a very kind of sharp distinction between us and them. . . . Either you are for Milošević, or you are against [him]. And all kinds of petty details were neglected at that time. . . . Now we are starting to think of students as all kinds of different, various kinds of young people. . . . [T]he idea was . . . that things done by the students are somehow pure and somehow not ideologically tainted. . . . Now we are starting to think about students as individual, various subgroups. So in that respect they are not homogenous and they are not so influential anymore.

According to this analysis, protest in the streets no longer signaled a collective will—us against him—in which "all kinds of petty details were neglected." Faculty, other students, and the press frequently represented protests as unproductive, immature, and silly compared to the pre–October 5 efforts. For example, a newspaper article that appeared in October 2002 referred to yearly autumn student protests over exam requirements in what can be taken only in an ironic tone as a revolution or uprising (*bunt*) in October. The piece unfavorably compared October "revolutions" over exam requirements, admissions, and tuition fees with the democratic revolution of October 5, 2000. Another young teaching assistant from the University of Niš in southern Serbia complained to me that students lacked a "consciousness" (*svest*) about bigger issues. He said that in his time as a student in the 1990s, "they fought for Milošević's resignation rather than another October exam period."

Quality Versus Quantity Citizenship

The quality protest took place within this broader context of changing meanings of space and citizenship with the arrival of formal democracy.
Protests are highly effective ways to frame and communicate meanings
about such embodied practice because they allow people to forge visible
links between abstract concepts like democracy and actual democratic
practice. If "embodied space is the location where human experience and
consciousness take on material and spatial form," it is also where specificities of citizenship are concretized, and state-citizen relations are configured (Low and Lawrence-Zúñiga 2003, 2). Participants must literally
take a stand on who they are, what they want, and why they deserve it. In
turn, they must enact and concretize aspects of representation rather than
merely invoking abstract notions of democratic representation.[10] Student
protesters at the quality protest were drawing on a long tradition of taking
to the streets as a way to both enact and demand certain rights as citizens.
At the same time, they were trying to reconfigure the meaning of that protest according to new conditions, described previously.

Student leaders in Student Union knew that it was not likely that
the protest would draw a large number of protesters. Why, then, would
students plan to stage a public protest when they knew it would be small,
and potentially embarrassing for the group, and when they had other
means available to talk with officials? What other kinds of effects were
the students hoping to achieve in the performance of the quality protest?
In addition, why should the protest event include a blockade of a busy
intersection in front of the university campus? The University of Novi Sad
has a fairly large and open campus where the students also might have
staged their event. A panel discussion or other informative event like those
often hosted by the group would probably have received the same (small)
amount of press. And a blockade of a busy city street seemed like an odd
site for the protest, when the real target was administrators at the provincial level who were not directly or obviously represented by the intersection. Indeed, the headquarters of the provincial-level administration was
only a few blocks away and seemed like a more obvious site. How, then,
was the protest a particular act of communication for different audiences,
and under what conditions would it been seen as such?

The blocking of traffic was a technique that was highly resonant with
mass protests against Milošević, in which controlling the flow of movement

on the streets was a counterresponse to state security's attempt to control the movement of citizens. But it had less immediate relevance in the post-2000 period, other than to inconvenience the many taxi drivers who passed through the targeted intersection. A conversation I had that day with Danica, who helped organize the protest, points to some of the reasons the students decided to use city streets and block traffic. I had asked whether she thought taxi drivers would be particularly angry (although students had called the taxi companies to tell them to reroute during the protest). Danica's response was, "I hope so." She said that the point of the protest was that nobody cared. They were just being ignored as students, and the point was to piss people off or make people pay attention. Danica was framing her fellow citizens as an audience, which is an important part of a public emerging in relationship to protest performance. This audience was not in a position to influence province-level budgetary decisions, nor was it symbolic of the power of the provincial-level state. The ability to stop traffic was less likely to be perceived as a blow to a centralized and dominating state authority (as it once might have been) than as a site for raising awareness, both immediately and in the pages of the press.

I also asked her in a later conversation why they hadn't just approached the ministry directly to try to negotiate the disbursement of student funds. They were, after all, a student advocacy group, and so that tactic might also have been effective. Indeed, only a few days after the protest, Danica told me that the regional minister of student welfare was quite angry at her because she hadn't approached him privately to handle the matter. I asked if that would have been effective. Yes, she told me, it might have been. But then she paused and grinned impishly. She thought the protest was a good idea anyway. They could have gone to the ministry, she confessed, but the protest showed that they had some autonomy from the government. From her perspective, as an organizer of the protest, the event was necessary not only to publicize state failures but also to establish an independent space for students to make that appeal. For one, student organizers of the quality protest were thus both trying to demonstrate and signal an independent voice through the protest and having to contend with the changing institutional and ideological conditions of protesting in a democracy that they themselves had helped to usher in.

At the same time, the existing channels of communication to ministers and the like raised questions about whether protest was appropriate or necessary after the 2000 revolution and in the new democratic

The minister's irritation at the protest was grounded in specific expectations based on ongoing relationships that student groups had developed over the course of their advocacy, as well as through personal ties. But it also touched on a deeper issue about how certain kinds of political action, and protest in particular, come to be understood as appropriate or inappropriate in newly democratic contexts. In the process, the students were trying to control the meaning of their bodies in space by framing the significance of the protest for very different audiences, including government officials, students and other student groups, and a wider public. The protest thus had to signal different things to different people in order to be effective as a performance of autonomy, as evidence that student groups were serving the needs of their student constituents, and as an event worthy of public attention and media coverage.

At the same time, the student organizers were concerned about the small number of protesters and the impression it might give that they lacked support from the general student body. In talking to the press, the organizers made a number of comments in an attempt to forestall this criticism. They must have anticipated the small turnout because the language of the quality protest was already in place in the flyers for the event. Having defined the event as one of quality, the representatives from Student Union could argue that their event was a de facto success, not despite the low turnout but because of it.

For example, the group's public relations officer, Ana—who later expressed to me real irritation at how many questions journalists asked about low attendance—explicitly framed the protest as one of quality and not quantity. In one interview with the daily paper *Glas Javnosti*, she said:

Perhaps it seems that the turnout wasn't big, but we in fact planned that the protest not be massive but that only representatives of all student organizations, deans, professors, representatives of the rectorate, and representatives of the student center [would] come out for it, which is what happened, and so it's possible to say the protest was a total success (*pa se može reći da je protest u potpunosti uspeo*).

Ana makes it very clear that Student Union defined the success of the protest as a small, quality affair, in which representatives of student organizations, faculty, and administration came to stand in metonymically for the large crowd of student-citizens usually associated with public protest in Serbia. Ana made several references to representatives as the key figures in the protest performance. In turn, those who were not present were unable to either stand in for constituents or perform the role of student representative. Indeed, Ana added, "the only ones not to respond to the protest were representatives of Student Alliance."

The invocation of Student Union's rival student organization on campus was a well-placed and targeted critique.[11] As student organizations shifted their focus from the streets to campus and the project of democracy, they began to compete for votes in elections. In the process, they often tried to publically represent themselves as the most democratic or most representative groups on campus, and they also increasingly differentiated their agendas, methods, and "brands" one from the other. Student Union members often dismissed Student Alliance as being populist, pandering to the masses, and lacking the necessary expertise to deal with complex issues of higher education reform. Alliance members accused Student Union of being overly politicized and elitist. Both organizations claimed to be the "most" representative of students' needs and interests. Different groups mobilized different kinds of rhetoric and produced different kinds of evidence to support their claims. In this case, Student Union's need to perform autonomy was part of taking control over commonly circulating narratives in which group members were represented as overly political and elitist.

These groups were thus trying to produce material evidence to make certain kinds of self-representations persuasive to audiences that included members of their own and other organizations, professors and administrators, the media, and other students. For Student Alliance to have shown up and swelled the numbers of protesters would have played into Student Union's ability to argue that the number of participants was evidence of the group's general support among the student body. Had they informed Student Alliance of the protest and built a coalition that would have brought more bodies to the streets, the protest might have attracted enough participants to give it the feel of a mass protest. In contrast, entering into coalition with its rival group would have undercut the careful work that Student Union had done to differentiate itself from Student Alliance. The logic of differentiation was, of course, the logic of a competitive election market, in which Student Union and Student Alliance competed for membership, scarce resources from the administration, office space, and the ability to claim "real" representation of student voices in faculty and administrative councils. Such competition, when translated into actual embodied performance, looked like a small, underattended protest. Given the lack of participants, Student Union had to find other ways to frame the protest as meaningful and representative of students' interests. It was in part this that prompted them to frame the protest as one of quality and not quantity.

Danica, as president of Student Union of Novi Sad, also explicitly defined the success of the protest in terms of a low turnout. But she directly contrasted the "quality" protest with the mass protest in an attempt to distinguish Student Union's efforts from other mass protests. She told a reporter from the paper *Dnevnik*:

Professors and students are gathering together for the first time in a struggle for their right to survival, and not to depose the government. For the first time students are not looking for additional exam periods or to decrease educational requirements. . . . We don't want to go out as a mass [*masovnost*], because we conceptualized all of this as a performance in order to animate the *academic* public [*Neće se ići na masovnost, jer je sve osmišljeno kao performans da bi se animirala akademska javnost*], and a statement of protest to initiate a new relationship with those responsible to the university and its students.

The reframing of the protest as quality was in part a strategic negotiation of everyday social realities of student organizing in postrevolutionary Serbia. The success of a quality protest requires only the presence of the leadership, which has real advantages in a context in which students are decreasingly interested in political engagement. Practically speaking, no student organization could compete with the sheer numbers of previous student protests. Rather, as Danica proposed, student representatives stood in for the general student population. In this scenario, representatives, not students in general, were responsible political actors, redefining the criteria for legitimate democratic mobilization. The relationship being modeled in the protest was not one of all citizens to a government that they held accountable. It was between a handful of student representatives trying to hold a state institution "responsible to the university and its students." In turn, the fate of the students was made to stand in for Serbia's own European future.

Both Ana and Danica emphasized quality over quantity and argued that mass presence was no longer the definition of successful political protest. Both women argued that the kinds of democratic mass protests of the 1990s aimed at deposing government were no longer relevant ways to organize citizen action. Danica also went out of her way to distinguish this kind of non–mass protest from the masses of unsatisfied students who gathered each fall at the beginning of the academic year to demand new exam schedules, reduced tuition fees, and an easing of academic requirements.

In the post–October 5 context, student protest had become suspect, particularly in comparison to the anti-Milošević movement. In this context, Student Union was able to frame its protest as successful for *not* representing what the mass of students wanted but for showing that its members, as representatives, could channel their authority into a quality protest. Student Union representatives also distanced themselves from the student masses by stripping their protest of the more obvious signs of youth protests from an earlier era. They relied on small numbers, they began with a press conference laying out their reasons for the protest, and they eschewed the colorful and confrontational style of previous protests. In so doing, the protesters tried to redefine the link between youth and politics through a new set of performance tactics and discursive frames. Indeed, this redefinition was particularly critical for Student Union. The carnivalesque and youthful energy of earlier protests sat in uneasy tension with the self-presentation Student Union mobilized to gain access to sites of decision making in the postrevolutionary period, when student activists tried to perform political maturity through the language of expertise. To this extent, the small, somber, and rather boring nature of the quality protest might be seen as political spectacle all grown up. It marked Student Union as representative of youth constituents but not necessarily like them. The use of protest thus signaled a break with former protests as much as continuity with previous uses of public space.

Similarly, if earlier protesters argued that youth in general were central to the democratic future of the state and the Serbian nation, the adjective *quality* points to a more exclusive subset of young citizens as the basis of this future. Indeed, the quality protest implied that not all student constituents were worthy of having a voice in an emerging democratic public sphere. What mattered was not how many students showed up but which ones.

So who exactly was a quality citizen, and why did a handful of them matter more than the democratic mass of students in general? During the initial press conference, the student representative at the university level, Boban, opened by saying, "Although Novi Sadians are valued as peaceful people, we aren't stupid and we have been compelled to react." Novi Sad is the capital of the Vojvodina region, which is associated in Serbia with not only greater economic prosperity and political stability but also greater civility and Europeanness than central and southern parts of the country. By referencing the peaceful nature of Novi Sadians and locating the protest specifically in Novi Sad, Boban drew on cultural and political associations, as well as narratives of civilization and backwardness that have been mapped onto Serbian regional identity. Indeed, on both the regional and the national stage, politicians from Vojvodina have frequently pointed to the multicultural demographics of the region, as well as its strong anti-Milošević base in the 1990s.

Boban was also responding to a darker genealogy in the history of democratic mass protest. Otpor used the "youth" idiom and calls for democratic change to distinguish itself from regime-sponsored, nationalist, populist protests. However, Otpor leaders and key opposition politicians used flexible repertoires to appeal to national and nationalist sentiment within the context of the prodemocracy movement. Reasons for an anti-Milošević stance varied widely, from a commitment to liberal democratic or progressive leftist politics to a nationalist desire to defend Serbia from further humiliation and territorial loss. The opposition and protest movements exploited the ambiguity of the anti-Milošević agenda as a key aspect of coalition building.

For this reason, many student activists with progressive leanings, like those in Student Union's Novi Sad leadership, expressed anxiety about their former ties to Otpor. Several whom I spoke with recalled that it was not uncommon to be marching side by side in protest against Milošević with young men holding aloft Serbian Orthodox religious icons (which have come to stand in for right-wing nationalist sentiment). Student Union leaders' discomfort with Otpor increased after October 5, when Otpor came out with a new national platform as a people's movement, with a more explicitly nationalist bent. Indeed, Otpor's membership rate, especially among young student progressives, dropped drastically at that point.

The ability to distinguish who was democratic and who was not in the context of mass protest was a source of anxiety more generally for progressive activists who knew that the anti-Milošević cause was enabled by their uncomfortable alliance with nationalist politicians and right-leaning citizens. This anxiety came across clearly in an interview I undertook with a leading member of a civil society nongovernmental organization in Belgrade. In addition to being a respected intellectual, trained as a sociologist, Rada ran a prominent civil society organization in Belgrade until about 2005. In an interview in which we were discussing the role of the middle class in Serbian civil society, she argued that the urban middle class had an inherently civic nature that was expressed in the protests of 1996 and 1997 after a period of dormancy in the early 1990s. She told me that after years of rapid impoverishment in the early 1990s, the protests made it clear that the middle class "still existed." She said, "In 1996, in the seventy-eight days of a democratic movement, suddenly you saw that they existed. The way they behaved, the way they looked, how they are dressed, everything. . . . [It] was suddenly clear that the middle class was there." In comparison, Rada distinguished this from a non-middle-class, and by extension, a noncivic basis, for the 2000 revolution:

In 2000, again the citizens forced the political opposition to unite in order to beat Milošević. . . . The public sent one single message: we will stand behind you, if you unite, and forget your differences. . . . [But 1996 and 1997 were] not October 2000. October 2000 was a kind of a revolution. You had the soccer fans, and you had all those people who you would not necessarily like to go to have coffee with. Of course, without them you cannot overthrow a regime.

Over the course of our conversation, Rada drew a distinction between civic mass protest and the transformative revolutionary protest of 2000 that relied on nondemocratic actors. In her analysis of the difference between the protests of 1996 and 1997 and the events of 2000, Rada defined non-middle-class actors as uncivil. She specifically cited soccer fans as standing in for people with radical and nationalist politics (Serbian soccer clubs were strongly linked to nationalist politics, and their fans were also linked to paramilitary organizations in Bosnia) and "people who you would not necessarily like to go to have coffee with."

The question for progressive, urbane, and middle-class people like Rada and the key leaders in Student Union at the time of the quality protest was how to reclaim the foundational democratic legacy of the 2000 revolution and yet excise the ties to nationalist belonging and violence at the heart of that legacy. The 2000 revolution was a moment of foundational political compromise in which nationalist "kinds of people" and imagery were essential to the production of a mass democratic form: the citizen protest.

Like the language of civil society, or class belonging, students used the language of "quality citizen" to draw distinctions among students who were democratic citizens and those who were not. By establishing the particularly democratic capacity of the quality citizen, student leaders underlined the importance and value of an urbane, educated elite for Serbia's future. In turn, the idea of a quality protest of quality people had greater rhetorical force because the protesters mobilized an implicit threat: if their demands weren't met, they would simply leave the country for a "real" European nation. As anthropologist Ildiko Erdei (2010) has argued, discourses of free movement (out of the country) are fundamentally connected to young Serbs' experiences of freedom more broadly, which makes the threat of brain drain a recognizable intervention into debates about Serbia's imagined political future. The protesters tried to stoke fear of brain drain, or university students whose departure would threaten Serbia's access to a civilized, European future. One of the few signs that students held during the protest read, "I'm leaving from here" (*Ja odoh odavde*), meaning from Serbia (Umičević 2003). One student leader told the press, "The Ministry of Education must realize at once that this country needs students, intellectuals, assistants and professors, and that the brain drain has got to stop" (Umičević 2003). As Danica told a reporter:

Our environment must change from its core, or brain drain, the marginalization of the university and neglected student dormitories will remain our reality. A society that wants to advance into the twenty-first century must invest in education, because knowledge is the most valuable resource of the modern age, or the beginning of transition toward a European system of education . . . [will] remain a distant dream.

Danica invoked a European temporality, positioning Serbia on a time line toward progress—"a distant dream." This time line justifies the demands of those students who already knew how to be properly European. As it turns out, the quality citizen emerges from a differential scale of value. The quality protest is a performance, as well as justification of, that exclusivity. Not only did the protesters represent "representation" rather than mass democratic will; their behavior, their mode of dress, their comportment, and their education represent an idealized performance of postrevolutionary democratic citizenship. In Rada's words, "The way they behaved, the way they looked, how they are dressed, everything"—these are the citizens you'd want to have coffee with and who you'd want to run the country. For the students, the embodied nature of protest became a critical strategic resource for reconfiguring the meaning of democratic citizenship in particular ways while positioning themselves as the rightful bearers of democracy more generally.

This task was all the more urgent because reform-minded student protesters weren't the only ones using public space as a site for protest. In mid-June 2003, a few months after the quality protest, riots broke out in Belgrade and Novi Sad after Serbia-Montenegro's national water-polo team defeated Croatia at the European Water Polo Championship. Large groups of young male fans ran through the streets of Belgrade and eventually attacked the Croatian embassy there. Sporting events, especially between former Yugoslav republics, were often tense events and opportunities for youth mobs, rumored to be supported and encouraged by nationalist political parties, to take to the streets.[12] In Novi Sad, young men ran through the center of town, screaming nationalist slogans and attacking and destroying public and commercial property. Among the objects of attack were Novi Sad's city hall, McDonald's, an ATM, a handful of stores, and a billboard advertising that year's Exit summer music festival.

The attack on the Exit festival's billboard was particularly telling. The Exit organizers had consciously crafted the festival as Serbia's entrée into global youth culture and cosmopolitanism. That year's festival slogan was "State of Exit," complete with a program designed to look like a passport and meant to encourage participants to feel like cosmopolitan "citizens of the idea of Exit," in the words one of the organizers who described the event to me.[13]

The June attack in downtown Novi Sad made clear that certain public spaces and commercial symbols continued to be significant terrain for contesting and performing ideological and social affiliations in Serbia. The students and university faculty with whom I discussed the attacks certainly read them this way. They attributed the targeting of the Exit billboard as a statement against the festival's internationalism and pro-Europe associations. Attacks on McDonald's and other multinational corporate chains are more commonly associated with a leftist, anticorporate, antiglobalization movement. That the festival billboard was an object of attack is an interesting and revealing clue to the reversals and unusual alignments between antiglobalization and rightist, nationalist politics in Serbia. Unlike the rise of populist and socialist movements in Latin America, in Eastern Europe it has largely been right-wing, nationalist political parties that have co-opted the language of social welfare against the encroachment of neo-liberal, global capital (see Kalb 2009; on the rise of nativist, antiglobalization rhetoric, see Holmes 2000).

The ties between a socialist welfare state and xenophobic nationalist agendas have placed those who identify as progressive in a complicated position. Positioning oneself as oriented toward "Europe" was a common way to distinguish oneself from nativist positions. Such alignments make critique of the European Union as a political project complicated. One can also trace the legacy of "civility" in the context of civil society activism playing out in the language of Europeanization. In this context, it becomes clear why students committed to democratic practice could embrace the trope of quality. The combination of protest and exclusion reveals the unlikely synergies between commitments to democratic representation and modes of policing the meanings of participation. As I discuss in Chapter 3, these associations also make it difficult to articulate an anti-neoliberal agenda when mandates for economic restructuring in the context of European integration are wedded to definitions of democratic participation that have emerged in response to nationalist forces.[14]

Conclusion

For all the thought and planning that the students put into their protest, it was not necessarily received in the way they had intended. The "quality" of those who attended was meant to serve as evidence that students were valuable citizens and should be listened to for that reason. And yet that same evidence could be mobilized and reframed easily using earlier understandings of what mass protest should look like. The comments of the rector of the University of Novi Sad were much more disturbing to the student organizers. The rector was extremely sympathetic to Student Union and worked with it directly on reform initiatives. She herself had a great deal invested in reinventing the university as a partner in European higher education reform, and she had done a great deal to promote the campus and its programs. Yet when asked publically to respond to the protest, the rector interpreted the protest through the commonly circulating lens of a tempest in a teapot. She told the local press:

That's their right and I don't have anything against it. It was a leisurely protest, without any intention of raising tensions. They did not have bombastic or revolutionary requests, but they wanted to show that salaries and stipends haven't arrived on time. I don't know that all their statements were one hundred percent accurate, but their observations were generally correct. I'm personally against blocking the intersection for a long time. At one point it was different, there was a revolution, but this is something else. Let them make waves a little and draw attention to something that's not functioning. [*Nekada je to bilo drugačije—bila je revolucija, a ovo je drugo. Neka malo zatalasaju i skrenu pažnju na to da nešto ne funkcioniše*].

Student Union stripped key elements of revolutionary protest from its quality protest to redefine the performance of student politics. Yet it was this process that allowed the rector to characterize the protest as small and inconsequential. The halfhearted blockade, the technical and limited demands—all played to common perceptions that students in the post-revolutionary period were using protest to make a fuss rather than to enact transformative social change. In this regard, Student Union failed to distinguish itself from the mass of students and their revolutions over exam requirements and tuition. The rector noted that the students had a right to protest, to be sure. Indeed, she even granted them the right to make waves a little, and to draw some attention to the issue. But her comparison of this small action as opposed to a revolution is a clear example of how postrevolutionary protest is judged in terms of an earlier student politics. It was also evidence of the fact that while students were able to play on their mythic associations with youth vanguardism and activism, they were also always subject to views that they were just kids, not to be taken too seriously.[15]

In the end, the small numbers of students on the streets that snowy day could not dispel the sense of disappointment in student politics after the revolution. Such protest performances made clear both problems in the new democratic Serbia and the fact that students were one kind of citizen competing in a crowded space in which other kinds of citizens also had rights.

Indeed, it was not taken for granted that other citizens would care about students' needs and concerns. Without the unifying goal of a strong anti-Milošević movement, students had long since ceased to stand in as vanguards representing a larger citizenry. Instead, they were viewed as a bunch of kids with specific needs and demands. When I asked a friend a few days later what he had thought of the protests, he commented, "Do you know how much a meal at the *menza* [student cafeteria] costs? Five dinars. What do they expect for that? They don't realize someone actually has to be out in the field doing work [for that food]." Thus, he framed students as one (already-privileged) group of citizens whose demands were different from and contrary to the interests of other groups (in this case, agricultural workers).

These seeming inconsistencies and paradoxes produced by the shifting and multiscale nature of political meaning is the terrain of both action and disappointment. Debates about the meaning of public student protest were fundamentally about what kinds of representation and citizen engagement were appropriate to Serbia's emerging democracy. Students drew on aspects of past political action even as they discredited the mass nature and youthful effervescence of the older street politics. Mass protest relied on the iconicity of the mass and the democratic will of all citizens. In contrast, the quality protest was an attempt to perform the representative relationship itself. In other words, the quality protest performed mediated democratic representation rather than mass democratic will. Categories of "mass" and "individual," "quality" and "quantity," were multivalent signs with which the students tried to strategically create spaces in which they could intervene as political agents. As one student described to me in explaining the difference between her group and Student Alliance, "They come out [to protests and events] as a mass; we come out as individuals." Finally, student protesters used discourses of quality versus quantity of the masses to claim that they were both representative of and outside of student constituencies. In this way, they justified their demands from the state as particular kinds of exceptional citizens.

3

Revolution and Reform
Citizenship and the Contradictions of Neoliberal University Reform

EARLY ONE EVENING IN BELGRADE IN 2008, I was out for dinner with two former student activists. Although they were still engaged in social activism, they had moved on to graduate school and a new stage in life. As we strolled down a cobblestone street on our way to one of the hip new restaurants that had sprouted up like mushrooms in the city, one of them began to complain about the administrative hoops he had to jump through at the university. I stopped in my tracks. "But that's all part of the Bologna Process," I objected. I was referring to the 1999 Declaration on European Higher Education reform that they had both worked to bring to Serbia in 2003. "It's what you guys were fighting for all those years," I said. My companions only laughed with characteristic good humor at the irony of the situation.

Three years later, I sat with another former student activist, Petar, sipping coffee at an outdoor café in town. It had been a few years since we had last seen each other, and I was surprised to see the streak of gray framing his otherwise-youthful face. We were also talking about graduate school, academic life, and the fate of the European university. Petar was no stranger to the Bologna regulations. He had been an expert on the European Credit Transfer and Accumulation System in his student group and a passionate advocate for reform. Now he was finishing a master's degree in education policy and applying to doctoral programs. He joked that he wished that two of his former activist colleagues (and still friends) had never been born, because they were instrumental to bringing Bologna to Serbia. Once again, I was struck by the irony. Only a few years earlier all these students had been defenders of EU-led higher education reform. They had seen it as the only path to Europeanizing and democratizing Serbia's university system specifically and the country more generally.

How did university reform go from being a rich site for imagining political transformation to a bureaucratic and administrative form of compulsion? Was this simply a misreading by students and other reform advocates at the time? Or does their story challenge our understanding of how and under which conditions scholars and activists experience politics as revolutionary or reformist, transformative or conservative, democratic or undemocratic? Such questions help us better understand why such binaries are never fixed in practice. Indeed, the meanings, and disappointments, of political activism lead to unanticipated consequences and alignments over time. The disappointment that these former activists later came to feel about the Bologna reforms was not born of an initial misrecognition about its implications for the university. Rather, it was the product of historical and contextual conditions in which a specific form of social activism made sense in response to a pressing set of local institutional relations.

After 2000, reformers in Serbia turned to the Bologna Process as a way to wield moral and political authority in a pitched battle over who would control the university's administrative resources and intellectual direction. The Bologna Process initiated the creation in 1999 of the Higher Education Area in Europe, which was intended to increase student mobility, rationalize higher education, and stimulate employment in Europe's lagging economy. In the intervening decade and a half, the Bologna Process has been the focus of intense critique across Europe (Shore and Wright 2000; Wright and Rabo 2010). Education reform has included massive cuts to higher education, the slashing of programs of study as part of a rationalization of education to fit bald market logics, and increasingly constrained labor conditions at European universities (see Wright and Rabo 2010).[1]

However, what these critiques often ignore is why the Bologna Process was once so compelling for students, professors, and policy makers, particularly at Europe's margins. As Cris Shore (2010) has argued, contradictory institutional arrangements and demands have produced a "schizophrenic" university in the era of neoliberalization. Higher education's project of producing citizens has been largely marketized, as universities have become engines for the new knowledge economy (Greenberg and Muehlebach 2007). In this context, students find themselves in a particularly difficult position.

I draw on expectations for the university as a space of "institutional redress" and social justice, and at the same time they want the university to provide a highly instrumentalized relationship to knowledge so that they can compete in changing labor markets (Oxlund 2010).

These "counter-tendencies" are critical to understanding the neoliberal university as a set of often-contradictory expectations and practices rooted in specific institutional contexts (Peck and Tickell 2002). The "schizophrenic" nature of higher education reform and the forms of critical activism and marketized desire that it invites, makes the university a particularly potent site for understanding how neoliberal frameworks come to be compelling to activists who have a range of political commitments. Indeed, as recent scholarship has shown, activists (and others) embrace neoliberal frameworks because they resonate with long-standing ethical, affective, and political sensibilities that might at first blush seem ideologically antithetical to market logics (Bockman 2011; Muehlebach 2012; Shever 2012; Song 2009). More than that, though, these critical contradictions help explain why the university has so long been a site of both student idealism and disappointment.

The current era of neoliberal higher education reform is one moment of many that reveals the more fundamental nature of the university as an institution shot through with contradictory social and institutional demands. The complexity of the university produces widely varying sets of social expectations, from discipline to education and employability. These are most frequently revealed in the contradictory roles that students take on. Although it is often taken for granted that universities are sites of political ferment, we less frequently interrogate why and how university-based politics is shaped by the institutional contours of the university.[2] As Serbian students moved from protesting against the state to working within a state-run, state-funded institution, their commitments to democracy persisted. But their ideas about what democracy entailed shifted in response to the institutional conditions. To this extent, the location of politics matters in understanding why and how certain frameworks seem well suited for articulating political commitments and goals.

The Desired University: Thinking Discipline and Popular Sovereignty Together

For advocates in Serbia, the compulsory nature of the Bologna Process was a powerful tool for challenging existing hierarchies in the university.

It was also a platform for articulating a vision of modern, European, democratic pedagogy and administration. Using administrative procedures backed by a set of binding, suprastate directives to force reforms in an institution still staffed with faculty who had been loyal to Milošević was not just a technocratic exercise. Many saw university reform as a continuation of the struggle against Milošević and his capture of Serbian state institutions. The earliest student protests had included calls for academic freedom and university autonomy, an issue that was tied up with the everyday experiences of students, from classrooms to dorms. Born of this struggle was a sense of students qua citizens that paved the way for later student activists' efforts to make the institution accountable to students by creating spaces for democratic participation.

At the same time that the university continued to be a space for popular resistance among students, many also came to see university reform as critical to creating conditions for a country in which they could live and work. These issues were all the more urgent given the difficult economic conditions after 2000. Students saw the Bologna Process as a way to create rules and regulatory regimes within an institution that could in turn make them into productive, functioning citizens and workers. The Bologna Process would ensure standardization of course workloads as well as evaluation and examination procedures. It would make the university more transparent by streamlining decision-making structures and by making clear legal statuses and lines of authority. Reform would also make pedagogy consistent across classrooms, eliminate opportunities for corruption, and regularize fee structures. In turn, students would become more mobile and employable, because their degrees would be recognizable in other European education and labor markets. This more normative project existed side by side with transformative political commitments to democratize the institution of the university. In both cases, the experience of citizenship was channeled through the university as the main state institution that structured students' aspirations and expectations.

In 2002, Student Union of Serbia's leaders compiled and issued a policy paper titled "What Kind of University Do We Want?" ("Kakav Univerzitet Želimo?").[3] The document synthesized Student Union's approach to higher education reform in Serbia and was exemplary of the group's policy recommendations and rhetoric in the period immediately after the October 5 revolution. Student Union's leadership wrote the document following the workshop "Take Off the Blindfold" (*Skini Povez*), which it organized with two hundred students at five universities in Serbia in December 2001. The resulting text dealt with education reforms and the university's relationship to social and economic development in Serbia. The authors advocated specific policies and programs, such as student and teacher evaluation, standardization of academic credits, anticorruption initiatives, and student participation in university administration. As the introduction to the document attests, the participants in the workshop "tried to present a vision of the university at which they would like to study and gave their proposals about how to go from the present state to the desired university" (*od sadašnjeg stanja do željenog univerziteta*).

The notion of the desired university drew together both transformative and normative approaches to citizenship that I discussed earlier. On the one hand, students used the language of university reform to call for increased participation in the university. Through tropes of choice, resistance, and critical thinking, they represented students as emerging citizens. It followed, then, that students ought to have a representative voice in the administrative and policy decisions that affected their lives. To this end, student activists drew on models of popular sovereignty and democratic participation to advocate for a unique role within university decision making.

On the other hand, student reformers demanded that university education and evaluation be standardized and objectified in order to produce consistent and systematic regimes of knowledge. They called for increased expertise in university administration. They promoted a managerial model for the university based on the European Union's higher education reform policies that had been codified in the Bologna Process. The policies centered on administrative procedures that would transform the university into an efficient mechanism of disciplinary power. The Bologna Process was designed to make students, professors, and administrators accountable to standardized procedures. Regulatory regimes were perceived as neutral because they exceeded the power of any particular group of actors. Bologna allowed for new approaches to pedagogy, codified standards for testing, a system of student evaluation, and standardized formulas for course credits (*bodovi*). This system, known as the European Credit Transfer System (ECTS), would turn courses into commensurate units of value that enabled student mobility across different European universities.

Students and other proreform advocates argued that such processes of evaluation and standardization would make Serbian students into particular kinds of subjects: mobile, employable, and attractive in wider European education and labor markets. To this extent, ECTS, and other Bologna reforms were quintessentially disciplinary. They produced intelligible subjects through the scrutiny of exams and the objectification of evaluation. Indeed, it is no coincidence that reform advocacy among student groups focused most intensively on policies of examination and evaluation. As Foucault (1995, 187) argues:

The examination is the technique by which power holds [subjects] in the mechanism of objectification. In this space of domination, disciplinary power manifests its potency, essentially, by arranging objects. The examination is, as it were, the ceremony of this objectification.

Within the disciplinary institution, subjects are produced through regimes of knowledge that classify and render subjects visible. In turn, these individualized subjects come to desire the "normalcy" that is the seductive promise of standardized calibration. The idea that "a pupil's 'offence' is not only a minor infraction, but also an inability to carry out his tasks," takes on a specific social meaning in this context (Foucault 1995, 178). At stake for students was their ability to be functioning and recognizable European subjects.

Students' demands for reform in Serbia, like their demands for the desired university, focused on mechanisms for "objective and constant evaluation" and the "establishment of scales of knowledge to enable objectivity in evaluation" (Student Union 2002). They also demanded "constant quality control." Such control, Student Union's policy paper argued, "must maximally protect students as individuals, and must be independent and objective." It was through such disciplinary techniques that students would be able to finally "carry out [their] tasks," in Foucault's words, after years of feeling like failed students, unable to graduate, unable to find employment, immobile in Serbia's borders. In other words, the university provided a space for enacting a particular model of citizen agency based on routinization, regulation, and standardization. In a context in which young people felt that the conditions for living a "normal" life were far outside of their control, the vision of agentive action was particularly appealing.[4]

Yet at the same time, many student activists felt that without their participation and expertise, such regulations would never be approved in university faculty and administrative councils. For one, students were often much more knowledgeable about the Bologna reforms than were many professors. In addition, the university remained a romanticized site of former 1968 protesters (many of whom were now professors) and anti-Milošević resistance, as well as an institution in which outside funders and observers had invested hope for expanding Serbia's democratic capacity. In calling for reform, students drew on their own active knowledge, the legacy of student protests, and the rhetoric of democratic participation. They argued that student voices should be represented in the faculty councils and ministry meetings.

These two strains of activism—regulatory regimes of discipline and objectification and participation grounded in models of protest and popular sovereignty—brought different understandings of citizenship and power into productive tension. Achieving the so-called desired university entailed unanticipated reversals in the trajectories of disciplinary power and subject formation. Although others have shown how tropes of participation often go hand in hand with new forms of neoliberal governance (Junge 2012; Leve 2001; Paley 2001), such analyses tend to elide what is compelling to local actors about becoming self-managing, self-regulating subjects. Rather than toss over one model of citizenship for the other, student activists embraced both. They reproduced the language of rights and decision making to facilitate the implementation of compulsive practices of evaluation to which they would be subject. They paradoxically used a politics of embodied protest and representation, grounded in logics of popular sovereignty and citizenship, to implement a politics of intelligibility through new regimes of governance. This would be enacted outside direct state control and through the university as a disciplinary institution.

As Student Union's policy paper demonstrates, it is precisely in the gap between being disciplined and participating in politicized matters of state intervention where students defined a new form of democratic and postsocialist citizen intervention. Those advocating for reform mobilized an entirely different model of active citizen engagement to create an institution through which they would become subjects of disciplinary forms of power. The emergence of disciplinarity in this case is not an inevitable historical process but an active project in the redefinition of Serbia as a democratic and European state. As such, forms of governmentality can paradoxically be the focus of intervention and activism, as well as of historically emergent effects of governmental forms of state power. Contrary to long-standing debates about why revolutionaries betray transformative agendas for reform tactics, it appears that Serbian student activists tried to embrace both simultaneously, if with unintended consequences.

The Contradictions of the University and the Contradictions of Citizenship

It is not surprising that the university was the place where student activists experimented with different kinds of citizenship regimes. The university is a state institution tasked with producing citizens who are critical thinkers and standardized, mobile workers whose skills have been pegged to new market logics.[5] This contradiction seems to parallel a more fundamental contradiction at the heart of modern citizenship: the dialectical relation of autonomy and self-regulation. Barry Hindess (1996) has argued this dialectic is central to liberal and neoliberal forms of citizenship and governance. It is particularly fascinating to examine this process in a postsocialist context, because the very contradictions of the university—to produce both critical revolutionaries and economically productive, self-managing subjects—were explicitly thematized as a unique form of political intervention by the socialist state.

As a key institution for Yugoslav ideological and state-building projects, the university crystallized both the many hopes and the many disappointments that people felt about the possible (and impossibly failed) modernist trajectory of their country. The socialist university was the site both for producing a new revolutionary generation and for redistributing the material and social benefits of the modernizing socialist state. It was thus a place for socialist experimentation and state control. In practice, it contributed to social advancement and to new hierarchies of political and elite power. Students engaged in practices of dissent even as they shored up state-citizen relations premised on citizen entitlements, as when they made demands for material resources. At the same time, university administrators were agents of direct and indirect state control. The university was thus a place of contradictions in which older social hierarchies were being upended and new forms of social value and expectations generated in the early years of postwar Yugoslav socialism.

The university as a space of ideological experimentation also reflected the Yugoslav state's careful balancing act of producing citizens who were active participants in decision making and nonetheless good citizen-subjects.[6] Ralph Pervan (1978) has referred to this foundational paradox as the problem of being "free and correct," although the paradox bears an interesting resemblance to how theorists of liberalism and neoliberalism have discussed the tension between autonomous subjects and naturalized social collectivities in the democratic liberal tradition.

In many ways, the socialist Yugoslav university concretized this paradox: it was an institution meant to produce modern subjects capable of actively and freely participating in the work of the self-managing socialist citizen, and yet it was also an institution tasked with educating and guiding students to be correct in their commitments to and interpretation of socialist principles. The university as a site of knowledge production took two seemingly contradictory forms. On the one hand, students learned to be correct through fundamentally hierarchical pedagogical techniques and surveillance—from the exam to soft surveillance by peers and faculty in order to determine their ideological correctness. On the other hand, students had, at least in theory, access to bodies of decision making through self-managing councils and the student organization itself, where they could express opinions as active and actively participating citizens and as youthful vanguards of the permanent revolution.

Ralph Pervan (1978, 12) has argued that students were central to how Yugoslavia negotiated this tension:

On the one hand it was stated that the basic associations of the Union of Students [here he is referring to the officially sanctioned socialist network of university students] were to be free to adapt their activities to suit the particular interests and needs of their members, because only in this way could there be a real involvement of the students and only in this way could they develop as responsible members of a self-managing community. At the same time, however, it was maintained that many of the young were immature and that there was a danger that they might fall under the influence of "hostile" forces; hence it was necessary to ensure that they developed in a "proper" climate.

Student leaders in the university were thus especially subject to scrutiny because they embodied both the vanguard (vis-à-vis other students) and the socialist citizen in need of guidance.[7] Indeed, the problem of students being both free and correct came to a head with the protests in 1968, when student protesters challenged the state's ability to manage dissent. The upending of the careful balance of academic and intellectual autonomy and state control resulted in particularly repressive measures against some faculty members in the 1970s. Despite the decentralized system of decision making and resource allocation, the state nonetheless reserved the right to directly intervene in university affairs at particular moments of perceived crisis. The history of the Yugoslav university included tacking back and forth between periods of greater and lesser autonomy (Popov 2000).

University Reform as Revolutionary Politics

Given the importance of the university in Yugoslavia, it is not surprising that Milošević saw the relative autonomy of the institution as both a threat and an opportunity to consolidate his power. During the 1990s the regime, and in particular Mira Marković (Milošević's wife and head of the Yugoslav Left Party, Jugoslovenska Levica), crushed dissent and appointed loyal supporters to administrative positions. Because deans had full budgetary and administrative control over their faculties, including setting tuition rates and fee structures, they often treated faculties as fiefdoms outside the control of central university administration. Regime control culminated in the 1998 University Act, which required that faculty sign new contracts, which functioned as loyalty oaths to the regime.

Student activism was thus shaped by the understanding that the university was a politically contested institution. Students active during the Milošević period attempted to open up new spaces for citizen participation, resistance, and decision making through university-based activism. Because the university was a contested space, they understood reform of the institution as integral to broader goals of creating a free and open society. Reform was thus frequently tied to a broader progressive political agenda, or at least to resistance to the regime. The modernization of pedagogy, the fair distribution of university resources, a fight against corruption, and the improvement of material conditions for students all became part of a broader struggle against Milošević.

For example, a conversation I had in 2004 with Lana, who had become a student activist in the early 1990s, demonstrates the dense entanglements between university reform agendas and coming of age as a political subject. Our conversation took place in an underground café not far from the center of Belgrade. The café, hidden behind an unmarked door—a throwback to a time when student activism was both subversive and dangerous—had remained popular with student activists of Lana's generation. It was an apt place for her to narrate her coming of age as a particularly active participant in the student movement.

Lana was thirty when I interviewed her, and she had begun university more than a decade earlier. She had formally joined Student Union at the Philosophy Faculty at the University of Belgrade in 1997, and she had been very active in the protests of 1996–97 protests, including being on the central board (*glavni odbor*) of the student protests. Like many people from that slightly older generation of students in university during the 1990s, Lana was betwixt and between—neither finishing school nor finding full employment at the time of our interview. Hers was a generation for whom the disciplinary aspect of the university was a false promise. She had not finished her studies because of the many problems at her faculty and because the demands of her activism had been too great. She was struggling to find work. She occasionally ran workshops for Student Union but had moved on from student organizations.

Lana's account of the moment she enrolled in the university demonstrates how the university as a specific institutional space shaped young people's experience of activism. For Lana, like others of her generation, democratic reform and resistance to state power were intertwined. This was clearest in their relationship to the university. Indeed, Lana described to me how becoming an activist was simultaneous with becoming a student:

I was first at the faculty when I enrolled in 1992 and the 1992 student demonstration had just begun, during the enrollment process. I waited for my name [to be called] to join the line . . . to go upstairs and quickly enroll and get my student ID [*indeks*] so that I could go join the demonstration. Because you could go wherever you wanted in the faculty with the *indeks*, you could go where students had locked themselves in. I longed for that student identity because I wanted to be socially active. In any way. Even though I sat the whole night at the faculty and didn't do anything, just to be able to sit there and create around me the illusion that . . . I am here now, a cog in the wheel [*šraf u mehanizmu*], or I don't know what.

For Lana, the moment of becoming a student was transformative because it gave her a framework in which she could become socially active. Enrolling in the university gave a form and social location to an activism that was already in her nature (*moja priroda je aktivistička*). Lana narrates her moment of self-realization quite literally through the space of the university itself: the experience of standing in line to go upstairs; her access to the forbidden recesses of the faculty, where only students were allowed to go; the link between sitting at the faculty all night; and her awareness of being part of something bigger than herself. The architecture of the university and the way in which it directed her body gave materiality to her student identity, most explicitly in the form of the student ID and grade record book (*indeks*). Students' everyday experience of the university was often expressed in such material terms—complaints about student dorms, food in the cafeteria, and the lack of updated resources such as books computer equipment. This materiality of the institution, the social status of students, and the experience of activism were inextricable.

The period of the 1992 student protests that Lana cites was a galvanizing moment in which student organizations and activists articulated their resistance to the regime through demands for reform and university autonomy. The protests in June and July in Belgrade (which would have preceded Lana's formal enrollment in the fall of 1992) culminated in a symbolic burial of university freedom in front of the Serbian parliament (Popov 2000, 323; Gordy 1999). Despite protests, in 1992 the parliament passed the new university law, which increased state control of the university by increasing government representation in university bodies and in the election process of rectors and deans. Student activism was shaped by these battles. Both the experience of becoming active that Lana narrates and the shape of political conflict were mediated by the specific institutional dynamics and the history of the university.

At the same time, students with progressive political leanings saw reform in the university not only as a form of anti-Milošević resistance but also as a site of redress for other issues of social inequality. Lana, who was avowedly a social democrat, was rare, but not unique in the ways in which she explicitly linked reform to these larger social issues:

In that sense my leading idea, my kind of mission was to follow the . . . decisions of ordinary people [*obični ljudi*], from one side, and from the other side, . . . to direct the intervention of the state toward ordinary people, toward a better life for ordinary people. Student organizing was important to me because it was some kind of world in which I could live in that moment, and naturally, I thought that it would first be necessary to change something [at] the state university. That was a terribly important thing, . . . I can say, because I think it is necessary to remain a state [institution], because it is the state that must dictate some kinds of needs for educated people.

Here, Lana expresses an urgency to reforming the university qua state institution. This understanding of reform as a means of antiregime activism was central to the development of Student Union and other groups after 2000. In addition, Lana framed the university as a site not only of state power but also of state responsibility. She was not alone in seeing herself as a student and fundamentally as a citizen, a sentiment best expressed by the term *student citizens* (*građani studenti*), which I heard activists mobilize. Student activists often saw their status as students as central to, and even constitutive of, their responsibility and entitlements as citizens. This self-understanding often clashed with the hierarchical vision of faculty, administrators, and parents that students were children to be disciplined or objects of pedagogical and administrative intervention.

The view of education as a site of active citizen engagement had broader roots in the growth of an activist and nongovernmental scene in the 1990s. Many student activists and student leaders had come of age in nongovernmental organizations (NGOs) that explicitly linked alternative pedagogy, critical thinking, democracy, and the anti-Milošević movement. Many of these alternative education organizations had roots in civil society initiatives of the early 1990s. Places like Belgrade Open School (Beogradska Otvorena Škola), Belgrade Circle (Beogradski Krug), Women's Studies (Ženske Studije), and the Center for Peace Studies (Centar za Mirovne Studije) offered alternatives to the standard ex cathedra pedagogy of state institutions. Their programs were interdisciplinary and incorporated cutting-edge theoretical and politically progressive education. Activists and academics (often one and the same) founded these institutions to offer young men and women a different vision of social, political, and economic relations in Serbia. They provided critical perspectives on the nationalist and patriarchal processes that shaped contemporary Serbian society. And they introduced students to collaborative education and emphasized critical thinking. Such centers became sites of organizing and refuge for activists, particularly in Belgrade's feminist and antiwar community. Many student activists came out of these institutions, and the staff and faculty of critical education groups continued to work in the NGO sector, or in some cases became opposition leaders.

For example, the Alternative Academic Education Network (Alternativna Akademska Obrazovna Mreža) emerged as a response to yet another repressive university law (the aforementioned University Act) passed in 1998. As a founder and professor at the University of Belgrade told me, the emergence of the network was as much a professional and social survival strategy as it was a political response to the increased oppression:

In 1998 we had the . . . University Act, and in fact a number of people were kind of running up and down the city, very desperate, and very miserable, not knowing what to do. Some of us decided not to sign that famous contract, and some others decided that something should be done. . . . And we have to try to create another alternative space for the professors, but for the students as well. . . . And out of that haze, in fact, in the autumn of 1998, came . . . the network. Without a very, kind of, particularly well-balanced and well-structured aim, objective, [or] mission. We were in fact discovering what we were supposed to be doing while we were doing it. . . . [T]he idea was to offer the programs that were not present in the curricula of the state-funded universities, and the idea was to . . . try very hard to bridge disciplinary gaps, which is not the case with the state-funded universities. . . . And we were trying also to think of the programs that would be . . . socially relevant and politically relevant at the moment. . . . [Y]oung people were very happy, judging by the fact that some eight hundred people applied.

As this professor narrates the founding of the network, the unstructured and frenzied response took shape simultaneously as an academic and a political response. Indeed, the two were inseparable. The political response of faculty forced from their positions and threatened by the regime took the concrete form of a particular educational agenda, including interdisciplinary education, new academic programs, and a space for students that would encourage socially and politically relevant learning and knowledge production. The elements of later reform agendas—particularly a more flexible, credit-based system—were in part an emerging response to academic and political conditions at the university. Faculty drew on their own experiences in the university as well as on the experiences of other universities abroad. By the late 1990s, both faculty members and students began to receive support for their antiregime initiatives from sympathetic student groups, academics, funders, and policy makers outside of Serbia. The repressive 1998 law galvanized public support for victims of repression at the university (Savić 1997–98). Tapping into a developed network of higher education reformers seemed a viable political survival strategy for increasingly isolated and beleaguered activists.

Administrative Logics of Reform

The European Higher Education Area, of which the Bologna Process was a key component, emerged in response to the economic recession in Europe in the early 1990s. Policy makers formulated the area as a strategic response that would make Europe a key producer of knowledge (geared toward the emerging knowledge economy) and stimulate employment by easing the mobility of students and workers across the continent. A key part of this strategy was the standardization of degrees via the ECTS credit system. In addition, advocates of the Bologna Process sought to produce a market for European higher education that would attract students from other regions of the world. The knowledge economy, lifelong learning, and student mobility were thus direct responses to European economic crisis.

At its heart, the Bologna Process is a deeply political process of reconfiguring the relationship between state and citizens, as well as the relationship between markets and knowledge production (Wright and Rabo 2010; Boyer 2010; Tomusk 2007). In the context of the knowledge economy, the university's role is to create marketable forms of knowledge and expertise for export. At the same time, the European Higher Education Area was meant to create a community in which standardized units of knowledge—credits—would enable the mobility and circulation of "European" citizens. The idea of the knowledge citizen and worker meant that students would be trained not only in particular areas of specialization; they also would be trained to be entrepreneurial and flexible, to consume and produce knowledge valuable in a global market.

In Serbia, particular features of the Bologna Process resonated for reformers because the process entailed restructuring the legal status and budgetary structure of the university system of the former Yugoslavia. Bologna reforms intersected with heated debates about how resources and power were allocated in the university system. The Bologna Process required that the university operate as a unified legal entity (*pravno lice*) by centralizing decision-making authority to create accountability. This was particularly significant because individual departments had long relied on the lack of centralized coordination to develop ad hoc policies in administrating their units. For example, individual faculties (i.e., schools within the university) set tuition rates and additional fees for enrollment and exams. Oftentimes, when faculties were unable to meet costs through direct tuition payments and state funding, they relied on the fee system, over which they had total discretion (for an explanation of funding structures and tuition policies, see Lažetić and Babin 2009).

Reform was not merely a technical exercise, but a fundamental restructuring of power and decision-making authority at a highly politicized institution. In this context, many professors and activists saw direct connections between European higher education reform and their own histories of university- and education-based activism. Student groups called for student participation in administrative decision making and higher education policies. Professors from alternative education programs advocated for reforms in traditional pedagogy and called for interdisciplinary approaches. While the Bologna Process is linked to broader processes of neoliberalization in education reform (Wright and Rabo 2010; Shore 2010), many reformers, especially those at the periphery of the European Union, saw it as a concrete means for achieving integration into Europe in both an economic and a cultural sense.

Indeed, I asked Lana, the founder of a previously mentioned alternative education NGO, whether the Bologna Process made a certain kind of sense to her from the beginning. She admitted that her long experience with Belgrade University (she had earned all her degrees there and had been teaching for eight years) had been mixed. She was "attached to it, emotionally, professionally," and yet had long been frustrated with "all kinds of unnecessary obstacles" to work and study, for which, she told me, she was always made to feel it was her fault.

Lana went on to describe her initial introduction to European reform processes as a moment when she first started actively theorizing her experiences and critiques of the Serbian university system. She saw alternative education as a space of experimentation for new Bologna reforms: "I started reading, and started listening to people, and started experimenting, and whatever we learned, all the knowledge that we gathered, then we tried to implement it over here. Introducing trimesters, introducing [the] ECTS grade system, all kinds of flexible curricul[a] in terms of lots of optional courses, in terms of possibilities for students to create their own path through the system, and so on and so forth."

Reformers like Lana thus recognized their own personal and professional experiences and aspirations in the framework of reform. In this context, it is hard to separate early forms of activism that gave rise to the 2000 revolution from the later directions of post-2000 reform. It is also difficult to refer to university reform in Serbia as a process wholly imposed from the outside. The Bologna Process always also included an alternative model of education and knowledge production that made sense given local obstacles and struggles within the institution itself.[8]

At the same time, this does not mean that were not outside pressures, both on reformers and on NGO members, and later on the Serbian government. Many reform-oriented faculty and students had seen the writing on the wall. If Serbia's university system was going to integrate into a greater space of European higher education in a post-Milošević world, then reforms would be absolutely necessary. Students and faculty saw the logic of the Bologna Process as a fitting response to particular conditions in Serbia and as part of a larger commitment for Serbia to rejoin Europe. Yet as time went on, and Serbia signed on to Bologna, what had been a strategic framework for resistance within the regime became a set of compulsory policy requirements, enforced by direct and indirect pressure to comply with new educational norms and neoliberal economic reforms in both Serbia and Europe more generally.

If Bologna was initially compelling to faculty and student activists, it was in part because reforms addressed existing institutional arrangements of power, resource allocation, and decision making at work in the decentralized structure of the university. It was also easy for professors and students with activist histories to overlook, or downplay, some of the implications of Bologna because of the vague and often-shifting meaning of the terms and discursive policy frames through which Bologna was articulated (Bačević 2010). Contradictory interpretations of reform emerged as people made sense of their own very different experiences through the narratives of reform. To this extent, the reform process was produced and mediated through the very interpretative frames brought to bear in debates around university reform. Productive confusions and tensions emerged as people made the institution meaningful through different interpretations of its history and its possible future.

This process was compounded by the fact that everyone involved was drawing from a similar vocabulary in discussing reform: *accountability*, *autonomy*, *responsibility*, *rationality*. As Wright and Rabo (2010) have pointed out, the chaotic nature of these "weasel words" has often meant that faculty and students who might otherwise be critical of aspects of university reform instead find themselves in unintended collusion with outside reformers. These weasel words were flexible and open to interpretation. When faculty formerly subjected to repression during the Milošević regime mobilized the notion of autonomy, they did not necessarily mean the kind of autonomy codified in the Bologna Process. At the same time, participants across political spectrums and institutional locations framed their claims in the language of reform itself, often giving key words very different meanings.

In addition, seemingly uncontroversial ideas, like reform of credit hours to enable more flexible programs of study, became stand-ins for larger debates about Serbia's relationship to Europe. The pro- and anti-Europe dichotomy fit into popular beliefs that the urban, NGO, activist, and intellectual scene (what was commonly referred to as *Druga Srbija*, or "the other Serbia") had betrayed the nation in favor of foreign interests and agendas. Some within the university read the push for pedagogical reform as a repudiation of Serbian national "tradition," as calls for reform were read in terms of long-standing tensions around Serbian nationalism. Those student activists with strong ties to the "pro-Europe" NGO scene saw pedagogical reform as a way to produce critical (and antinationalist) thinkers who would bring young people closer to Europe. I encountered other activists critical of the Bologna Process as a European import that ignored Serbia's own long-standing educational traditions. It was also a claim that I frequently heard from faculty and administrators resistant to the Bologna Process and the curricular and administrative reorganization of the university that it entailed.[9]

Like any arena in which people took a stance on Serbia's relationship to European (i.e., EU) norms and standards, such distinctions became a way for students, faculty, and administrators to differentiate themselves in subtle ways. Higher education reform thus became a proxy arena in which people tried to carve out alternative ways of talking about Serbian national belonging while avoiding more controversial issues such as complicity with the Milošević regime, among others. The language of preservation and tradition and charges of elitism were ways to figure a kind of patriotism that sidestepped, though could nonetheless be resonant with, other kinds of nationalist frameworks.[10]

By the late 1990s, and certainly after 2000, these leaders in both reform and alternative education were coming to terms with the Bologna Process and with the range of European institutions, educational groups, and policies that made the process a complex social field. What was emerging out of reform efforts and new higher education policy initiatives was a "contested space, where students, academics, university managers and policymakers, all have ways of imagining the future university, and where they engage, albeit with unequal resources, in trying to shape their institution" (Wright and Rabo 2010, 11). But what was also emerging were different models of citizenship in relation to the university, as well as different expectations for how (and why) the university ought to function as an institution with specific social relations and relations of power and authority. Students continued to want various things from both their education and their activism within the university, and they had goals and demands that drew on histories of student activism in the 1990s, alternative education and reform initiatives, and the emerging language of Bologna-style approaches to reform.

Conditions at the University

For student activists, reform could not be unlinked from a litany of complaints about the material and social conditions of the university itself. From rising tuition costs to outdated pedagogy, Bologna-style reforms were appealing as responses to an institution that many students felt failed across multiple domains. Chief among the complaints I heard was the length of study at the university. According to administrators and student activists whom I spoke with, the average length of study for what was presented as a four-year program was approximately eight years. Because programs were entirely fixed and did not include elective courses, students were required to pass exams in subjects within their broad fields in which they might have had little interest. Medical students complained that they were forced to memorize every aspect of medicine from textbooks while they had few opportunities for practical study and application. Literature majors lamented that they were called on to reproduce facts and dates from the novels that they had read rather than engage critically with the texts. Given the rigid institutional organization of the universities and the huge course burden for students, interdisciplinary classes were virtually unheard of. Students often felt imprisoned by the sheer amount they had to learn to pass exams.

In addition, students often complained about the dominant approaches to pedagogy. Lectures were largely ex cathedra, with little opportunity for class discussion. Hierarchies of authority within classrooms and departments were strictly maintained. At the same time, those professors who did try to implement new pedagogical practices were often met with indifference, at best, or even open hostility from their colleagues. These problems were compounded by a testing system that produced an extremely high failure rate. Grades were often given with little transparency as to the evaluation criteria.

Students told me that these problems were compounded by corruption at the university. The combination of extremely low salaries and high rates of failure on exams led to rampant bribes and outright grade buying. In addition, students frequently cited sexual harassment as a persistent problem. On top of these more serious allegations, many students also felt that professors could be cruel and arbitrary in their dealings with students. Although it is difficult to determine the extent of the problems—much of the information is anecdotal, and students were often reluctant to come forward—I heard these problems cited consistently across three universities over my period of research.[11]

Tuition continued to rise from 2000 on, in order to fill the gap left by decreased state funding (Lažetić and Babin 2009). Tuition was set from faculty to faculty, as were admissions policies. Thus, costs varied widely across faculties and universities, and cash-strapped departments relied on that money for their expanding programs. Fees for exams were relatively unregulated, and though not prohibitive on a case-by-case basis, they could add up to a significant amount. Those students who had been granted stipends from the state budget were also eligible for housing in student dormitories and food at the student cafeteria. However, the number of rooms available for students in the dorms was not nearly enough to cover the need, especially for the University of Belgrade, where there were many students from other parts of the country and rent in the city was prohibitively expensive. Keeping libraries current and well stocked, especially with new texts or journals, was virtually impossible given the costs. In addition, technological resources were scarce, and even computer science courses relied on chalk, pencil, and paper to teach computer programming.

Overcrowding in departments was also large concern for students. Policies of virtually open enrollment during the 1990s meant that the university was severely overburdened going into the 2000s. In addition, young men continue to stay enrolled in university to avoid or delay mandatory military service, as an earlier generation had to avoid being called up during the wars of the 1990s (Milićević 2004). At a broader level, a sluggish labor market provided little incentive for students to graduate, especially when they were entitled to student discounts, benefits, and other perquisites.

The question of the university's relationship to the labor market raised many concerns for students, both in and out of the reform movement. Students bristled at the lack of practical knowledge and skills they were learning at the university. The struggle over which kinds of education would create employment opportunities was not only a personal one for students. By the late 1990s and after 2000, there had been a shift in the faculties that were the most attractive and competitive for incoming students, from the hard sciences and humanities in the 1970s and 1980s to law, English, business, dentistry, and tourism in the 1990s. These faculties were viewed either as advantageous in a difficult labor market or as tickets to emigration. The general rhetoric of business and entrepreneurship was dangled before students and their parents as some utopian employment solution guaranteeing if not wealth, then middle-class stability. I met many students who were interested in marketing or public relations, even though they had trouble specifying exactly what kind of work those fields might guarantee them.

Some students simply chose to flee the state university to enroll in one of the private faculties or universities, which were opening in droves. Although many of these institutions have become staples of higher education in Serbia—particularly once an accreditation system was put in place to deal with previously nonexistent private higher education—the schools were often dismissed by those at the more prestigious state university. Many felt that they were there for rich kids who simply wanted to buy a degree. However, most private faculties were staffed by the same professors who taught at the state institutions.

In part, frustration with the state university lay in its inability to deliver on the promises made by older generations to younger ones. When talking to a good friend one day in 2003, he told me that his biggest regret was staying in Serbia to finish university in Niš, a process that took him nearly a decade. Both he and his wife had struggled to find work in Serbia that paid decently and that they enjoyed. They eventually left Serbia to move back to Banja Luka, in Bosnia, where they felt the prospects were better. My friend compared himself to his brother, who had left university to move to Sweden and had found a good job in telecommunications with Ericsson. His brother was living there happily with his wife and children. My friend told me that his greatest regret was that he didn't go to Sweden when he had the chance. He looked at his brother's salary and lifestyle and imagined what he could have had. But as he told me, it was too important to him to get the university degree. As he put it, he had been "brainwashed by that kind of thinking." For my friend, who was born in the mid-1970s, a university degree had held value and prestige, and it was supposed to guarantee employability. In these ways, the university system had totally failed his generation—those who started university during the Milošević period and often did not finish until a decade later, if ever. Younger students just entering university at the time of my fieldwork were perhaps less reflective than their elder peers, who felt that much of their youth had been wasted in war, isolation, and lost opportunities. But those young students also experienced disappointments in everyday, often material ways.

For members of student organizations, such experiences and disappointments were very real and very personal. Many student leaders struggled to graduate for many of the same reasons as their peers, and these problems were compounded by the intensive time they committed to student activism. Indeed, some of the brightest, most talented, and ambitious young people I met in student organizations, or later in the NGO sector, either never finished their studies or took years to do so. But in translating their own experiences into another register appropriate for organizing and activism, student leaders framed their experiences at the university as issues of greater import and urgency. The realities of corruption, lousy cafeteria food, crowded classrooms, and outmoded testing methods were not far from their minds. But the question of reform was also about becoming members of a larger European community, developing students as democratic citizens, and making Serbia an economically and politically stable place to live for future generations. The passion, thrill, and importance of student activism during the authoritarian period was still quite real for student activists, who were hoping that their work at the university would contribute to political and social change in Serbia more broadly.

Employment: Revolutionary Tactics and Reform Logics

It was in this translation from personal experience of conditions at the university to a programmatic agenda to make the university function "as it should" that models of active participation and technologies of discipline came together. This fusion was perhaps clearest when students confronted the issue of the university's responsibility to make them into employable subjects. In dealing with this question, student leaders most explicitly formulated their vision of the university as a disciplinary institution designed to produce particular kinds of (employable) citizen subjects. Yet as I show here, this model of a disciplinary institution drew from language of the Bologna Process reforms even as it held on to certain tenets about the responsibility of states to their citizens. What students developed was a unique approach to governmentality as a strategic instrument of state and citizen advocacy.

Unemployment was extremely high in Serbia post-2000, especially for younger job seekers. According to an employment policy report issued by the Council of Europe and the International Labor Organization, Serbia's youth unemployment rate in 2004 was 48.8 percent, and for young women it was higher still, at 51.2 percent (COE and ILO 2007, 17). About one-third of the unemployed had either higher education or tertiary or secondary vocational education (COE and ILO 2007, 25). In addition to slow economic growth overall, the policy report cited the poor quality of university education and vocational training as a barrier to youth employment, noting frequent complaints from employers about "lack of problem-solving skills and ability to deal with real-life situations, lack of entrepreneurship, excessive theoretical knowledge and inadequate practical technical skills" (COE and ILO 2007, 28). Not surprisingly, these kinds of complaints echoed many of the frustrations and shortcomings that university students cited from their own experiences. University reform, including curricular reform, overcrowding, lack of resources, and outdated pedagogy, was at some level tied to questions of possible future employment.

At the same time, the state's role in managing unemployment was an area of debate among students. Some students thought that the university should develop quota systems in which enrollment was calculated against the need and availability of slots for particular professions. This kind of labor market planning was in use during the socialist period, although it was unclear whether those students making such suggestions knew that. For many students, planning made sense as a response to overenrollment, especially in the most popular faculties, such as law. Surely, if there were limits on the number of students enrolled, there would be more opportunities for those who graduated. In talking in May 2003 at the University of Novi Sad to a group of law students, all members of the student group Savez Studenata (Student Alliance), I got a strong sense of the frustration with overcrowding and the overproduction of particular professions. Over the course of the conversation I posed the question, "Who should be responsible for the problem?" "I'll tell you who," one young man responded, "the state" (*država*). The others agreed, suggesting that the state should determine the necessary number of lawyers and corresponding quotas for university admissions. These students, like others I spoke with, made a direct link between overenrollment and their future job prospects. Although they identified the state as the actor responsible for addressing the situation, the mechanism they invoked was regulation within the university itself (rather than, for example, stimulating greater demand for lawyers). In other words, these students understood their status as citizens and workers to be mediated through the university itself. Nitty-gritty questions of reform, such as faculty enrollment policies, were more often than not also questions of citizenship.

Whether or not they believed in a quota system, many students felt that the university was responsible for making them employable, although the specific mechanisms for doing so varied. Some students believed that direct state intervention was the key to regulating and enabling employment, and others embraced the idea that the state's role was more indirectly regulative. Those student leaders who promoted the Bologna reforms at the university often focused on improving the quality and marketability of education, in line with the broader agenda of European higher education reform. Calls for curriculum reform often centered on making knowledge more practical, to ensure that students had marketable skills upon graduation. The ECTS credit system and student mobility were also mechanisms for employability that would open up labor markets outside Serbia to students. Students hoped that the Bologna requirements to "rationalize" the university would create accountability by taking enrollment policy out of the hands of individual faculties, which would in turn address overenrollment and improve the quality of education and marketability of degrees.

At the same time that some student leaders wholeheartedly embraced the Bologna Process, their interpretation of the relationship between a knowledge economy and employment did not always jibe with that of outside authorities. Ultimately, student activists continued to hold on to the idea that the state had some responsibility for students in the labor market. In contrast, outside Bologna Process advocates mobilizing language of the knowledge society, risk, and entrepreneurship argued for the autonomy of the university vis-à-vis the state. People speaking the "same" language—that of reform and rights—wound up arguing for very different models of state power and responsibility. This distinction is important because it sheds light on the way large-scale reforms are ultimately given force and meaning through subtle, often minor negotiations around the interpretation of terms. A commonality of terms often masks much larger questions about the relationship between power and knowledge and between state, market, and society.

I saw this dynamic play out directly on a sunny May morning in 2003. I attended the "University Autonomy and the New Law on Higher Education in Serbia," organized by the rector of the University of Novi Sad. The forum brought together faculty and administrators with two representatives of the Magna Charta Universitatum, Observatory of Fundamental University Values and Rights, in Bologna, to which the University of Novi Sad had become a recent signatory. The event was intended to be an open conversation about issues related to university autonomy and legal reform. The final report by the two Observatory representatives declared that the conversation was about "the situation in Serbian higher education at present and participants' views on how arrangements might be made so that Serbian universities can reclaim their full place in the European academic community."[12]

The event took place over the course of a full day around a large, stately oval table at the central administrative offices of the University of Novi Sad. Over the course of a morning and an afternoon session, the participants—outside observers, faculty administrators, and professors from around the country—engaged in sometimes heated debate about the meaning of university autonomy, the necessity of legal reform, and the relationship between the university and the labor market. On this last point, the one student representative present, Petar—the student leader whom I mentioned at the beginning of this chapter—was most forceful. One particular exchange illustrates particularly well the different interpretations of the role of the state in the context of neoliberal risk. Although this was part of a larger conversation, the exchange was among Petar; the rector of the University of Novi Sad; and one of the observatory representatives, a middle-aged German man named Michael.

The exchange was sparked by Petar's concern about the material and educational impacts of overenrollment at the university, a familiar theme for Student Union, of which Petar was a key member. He raised the issues almost immediately in the afternoon session.[13] He began by insisting on the importance of student participation and representation in reform processes. In response, the rector told him that while she was supportive of his position, she felt that student organizations had overstepped their bounds by gathering specific data about material conditions at the university (they had collected information about the lack of chairs available in faculties to bolster their argument of overenrollment). Petar responded:

I understand you think we should ask the university to count the number of chairs. But at least in the last three years, I haven't noticed that the university is doing that. . . . Some faculties—and our local unions counted [them]—don't even have the basic number of chairs. Every student, budget or not, should have equal rights. The enormous number of enrolled students affects the quality of teaching.

In his retort to the rector, Petar framed the question of enrollment using material evidence—the number of chairs—to argue for two different rationales for limiting enrollment: quality and rights. Students have a right to equal access to certain material conditions and consistency in material standards among faculties (some had enough chairs, and others did not). Rights here refer not necessarily to open access to university education but rather to a certain level of quality once a student is within the institution itself.

While other professors tried to move on to other topics, some visibly annoyed that a student had hijacked the proceedings, the issue of quality continued to come up. Another professor from the University of Kragujevac raised the issue of chairs again as an example for lack of regulation of how many students could be in a classroom. Petar seized her comment as his chance to again bring up the link between enrollment and quality of education. He demanded that the Ministry of Education provide basic procedures for enrollment linked to specific information about a faculty's capacities. Such rights would be tied to specific procedures that assessed material conditions at the university as the basis for enrollment policy. At heart, Petar was arguing that limiting the number of students in accordance with material conditions would help produce quality students with equal rights. These rights were defined in terms of the institution's ability to effectively train and educate students across all departments (known as *faculties* in Serbian).

As the conversation threatened to turn once again in this direction, Michael, the observatory's representative, intervened. He acknowledged that Petar was talking about the "lifeworld in academia," and that indeed this was an important topic. But he went on to say, "In a poor society, you shouldn't ask 'are there too many students?' Because, I ask you, what are going to do with the rest? Professional and vocational education are as expensive as the university. . . . The question of how many do we allow to get a degree [doesn't work] when this country doesn't have enough academics." He went on to critique Petar for the idea that "bureaucrats" should be counting chairs. Instead, he argued, the role of the state was to create conditions for the university to put procedures in place, not to intervene in such a direct way.

For Petar the university was a space in which to enact particular kinds of rights—the right to equal standards and quality education—but Michael was blatant about the role of the university as a pressure valve for an overburdened labor market as well as a crucial mechanism for creating the experts critical to Serbia's economic development. Petar tied material capacity to the rights of students to receive a quality education. Michael countered by situating the university in a broader socioeconomic context. Although enrollment policy was important at the university level, increasing the number of university-educated students was critical to Serbia's economic health. Michael also voiced skepticism about extending the state's power to regulate conditions in the university. The state's job was to set baseline criteria and the leave the university to manage its affairs. It was most certainly not to dictate enrollment or count chairs.

Both Michael and Petar were advocates of the same set of Bologna reforms. They both sought to rationalize enrollment policy, to bolster Serbia's economic development, and to ease its entry into a knowledge economy. Yet Petar found Michael's logic of state withdrawal from direct regulation of conditions at the university infuriating:

We also get this argument at the Council for Development of Higher Education[, that] we don't have enough academics. But this argument doesn't stand. It's also true that only thirty percent of enrolled students finish their studies—other students are simply lost. If we want to double the number of academics—should we enroll double the number of students? Or should we enroll fewer students so that sixty percent of them actually finish their studies?

Here Petar framed the role of reform to make the university an effective institution that would produce employable, high-quality graduates. The responsibility of the state, vis-à-vis reform, was to make the university function well. Students who entered had a right to finish. The goal of reform was not only to produce more graduates but also to force the institution to function, and to function well. This necessitated direct intervention in ensuring standardized quality conditions across the institution.

Michael's response to this comment was to shift the responsibility from the state or the university as an institution to the students themselves:

[The question is,] who should bear the risk? If a student wants to study astrology [said sarcastically] then they have the right to bear the risk. There is a lower risk to becoming a dentist. Should the university take the risk? If I'm hiring five new professors in dentistry, then I risk having a surplus in dentists? Should the ministry bear the risk? . . . How do we get a basically rational model respecting individual choices that is reasonably affordable?

Counter to Petar's assertion that a student's rights are realized by limits on enrollment, Michael asserted that their rights are constrained by over-legislating enrollment policy. Here, citizen choice lies in the right to take on risk or not, and it is secondary to employment itself. The very notion of a knowledge economy positions the university as a central engine of employment in the European imaginary. The question is, what kinds of policies produce employability, and what are the role of the citizen and the responsibility of the state in this process? Should citizens, as freely choosing individuals, take on risk? Should universities maximize the number of enrolled students, as Michael suggested? Or should the university be institutionally responsible in producing students who are employable? If so, shouldn't universities use administrative tools, such as enrollment policy, as Petar demanded?

The difference in Michael's and Petar's positions is subtle. For Petar, the university makes students into productive and employable citizens by upholding specific policies. For example, enrollment policies limit the number of people in the labor market and so ensure that the quality of education, the knowledge received, is actually of value. In this view, the state, via the university, should act as guarantor that those who are already enrolled will graduate and find jobs. For Michael, it is students' right (and obligation) to bear the risk of a competitive labor market. If the university is a relay point for employment, then the role of the university is to allow as many students access as possible. Citizenship is defined by the choice to enroll, such that access to the university becomes a locus of rights. For Petar, the definition of rights is linked to the quality of education itself. Citizenship is a productive relationship of becoming a subject who works through the disciplinary regimes of the institution.

This logic is echoed in other student activists' reactions to changing labor market conditions and legal regimes. Many students had grown up with the sense that they had a "right" to find employment in their area of interest. To this extent, the degree was a social contract with the state that allowed students to find employment of their choosing. The university degree was a path for students to become who it was they imagined themselves to be: lawyers, doctors, economists, chemists. At the same time that students wanted to develop entrepreneurial skills, many felt that the greatest shortcoming of university education was that a degree did not guarantee students such employment. This sense was exacerbated by the 2003 Law on Employment and Unemployment Insurance (adopted in July of that year), designed to provide incentives and training for those registered as unemployed to more actively seek jobs (COE and ILO 2007). The law tied receipt of benefits, including those social benefits that accrued to the registered unemployed, to an active job search. It stipulated that those seeking work could not refuse job offers or training, even outside their area of expertise or previous training (Stojić 2004, 25). Such policies of active versus passive labor market regulation were new to Serbia, though not unprecedented in Europe, and they were part of a larger approach to labor market policy in Europe that emphasized the "obligations" of workers as well as their rights and entitlements vis-à-vis state employment benefits (COE and ILO 2007).

The state thus managed young people's entry into a sluggish labor market through new legal regimes. At the same time, administrators and university reformers embraced the idea of the entrepreneurial university. These institutional and ideological factors chipped away at a long-held belief that the university guaranteed employment in one's area of study. Indeed, the rector of the University of Novi Sad complained to me once over lunch that students were overly rigid about the kind of work they expected after graduating. She told me that students come in to train as one thing and expect to be able to do that one thing after graduation. But, she noted, that kind of guarantee didn't exist anywhere anymore. At the heart of this complaint was annoyance at students' lack of flexibility regarding their studies and a concern that the university become an institution capable of producing more flexible workers and citizens.

Indeed, I had heard the rector make similar remarks at a forum held at the University of Novi Sad in response to the proposed law on employment and unemployment insurance. The flyer for the event advertised that it would address "everything that you want to know about your future employment but are afraid to ask" (*Sve što ste hteli da znate o vašem budućem zaposlenju a niste mogli da pitate*). It was attended by about fifty students and sponsored by the Youth Council of Vojvodina and Student Union of Novi Sad. The speakers for the event included representatives from provincial offices, including employment and youth and sport. Anticipating what she would later explain to me, the rector lectured the assembled students on the proper relationship between a university degree and a future career.

She insisted to them that nowhere in the world was it a guarantee that you could have a career in your area of study. Students needed to lower their expectations, she informed them, and to be more entrepreneurial.

Such comments seemed cold comfort for a room full of anxious undergraduates facing one of the worst labor markets in Europe. Indeed, one of the activists who helped organize the event felt that the panelists made such comments because they knew they couldn't really do anything to help students. Like Petar, this student saw the state's refusal to intervene as incompetence and impotence rather than as a particular ideological arrangement among the state, the university, and citizens. The 2003 law met with similar angry reactions from other students I spoke with. In a conversation I had in Niš with two student leaders, Dušan and Ljilja, they explained to me that if people couldn't find a job in their field after three months, they were obliged to take some other kind of work. "What kind of freedom is that?" Dušan angrily declared to me. In an attempt to assuage her colleague, Ljilja told him that he had to take into consideration where they lived and the situation in Serbia. Dušan replied sharply, "I'm sick of being understanding." Dušan was expressing a tension between "freedom" and "being understanding" of the economic realities in Serbia. It is the same tension that runs through the debate between Petar and Michael and that shapes two very different approaches to university reform in Serbia. What kind of citizens should the university create? Do students come to university as already-formed subjects ready to take on risk and become entrepreneurs in a tight labor market? Or is it the state's job, via the university, to produce subjects that "work"? Here the idea of work echoes Foucault's description of the subject with the ability "to carry out his tasks" and the idea of employability. Rights were configured around the "freedom" to make choices (about career or education) and the corresponding "right" to bear risk for those choices. For many student activists, they subjected themselves to the disciplinary regimes of a university education precisely to become a certain kind of citizen-subject. University reform was a mechanism by which student activists could put conditions into place to restore that link, at least in theory. For many students, such as Petar and Dušan, freedom resulted from the university being a successful disciplinary institution; it was not prior to reform.

These practical interventions form a model of citizenship in which the state continues to bear responsibility for its citizens but through regulation of the institution rather than the individuals themselves. It is a model that produces citizen rights in a juridical sense, realized through practices of regulative governmentality. And it is a model that fuses a long and specific history of student subjectivity and citizenship, both of which are grounded in participation and discipline. Students advocated for disciplinary techniques of governance to produce themselves as sovereign citizens. In turn, student activists could use formerly revolutionary tactics, such as protests or demands for democratic participation, to force universities to provide "quality" education, small classes, practical work experiences. The practical entanglements of different kinds of student action reveal a dialectic of resistance and complicity—a dialectic that provides room for students and others to take up different, seemingly contradictory discursive strategies to justify their demands for institutional reform. In turn, institutional reform becomes a productive discursive field in which the meaning of citizenship is worked out in relation to debates about what the university is supposed to do and how it is supposed to function.

4

The Ethics of Knowledge
Expertise, Branding, and (In)visibility as Forms of Democratic Representation

ONE JANUARY AFTERNOON IN 2003 I strolled across campus to attend the weekly board meeting in the drafty offices of Student Union of Novi Sad. I wandered in and found a place to perch on a rundown couch with saggy cushions that was a hub of office activities and socializing. As it turned out, there were not enough members to make a quorum that afternoon, and the planned meeting turned into an informal chat session. A heated debate ensued about whether one of the executive board members (who was not present) was pulling her weight in the organization. It was a conversation that brought together personal animosities, gossip, and insider knowledge, and it revealed many of the ways in which organizational and intimate worlds intersected. Membership in an organization constituted a social fabric crosshatched with personal intimacies, rivalries, and friendships. Shoptalk provided social scripts in and through which young men and women navigated their world. And slippages in those performances revealed the social as well as political stakes of the kinds of solidarities and exclusions that successfully taking up these registers could produce.

At one point in the conversation, the door opened and a student who was not a member of the group walked in. He had come to the offices seeking input on a proposal for an Internet café that he wanted to submit to an American funder. The atmosphere in the room changed suddenly. The students went from an informal, if intensely heated, interpersonal debate, to being "on." They sat up straighter, all facing toward the outsider. The buzz of multiple overlapping voices gave way to a unified, interviewlike style of talk. They peppered the student with pointed questions about his proposed project. Where before there was discord, all of sudden there was unity—in voice, tone, and focus. The students then proceeded to criticize the hapless appellant for being unfocused and not being able to articulate how or whether the project would be profitable and sustainable. Using their own vast expertise in proposal writing and project development, they mobilized disciplinary discursive frames to position themselves (and the student) as authorities in relation to particular audiences, both in the room and in an imagined world of foreign donors. This disciplining happened in two senses. In scolding the student and telling him to come back when he had a more formal plan, they attempted to educate him in the world of foreign donor organizations. They also positioned him as a certain kind of subject vis-à-vis their own knowledge and authority. And they disciplined themselves in their change of bodily stance, attitude, and register. They collectively and seamlessly took on a familiar role as experts.

At the same time that this process went unremarked, the student activists clearly understood themselves to be performing a particular role, with which they were more or less comfortable. Indeed, after the student making the appeal had left, there followed a moment of silence. Then everyone in the room looked at one another and burst out laughing. The laughter might have been at the young man's expense, but it seemed more likely to be an expression of awareness of the collective shift in their demeanor. The students had been engaged in lively and highly personal insider argument. They then suddenly took on the role of detached, formal, experts. This isn't to say that that performance was somehow inauthentic. Many of the students were indeed experts in proposal writing and other matters. But the laughter was an acknowledgment of the disjuncture between the moment before and the moment after the student had entered. His presence had changed the feel of the office—from casual to formal— and the relationships among everyone in the room. If the debate beforehand had blurred the lines between the personal and the organizational, the presence of an outsider had reconstituted the lines between public and private knowledge.

In switching from one genre of talk to another, the students in the room had transformed the relationships among everyone present by taking on the authority of experts. Expertise is accomplished in socially and discursively mediated interactions rather than being an expression of already-existing knowledge (Carr 2010). It is signaled, produced, and performed through registers of speech; embodied practices, such as gesture or tone of voice; and the use of particular codes. At the same time, in many contexts, producing expertise involves rendering invisible the ways in which knowledge is a socially mediated achievement. Expert knowledge—often constituted against the specific populations to which expert knowledge is applied—comes to appear objective, universally relevant, generalizable, and inherent in the expert him- or herself (Mitchell 2002). The student who had come to Student Union for advice was opening himself up to pedagogical intervention. He believed that the students present possessed specialized knowledge and access. He most likely did not experience that such expertise was enacted in and through his presence as an object of intervention—although the laughter on the part of the student activists in the room may be a trace of that process.

This brief scene raises similar kinds of questions to those of protest (chapter 2) and proceduralism (chapter 5): how can a group of activists who understand themselves as fundamentally committed to democracy produce practices that at first blush seem so exclusionary? I knew the students involved in this opening scene well enough to know that their shift in tone was well meaning. They weren't trying to bully the student simply to reassert hierarchies. They had slipped into roles that corresponded with their beliefs about the ethics and responsibilities of student activism. They saw their role as student leaders as helping students become more skilled and knowledgeable about the complex world of university reform. With the new focus on university reform after 2000, taking on the role of experts in matters of higher education policy and reform became a critical way in which students could justify their continued involvement in different spheres of decision making, from faculty councils to ministry working-group meetings. Student activists learned to talk in a particular ways that marked them as people to be taken seriously. By asserting themselves as experts on the technical aspects of higher education reform, students could justify that they, too, deserved a seat at the table. What better way to be able to represent student interests?

In other words, these student activists saw their mobilization of expertise as transformative—both of conditions at the university and of students more broadly—and representative of the long-term needs and interests of student constituents. These were interests that ordinary students could not fully know or understand without some guidance. Expertise was not just a technology of authority making. It was a particular ethics

of knowledge that structured the relationship between student representatives and the population they were meant to serve. Expert talk was an
example of the ways in which highly politicized and socially embedded
relations are mediated through technical registers (see Masco 2006; Riles
2011).[1] Disciplining students to behave and think like experts—or refusing
to do so, as did some of the activists discussed in this chapter—was part
of the broader encounter with democracy. Student leaders struggled with
how to actually represent the general will of student constituents and how
to further produce evidence of that democratic representation.[2]

Student activists, like other politically engaged actors, were thus
struggling with central questions and contradictions of democratic representation. What is the evidentiary basis for democracy? What is the difference between educating versus representing constituents, and whose
knowledge matters most? Processes of representation necessarily rest on
forms of exclusion and abstraction, because they require "making present *in some sense* that which is nevertheless *not* present literally or in fact"
(Pitkin 1967, 11). Given this contradiction, it is not self-evident how democratic will translates into particular kinds of artifacts and practices. Expert
knowledge provided one framework for producing evidence—textual, discursive, and otherwise—that representation had taken place. Policy position papers, surveys, and glossy and informative promotional material
showed the kinds of knowledge that student representatives could offer
their constituents. Taken this way, one can see expertise as a strategy or
mode of political representation that deals with the complexities of translating "voice" into textual and semiotic artifacts, organizational forms, and
modes of sociality (Agha 2005).

This key relationship between knowledge and representation echoed
long-standing debates in Yugoslavia.[3] The category of "expert" was central
to visions of democracy within the Yugoslav self-management context, a
figure that would disinterestedly guide, but not trump, decision making
by all citizens. This figure of the technocratic manager was valorized as a
coordinator of knowledge, necessary to mediate and respect local practices,
particularly in the context of the self-managing Yugoslav firm (Pateman
1970). Indeed, carving a space outside of politics for technocratic managerial practice was to recuperate a potentially democratic-socialist project in
state-socialist contexts. The expert was somehow above the fray of messy
political and ideological life, and thus better able to represent the interests

of the people. As such, expertise was understood to be a form of democratic representation within a socialist idiom.

The legacy of the disinterested expert left its mark after 2000. Expertise fit neatly into other kinds of political and social transformations taking place in Serbia, including a reaction to the hyperpoliticization of everyday life under Milošević. For example, it is not a coincidence that G-17, an independent group of economic experts, was one of the most highly respected institutions in Serbia in the 1990s, particularly among young people and student activists. When it became the political party G-17 Plus (after a brief stint as a nongovernmental organization) in 2002, it enjoyed initial popularity. Young people in particular were drawn to the party's proreform stance and credibility as experts.[4] Within a few years, though, infighting within the party, a series of political compromises, and the wear and tear of the election process stripped G-17 Plus of its initial popularity. The credibility it had gained as a group of "neutral" experts was no match for the messy realities of the election process.[5]

In addition, the importance of expertise to student groups was tied to processes affecting higher education institutions globally. With the rise of university audit cultures in Europe (Strathern 2000), Serbian students' efforts to professionalize their activities paralleled emerging practices in higher education reform—standardization, commensurability, transparency, and mobility. The material forms that students produced, such as glossy pamphlets, white papers, and surveys, echoed in both content and form the will toward standardization. However, stopping there would miss much of what was productive and interesting about expertise as a particularly democratic technology of representation and knowledge production.

Producing Evidence of Democracy

What exactly does it mean for expertise to be a kind of democratic representation? And what does expertise look like in the context of student activism? For some student activists, the pamphlets, policy papers, and participation in high-level meetings on university reform proved that they were representing student interests. In other words, these practices, as artifacts, served as a kind of evidentiary basis for democracy having taken place. This is evident over the course of an interview that I conducted with a member of Student Union in Niš. The exchange demonstrates how representation, like ethics, invites particular evidentiary practices, which increasingly take the form of visually and textually mediated "artifacts of modern knowledge" (Riles 2006). That such artifacts, like documents, surveys, graphs, and even color-coordinated promotional material, can be made to circulate (or to seem to circulate) is critical to the authority they accrue (Hull 2003). This is especially true in the context of democratic ideologies of representation that are premised on the production of universal forms of political will (Greenberg 2012).

Sanja joined Student Union in 2001 and, as a student of economics, was particularly interested in the marketing and public relations aspects of the organization. She served for a few years as spokesperson (*portparol*) and moved up in the ranks of the group, to the university level and later to the executive board of the national group. She told me that the first time she read the brochure describing Student Union's activities, she was immediately drawn to the importance of higher education reform. She expressed an urgency about the need for Student Union to translate its activities and policies into visible action about which all students would be aware. As Sanja explained, reform was in the interests of students, but students weren't aware of the efforts of Student Union to represent them. "We aren't visible and students don't know what we do" (*Nismo vidljivi. S druge strane, studenti ne znaju šta radimo*), she told me.

How, then, could the group translate its efforts into visible practices that others would recognize as evidence of democratic representation? For Sanja, this entailed a process of branding. Student Union was commercializing its activities (*komercijalizacija svojih aktivnosti,*). But this also required a total shift in students' consciousness and ability to recognize that Student Union was representing their interests. The problem Student Union faced was the populist approach of other competing student groups and a low level of student awareness about their needs (*neka svest, znaš, studenata u situaciji je na jako niskom nivou*).

Such branding was not unprecedented among student groups. Otpor had relied heavily on the symbolic fist, represented in spray paint across public spaces and city walls in Serbia, as well as on T-shirts, buttons, and other paraphernalia, creating an instantly recognizable membership and sense of solidarity among young people (and others) across Serbia. Otpor and Student Union members, among others, were also particularly adept at creating events that both drew people and demonstrated popular support. They created iconic images, experiences, and sounds (particularly music) that continued to inspire over time. Otpor's raised, black fist was a kind of political branding, meant to represent the ubiquity of the organization and to provide a mechanism of easy identification with the movement. But Student Union was innovative in tying that branding to expertise and to visually representing its more universal relationship to its student members.

Student Union's method of branding entailed a translation of local knowledge and conditions into a coherent, strategic approach to reform. The act of translating local to universal experience required leaders to be able to simultaneously ground their knowledge of the particular aspects of the university as an institution and to imagine those particularities in relation to a larger vision of "the European university." According to Sanja, branding and commercialization were not a populist way to pander to the masses. Brands were key to both making students aware of their interests and representing those interests. Invoking the problem of "visibility" several times, Sanja told me how important certain kinds of artifacts and practices were to the process of representation. These included media appearances, brochures, parties, and excursions. At the same time, Student Union needed to teach students to recognize these forms of branding as evidence that their interests were being represented.

In a strange twist on the temporality of representation, such consciousness raising was part of the democratic process itself. Awareness of one's own interests both preceded and enabled democratic representation to take place. Student activists thus incorporated such processes of learning to recognize the practices of democratic representation into their vision of activism. Sanja explained:

We are the only student organization which has a vision and a mission. And from one side that's our internal strength. But from the other side it's also our deficit, as I told you, this [lack] of commercial things targeting a wider population. We've never been a populist organization, you know? . . . So from that side, I do think we represent students, not a huge number. But from [the perspective of] Student Alliance [Student Union's rival organization on campus], Student Alliance represents a larger number, because [membership] used to be by default.

Here Sanja makes a twofold case for Student Union's representativity. The first refers back to Student Alliance's role as the only official student group in socialist Yugoslavia. Sanja is implying that because membership for all students was at one point mandatory, belonging to Student Alliance was not a choice, and thus couldn't be seen as democratic. But more importantly, Sanja argued that despite Student Union's smaller membership, its representativity was more genuine, because it dealt with problems that truly affected students. Student Union's representativity lay in its ability to effectively articulate and represent what students really need, despite their low level of awareness about those same problems. And yet the difficulty of translating such issues into visible practices that drew large numbers of students confounded Sanja and her colleagues.

This is not to say that Sanja and others weren't deeply concerned about whether their organization really was democratic. Indeed, Sanja spent time describing to me the complex democratic principles by which Student Union was organized, including its semiannual congress and elected representatives. But the things that Student Union needed to do to gain broader public influence were in some ways at odds with the activities that would make the group popular among its own constituents. She described to me the importance of her work in public relations as creating an image or brand that reached various "stakeholders," from deans, rectors, and other student groups to the media. This was absolutely necessary to being effective, from her perspective, especially in areas like university reform, or to being able to pick up the phone and negotiate with people in power and also be present in the media representing students' needs and opinions.[6] But, she noted, those messages didn't always translate to being heard and seen by "regular" students, or the vast majority of nonaffiliated students, who rarely felt that student groups were really representing their interests.

It was for those reasons that Sanja told me that the recent emphasis for Student Union was on branding (*ove godine akcenat je upravo stavljen na brendiranje*), to deal with the group's lack of visibility at the departments (*nismo vidljivi na fakultetima*) and to increase the number of students familiar with Student Union. This process required making a recognizable identity for the group. Sanja told me:

We had an old brochure on which was written "What is it for, and besides that it also works" [*čemu to služi, a uz to i radi*],[7] which, in my opinion, was a really good slogan. It got you interested at first sight, and then you read it and saw and recognized [Student Union] in some way. From the other side our reputation has been destroyed, these past years. . . . I don't want to say that students are stupid, you know, in that sense that they think what people tell them [to think], but again you have public opinion, you have in all spheres of public life when someone says something terrible about you, in some ways you have to carry that, like it or not. . . . In that sense, I think that it's really more important to . . . create some image and identity [*imidž i identitet*], . . . to have an existing identity . . . that they immediately think, Aha, those are the ones that are fighting for, I don't know, opening another student dorm in Niš, let's say. Or those are the ones introducing ECTS [European Credit Transfer and Accumulation System], and because of them I will more easily be able to pass my exams. In that sense, that kind of identity.

Producing visibility for the group meant creating a set of images and artifacts that could circulate across departments and universities. When mobilized within a specifically democratic idiom, artifacts of expertise (e.g., brochures, media appearances) are important because they become evidence of representation having taken place. Experts produce knowledge of students' needs and interests, which they package as brands of activism. In turn, activist-experts educate students to recognize their own interests in those identities and images. The group can then truly represent (and produce) the interests of its constituents.

Expertise—about university reform, for example—produced policies that translated local concerns into general student interest. Sanja believed that expertise helped student leaders to know what was best for their students. To represent their constituents, student groups had to see the bigger picture and help students see it, too. At the same time, it was important that people learn how to recognize the signs of the "big picture." The more easily promotional material could be standardized and decontextualized, the faster and more widespread its uptake would be, thus creating the effect of circulation.[8] Material could come from any local union and thus represent all unions. This is not to say that Student Union's material did not reference the local. The organization remained committed to its roots as a locally based, department-driven, syndicalist organization. But specific local needs and interests were often represented as aggregate sums of knowledge, like those generated in surveys, which were reliant on universal perspectives of those who administered and analyzed the data.[9]

This process of producing and translating knowledge was essential to some activists' understanding of their work as democratic. However, this version of democratic representation did not go unchallenged. Indeed, there are other ways to define democratic representation in relationship to local knowledge and expertise. What if democratic representation meant *not* translating local concerns into a more general form of interest? What if being truly democratic meant *not* trying to move beyond local concerns? In this case, democratic representation required evidence of being place bound—that is, voicing, rather than translating, local needs and concerns. Indeed, some student activists felt that the work of student groups ought to be more localized and place bound in order to truly be representative.

For example, in 2004 I met with Toma—then the president of Student Alliance—in the group's small, overheated office on the campus of the University of Novi Sad. Toma was eager to compare Student Alliance and Student Union and to demonstrate how very different the approaches of the two groups were. Toma specifically emphasized the local focus of Student Alliance, its direct service to students, and its much larger membership. Like others I spoke to in Student Alliance across three universities, this attention to department-level needs was a strong point of pride. In comparing Student Union and Student Alliance, Toma told me:

We are really different. I think . . . we [Alliance] are the definition of a student organization. We're present at every faculty and technical college [*viša škola*]. Student organizations need to solve the everyday problems which go on, and let's say all other organizations aren't comparable because they aren't present everywhere [at all departments].

He went on to tell me, "Student Alliance is somehow, in my opinion, more a student story [*studentska priča*]. If you deal with students' problems, then you need to work in the most studentish way [*radiš u najstudentskijoj*]." For Toma, the most "studentish" way to work meant dealing with everyday problems. It also meant having an ongoing physical presence in every department, as opposed to being present in high-level ministry meetings or national level events. This sense of locality and physical presence was key to how many Student Alliance members understood the role of the organization. Rather than translating specific concerns into a general student interest, they saw their job as providing highly localized forms of service.

This emphasis on the local was not a "purer" form of representation, although some student activists might have framed it that way (indeed, I often heard student activists from all groups complain how their rivals on campus weren't really representative). Strategies that used brands to both transcend and shape local student concerns and strategies that emphasized locality differed in how they configured the relationship between knowledge and democracy. Student activists like Sanja at Student Union believed that democratic legitimacy rested in the foresight granted to student experts. Expertise was thus key to representation. Those like Toma believed that democracy entailed a channeling, rather than a guiding, of knowledge.

The Ethics of Knowledge

These different attitudes toward knowledge and representation shaped practices within organizations and student campaigns. Sometimes an emphasis on brand or an appeal to "local" voices was a strategic move in a larger struggle over material resources at the university. But the differences in the approaches were also deeply heartfelt. The emphasis on expertise or localized forms of knowledge was an ethical commitment. This came across in a two-hour conversation I had with a twenty-three-year-old student activist, Nada. We met in a dark, crowded, and cramped café in Belgrade, near the Philosophy Faculty, where she was finishing her degree in sociology. Nada was involved in a student group for aspiring sociologists, which began at the Philosophy Faculty in Belgrade in 2000. What was fascinating about the exchange was how Nada seamlessly combined (and represented the group as combining) a commitment to progressive politics and to expertise. Indeed, the role of the group as young professionals, interested in making connections with other sociologists, seemed to be the condition of their progressive political commitments.

Nada had been involved in student protests in the 1990s. She recalled, in rushed and excited tones, her experience of being sixteen years old and marching every day in the protests of 1996 and 1997 in Belgrade. She characterized herself as a leftist (*levičar*) and a humanist. But at the same time, she emphasized that her interest in Stalkeri (the name of her student group) was as a sociologist. She described the group as the future intellectual elite. Stalkeri engaged in political work through the idiom of professional development, holding seminars and other kinds of professional training. At the same time, it had developed ties to organizations within Serbia working on human rights, transitional justice, and feminist issues. Stalkeri was one of few groups to maintain active connections to its Kosovar Albanian student counterparts in Priština, inviting them to Belgrade for a seminar. This was a bold and even risky thing to do for all participants, given the still-tense atmosphere in Belgrade around the issue of Kosovo's independence.

Yet its members' identity as professionals and experts seemed to be what enabled the group to take such risky moves by creating a space for identification and connection outside political and ethnic forms of identification. Indeed, Nada's response to my question about the role of student groups was to emphasize that Stalkeri was politically oriented but that its value lay in not moving outside of its personal and professional frame (as students of sociology). She explicitly drew a distinction between Student Union as a syndicalist organization and Stalkeri as a group of experts (*stručnjaci*). Although this may have been at odds with some of Student Union leadership's own self-understanding, the distinction is important.

The combination of activist, self-proclaimed leftist, feminist, and professional sociologist is an indication of the kinds of contradictory personae bound up in the notion of the expert in post-2000 Serbia. The role of expert could be mobilized to authorize a variety of different activist engagements and political positions. In addition, for Nada, as for others of her generation, this professionalism was a response to and a path out of more intimate encounters with violence and nationalism, as well as the kinds of ethical and social dilemmas that history (and the present) posed. For example, Nada confided that in addition to working with fellow students of sociology in Priština, she had also begun a romantic relationship with one of the participants from Kosovo. It was a relationship that they felt they had to hide, to protect his safety, when he came to Belgrade. But the space that the professional organization afforded opened up worlds for more such intimate connections for young student activists.

These crosshatched understandings of politics, professionalism, and an ethics of knowledge allowed student activists to negotiate highly contested political and social fields. As did other student activists, Nada saw expertise as an important way to be actively engaged but not "political." It was politicians who were "guilty for everything" (*političari su krivi za sve*). Nada, exuberant throughout our conversation, became quiet and began to tear up when I asked her more directly about her experiences during the conflicts of the 1990s. Her father was of Croatian background, and she told me that her response to the difficult experiences during the war of the 1990s was to take a humanist perspective. This combination of expertise and humanism allowed her to come to terms with Serbia's legacy of violence. As with the language of procedure (chapter 5), Nada's mobilization of expertise was an "etiquette of political participation" (Eliasoph 1998, 17) that allowed Nada and others of her generation to create a space for ethical social action.

As Nada's example demonstrates, it was difficult to clearly categorize rhetorics of expertise as left or right because they could be mobilized in the service of elitist or populist understandings of democratic representation. Nada saw herself both as a progressive leftist and a member of an elite cadre of educated, urban, and urbane youth. At the same time that she embraced her self-understanding as political, the positionality of expert or professional allowed Nada to distance herself from formal political processes.

For some students, the stakes of such positions were high, especially in light of Serbia's history of populist nationalist political mobilization. Expertise thus tied into a tradition of vanguardism and a mechanism for developing student consciousness. I heard this position from Jasna, a prominent member of Student Union in Niš, who was active at the faculty, university, and national levels, as well as in the arena of human rights non-governmental organizations. In addition to a deep commitment to human rights, Jasna had no tolerance for nationalist positions, and particularly homophobic ones. She associated such positions with a populist politics that had destroyed Serbian values. Correspondingly, her faith that the general voting constituency would make informed and progressive decisions about these issues was low. She once told me about a conversation she was part of in the executive board of Student Union's national branch in which she strongly advocated the position that the student constituency could not be trusted to make the right (i.e., progressive) decisions. Her colleague on the board, himself a student of political theory with a wicked sense of humor, jokingly called her Lenin. Suffice it to say that the debates in Yugoslavia around party centralism and vanguardism live on in the memories of Student Union leaders, even if expressed in the form of a joke.

According to Jasna, students could not be trusted to make informed decisions as a voting body. As she told me one day during an interview, "Our voting body is still not sufficiently developed or on a high enough level of consciousness to go and out vote" (*naše biračko telo još uvek nije dovoljno razvijeno i na dovoljnom nivou svesti da izađe i da glasa*). Like Sanja, with whom she worked, this low level of consciousness was exemplified by populist approaches to student organizing that pandered to students' most material interests: loosening exam requirements or hosting parties. Jasna told me:

Student Union is one organization which . . . for example, doesn't promote reducing exam requirements [*smanjenje uslova*] at the end of the year . . . because it's aware that in three years, these students will have extended their faculty another two years. I think we see further than all these organizations which fight for requirements in order to draw some larger number of people who support them.

Jasna did believe that material issues like decent food at the student cafeteria were fundamental building blocks of the overall reform effort. But these activities needed to be combined with a long-term perspective and a certain level of consciousness to be meaningful. If the level of student consciousness was low, students could not be trusted to have a long-term perspective or to make informed and intelligent decisions. From her perspective, a populist politics was antithetical to the mission of student groups. At stake for Jasna was a set of ethical links among knowledge, student organizing, and social change.

Yet at the same time, other student activists passionately defended the policies that Jasna referred to as populism on similarly ethical grounds that linked knowledge to the practice of democracy. For example, Dušan and Ljilja were leaders of Student Alliance at the Mathematics Department in Niš. Both knew Jasna well and respected her work. The three student activists had at some point informally approached one another about combining forces. However, Dušan and Ljilja decided against it because they saw Student Union as overly focused on "expertise and programming," with not enough focus on membership. Like Toma in Novi Sad, they saw themselves as more truly committed to representing students' most clearly articulated needs and demands.

If Jasna sought to use student organizing to educate and guide students, Dušan and Ljilja struggled with how to fairly and accurately represent students' voices, even if they (student leaders) knew better. Dušan and Ljilja, like other student representatives I had spoken with, felt deeply torn between their obligations to what they called a "syndical struggle" and their own better judgment about what was best for students. Dušan and Ljilja explained to me the bind they were in when students began to demand that their representatives advocate for a reduced number of exams required to pass to the next year of a faculty. In anticipation of this demand, Dušan, Ljilja, and other members of their organization tried to negotiate with students beforehand, to prevent having to go to the administration with the request. And yet in the end, they had to represent the demands of their constituents to be true to democratic and syndicalist principles. Despite the fact that they didn't agree with the students, Ljilja told me:

When September came they all swarmed here, I don't know how many of them, [saying,] "We want the reduction [of exam requirements]." Which meant that, although we didn't support it, it was our duty to go out in front of [represent] these students [*naša je dužnost da izađemo ispred tih studenata*]. . . . Although I wasn't personaliy for that. You have to because there was a huge number of students and you are here to represent them [*da ih predstavljaš*].

Dušan added, "And that's the biggest problem, as Ljilja said. It wasn't a small number of students. It was a huge number. And then you ask yourself, who is right? Maybe I'm wrong to be against this." Later in the conversation he added:

Here we have this kind of situation in the country that there are two sides: a syndical struggle, and that, the way [Student] Union works, unconnected [*nespojive*]. . . . Syndical struggle implies, in some ways satisfying the majority . . . [*zadovoljava većinu*]. That's the essence of democracy. That means that you try to enable what the majority wants. However, here we have this kind of situation of a country in transition, and the level of consciousness isn't really on that level that you can always do what the majority wants. . . . [T]here exist some things which we have to accept from one side. . . . Whether we like it or not, it simply has to be that way.

The brief narratives of these students demonstrate the aspect of moral compulsion that ran through talk about knowledge and its representation. Although sometimes students explicitly thematized these struggles, more often than not the struggles came out through other debates about the structure of organizations. But in each instance, the stakes of codifying and representing knowledge were about the most democratic way to ensure that student interests be represented and student voices heard. Of course, these practices were shot through with all kinds of social dynamics, struggles for power, and personal intimacies and animosities. Talk of knowledge, performances of expertise, and locality were also registers with which students constructed senses of self and community. And in very real ways these struggles created possibilities for new kinds of political formations and disappointments—in friends, in organizations, in the students whom activists were meant to be representing.

Knowledge Practices and Evidence of Representation

These tropes of locality and expertise captured particular ethical and political relationships among knowledge, power, and democracy. In turn, these ideal relationships informed specific student practices and organizational structures. As in the previous examples, the way in which student groups channeled the interests of their constituents produced very different evidentiary practices for establishing that democratic representation had taken place.

Processes of representation are thus inextricable from the textually and semiotically mediated artifacts that both produce and signal the publics to which they refer (Paz 2009; Cody 2009). For Sanja and other student activists, branding was a way to produce and circulate artifacts that produced evidence of representation having taken place.[10] Brochures, pamphlets, and policy papers were the concrete manifestation of expert knowledge. More important, these artifacts could move across local organizations, in between national and local leadership, and from student groups to other interested stakeholders (a term that Sanja used). The circulation of these artifacts laid the groundwork for others to consider and take up the language and ideas of student experts. For some students this circuit was itself evidence of their ability to represent and shape student interest. For others, it violated student groups' mandates as syndicalist organizations tied to local needs and voices.

Members of rival student groups often made counterclaims that experts couldn't possibly represent university students' needs and interests. These students argued that the knowledge required for democratic action and representation was necessarily located and irreducibly particular. Knowledge here included "local" needs of individual institutional units: how many chairs a department still needs, which deans are sympathetic to student concerns, which professors should be avoided because of corruption or harassment. Student leaders who took this position often tried to make explicit the relations of power underlying expertise by pointing to the way that some kinds of knowledge come to mediate or displace others.

These debates came to a head around attempts to found universitywide student parliaments in 2003 and 2004. The student parliament was intended to be a neutral body on each university campus to which student constituents would elect representatives to negotiate their interests. Negotiations between Student Alliance and Student Union about the structure of parliament hinged very much on the links of locality, representation, and knowledge. A student commission made up of student organization representatives and vice deans from the universities in Serbia was formed in Belgrade in 2003 to draft rules and regulations for a student parliament. The hope was that students could lobby to have the rules included in legislation concerning student organizations.

I was not present at the negotiations, but some key points were explained to me a year later, in March 2004, by Goran, then a member of the top leadership of Student Alliance at the University of Belgrade. Goran had been present at the commission as the student vice dean of the Philosophy Faculty. He was a member and supporter of Student Alliance, although he was also sympathetic to Student Union and had friends and close colleagues in the organization.

As Goran recounted, a key issue in the negotiations was the way representation and elections would be handled for the student parliament (SP). There were two sets of thinking on this at the time of the commission. The first was that the SP should be made up of delegates who were elected at their faculty through faculty-level student parliaments. In turn, faculty representatives would constitute SP at the university level. In the other model, the SP would be made up of delegates chosen in elections at the university level. This would bypass the faculty-level elections altogether for the university SP. In general, Student Alliance was in favor of the first proposition. Its argument, according to Goran, was that it made sense for faculties to choose their representatives because the issues and concerns of each faculty are different. In turn, it would be important to have delegates in the student parliament who understood the needs of each faculty.

Student Union representatives were generally in favor of the second model, elections at the university level. In this scenario, faculties would have elections for an SP that would operate only at the faculty level. In addition, there would be separate universitywide elections for a university SP. The two levels of parliament would bear no direct relationship to each other. As Goran presented it, Student Union's argument was that a university-level student parliament should deal with issues of universal, broader concern to students. This included the general direction of reform and other issues that affected all students. Student Union's position, again according to Goran, was that university SP delegates shouldn't be elected from faculties directly, because that would present a conflict of interest. Faculty delegates would feel torn between their duty to serve and to represent their faculty's interest at the university SP, thus compromising their ability to represent students' general interests. Here, the argument from Student Union emphasized that a delegate from a faculty parliament "can't have a mind of its own" (in Goran's words) but instead would be beholden to the department.

Goran's counterargument for this position was that direct university elections for an SP would mean that some faculties wouldn't be represented in the university parliament at all. Without faculty representatives, particular and locally defined needs of individual faculties might never get a hearing at the universitywide SP. When this issue was raised in the negotiations, Goran said Student Union's answer was that, though it might be true to an extent, the universitywide SP would have experts in the parliament who knew about the university law and how the university should be governed more generally. In other words, Student Union's position was that it would not matter if faculties weren't individually represented; the SP would be made up of experts who would deal with broader legal and organizational issues relevant to the university as a whole, regardless of specific faculty needs.

The stakes of these debates weren't purely ideological. Goran pointed out that a system of university elections for the SP would be much better for Student Union. He was sure they would run a better campaign and that they had a number of student experts skilled in public relations, campaigning, and so on. He noted that Student Alliance had "a deficit of student experts." However, he reasoned that because Student Union had less of a presence in most faculties, if the elections were held at the faculty level, Student Alliance would do much better. People in these organizations were certainly aware that pitching elections at different levels of the university would complement their different organizational structure and talents. At the same time, these strengths are in part linked to the operating ideologies and values of the groups, as well as to their institutional histories and the interests of the students they attract to their membership.

At the same time, the fact that these debates were coded in spatial terms is no coincidence. The debates reveal how particular knowledge practices within the context of democratic representation often rely on coding the particular into the universal. In his examination of literacy and democratic practice in India, Akhil Gupta argued that one reason state bureaucracies focus so much on the production of texts is because they are seemingly circulated more readily and easily (Gupta 2008). This process has a spatial dimension insofar as the networks of circulation create a sense of state presence that both saturates and encompasses localized spaces (see Ferguson and Gupta 2002). While he doesn't theorize the specific materiality of these semiotic forms, Gupta's (2008) insights are helpful in understanding the particularly spatialized dimension of expertise talk and why students find it a powerful way to both represent and enact relations of power and knowledge. Making knowledge seem transcendent, through discursively mediated forms like public relations material or the seemingly technical organization of elections, was one particular approach to dealing with the contradictions of representational democratic processes. At the same time, Student Alliance's interest in organizing elections grounded in local knowledge relied on precisely the inability of the specific to transcend contexts, a very different model of both knowledge production and circulation at the heart of democratic representation (see Greenberg 2012). For Student Alliance, this was fundamentally a localized vision in which particular student interests were irreducible across specific faculty units. For Student Union, it required a universalizing perspective. However, not all students were able or willing to act as such sites of translation. The refusal of circulatability (i.e., the refusal to remove pragmatic markers that linked particular texts to specific and nongeneralizable locales and groups) also had its own appeal.

Representation, Circulation, and Locality

Student organizations enacted linkages of locality and transcendence through specific performances and material artifacts. A particularly telling set of examples involves the very different approaches of Student Alliance and Student Union to publically representing themselves as syndicalist organizations with ties to a broader labor movement.

The first event involves Toma, the president of Student Alliance in Novi Sad, at a local labor rally in June 2003. The labor rally took place at the corner of Mihajla Pupina and Stražilovska streets in the center of Novi Sad, near the headquarters of Vojvodina's provincial government. It was part of a series of protests across the country demanding a "social dialogue" (*tražimo socijalni dijalog*) about the effects of transition, including unemployment, privatization, and cuts in social benefits. There were maybe a thousand people there, largely men and almost entirely older, in their mid- to late thirties and older. As I approached the crowd, I could hear loud chants of "Thieves, thieves" (*lopovi, lopovi*) and placards and stickers proclaiming, "I don't want to be a victim of transition" (*Neću da budem žrtva tranzicije*).

The act of creating solidarity and locality throughout the protest took several forms. The fact that this protest was one of many across the country under the rubric of searching for a "social dialogue" lent it the feel of a broader movement. But at the same time, speakers marked locality by making specific mention of Vojvodina (the region of which Novi Sad is capital) and the particular plight of its workers. In demanding recognition, one speaker told the crowd, "We don't want to become numbers; we have a name and a last name" (*ime i prezime*). He referenced ties of local solidarity and their undoing by economic transition, saying, "We don't want to hate our neighbors because they have work and we don't."[11] On some level, comments like this mobilized cultural knowledge and sentiment, even as they pointed to the desire for continued social ties that linked people to one another. Another presenter called out the names of cities from which he had received telegrams of support, again linking Novi Sad and Vojvodina as a specific place to a network of other sites of solidarity across the country.

It was with this context of making use of locality to forge solidarity that Toma got up to speak. As with the speakers that preceded him, his brief comments were framed in terms of a connection between students and union members that was reliant on highly contextual features of talk. In other words, Toma's bid for solidarity was highly dependent on his actual presence at the rally, and his attempts to produce solidarity entailed a highly context-specific (indexicalized) language (Silverstein 1976). This is not to say that Toma's bid for solidarity could not be circulated in media representations of the event. But the performance of solidarity relied on his presence at the event, on stage, addressing those gathered. The act of making solidarity could be represented or invoked, but not reenacted, as it circulated.

In part, Toma was reacting to other modes of creating localized forms of solidarity already at work in the event. He joined other speakers on a raised stage at the front of the rally. He told the group that he had come to express student support, and he invoked the unity (*jedinstvo*) of students and workers. He directly linked the fate of students, in terms of both space and time, by telling the group, "Your appeal today will be our appeal tomorrow," and he mentioned both the large numbers of unemployed workers and the thirty-six thousand students at the University of Novi Sad (presumably both future workers and future unemployed). The language of "your [*vaš*] appeal today" and "our [*naš*] appeal tomorrow" (*vaš zahtev* and *naš zahtev*, respectively) linked students to workers, binding them together in relationship to a common cause and a common fate. It was also likely that Toma was relying on his own family network (his father was heavily involved in the workers' union) to signal insider status. Toma spoke for just a minute or two, but by being present at the rally, he attempted to embed his presence as a student leader within the frame of a larger labor event. At the same time, his participation in such a localized event echoed his comments to me in my interview with him about the importance of being truly present in order to be representative.

By contrast, the press conference during which Student Union signed the Agreement of Cooperation (*Sporazum o saradnji*) with the union Nezavisnost (Independence) was a markedly different event. The two Student Union representatives at the event also tried to produce a kind of solidarity between students and workers. However, if Toma's appeal hinged on the fact that the problems of labor today are the problems of students tomorrow, the language of "agreement about international cooperation" focused on common objectives and conditions that affected both groups. The language of solidarity was couched in the mutual interests of the two sides rather than their common fate.

In addition, the act of solidarity focused on a different kind of co-action—not the presence of students at a labor rally but the mutual production and signing of a document that bound students and workers to a common cause. The document itself was easy to put in motion, with websites, press statements, and resulting newspaper coverage. In other words, the solidarity produced in the document was not wholly contingent on the context of its signing. The terms and conditions of solidarity were written into the document itself. Although the signing ritually performed the agreement of both sides, the language of solidarity itself was enacted any time the document was represented, read, cited, or put into circulation.

The press conference to announce the signing took place in a small room in the office of Nezavisnost on March 10, 2004, only a few months before the protest at which Toma spoke. Two representatives from Student Union, Aleksander and Zoran, sat at a long table at the front of the room alongside a representative from the labor union, facing the press and a few guests in attendance. As the "most representative student union," Zoran told the assembled group, it made sense for Student Union to work in conjunction with Nezavisnost. He listed the values the two groups shared, "typical syndicalist questions." This included the economic and social role of students, as well as the reform of the labor market. When he finished speaking, one of the two Nezavisnost representatives talked about the international dimension of the two groups, both of which were "on the road to Europe." The second representative added that it was in everyone's interest to participate together in the reform of higher education and that "a modern syndicate should be open to the presence of young, educated people."

Aleksander went on to add that Student Union was already in a network of student unions (the National Unions of Students in Europe, or ESIB). They didn't want to be part of the union, he noted, because "we are a student syndical organization." While all the speakers emphasized the commonality of their fight, the strategic interest they had in common, and the future of "the struggle" (*borba*), the representatives from Student Union were nonetheless careful to distinguish the organization as independent, with its own goals and connections.

The Student Union website later reported that the agreement "implied joint activities to develop and advance relations, and also worked to address all problems in which [Student Union] has engaged up to this point, and will engage in the future, to activities that connect with the democratization of society and the university, syndical and other student groups." The language of the actual agreement is similar, focusing on the "democratization of society, the establishment of principles of good governance, creation of reform and stabilization of development, the development of tolerance among people and the further development of civil society."[12]

What made both these groups syndicalist, within the framework they cocreated at the press conference and within their document, was a common focus on objective conditions that affected their members. In other words, the local needs of students were articulated in terms of broader social questions and trends that linked workers and students. The value of the groups' solidarity was that it expanded their capacity to channel those needs toward a broader program of social change and democratization. The syndicalist project relied on localized and specific concerns, but it transformed those concerns into joint initiatives and programs that superseded local conditions and context.

So, the point is not that Student Alliance or Student Union represented student needs better or in a "more studentish" way, in Toma's words. Rather, the evidentiary basis of representation—what we might call indexicalized locality versus objectified circulation—was completely different. Evidence of solidarity was produced in accordance with different organizational practices for representing and servicing student needs. For Toma, his presence at the labor rally intersects with his emphasis on being "present everywhere" at the faculty. This is the condition of being the "most studentish organization." For Zoran and Aleksander, the signing of the agreement fit with the idea that Student Union was a syndicalist organization that articulates broader student interests on the basis of more universal knowledge practices. The agreement with Nezavisnost enacted the erasure of the specific conditions of the agreement's contextually bound production, thus allowing it to move across, and bring sense to, specific contexts and problems. In other words, it operated parallel to the logic of branding and visibility.[13]

The Bogeyman of Freedom: The Paradox of Visibility

Paradoxically, visibility to the outside world did not necessarily mean transparency for organizations. As students struggled with how to represent student constituents (in the democratic sense), they also confronted the problem of how to represent their own organizations. As in the example that opened this chapter, presenting themselves as experts entailed a staging of public and private spaces, as well as insider and outsider relationships to knowledge about and within student organizations. In addition, the idea of branding and controlling image necessitated turning into private spaces those spheres of the organization that had previously been open and available to the public. In other words, particular kinds of visibility in one domain required other kinds of silencing, including that of internal dissent. In the process, what some student leaders saw as necessary to maintaining student influence after 2000 felt like betrayal of central democratic principles and ideals to other activists. These acts of boundary making had profound effects on the structure of Student Union and on the way in which students redefined the most fundamental definitions of student activism.

In late summer of 2003, an article by a member of a local Student Union branch at the Philosophy Faculty at the University of Belgrade appeared in the faculty's own zine, *Bogeyman of Freedom* (*Bauk Slobode*).[14] The article, titled "The Poverty of Centralism [*Beda centralizma*]: SUS from Network to Organization" (*Beda centralizma*), included the following critiques:

Have you noticed that in every organization, as well as in student organizations, there always exist those who have the right to vote (those who call themselves the Executive, Administrative, Main, . . . Board) and those who don't have that right? Why, then, would someone who is never asked about anything be motivated to work on anything? . . . In place of those who have and don't have the right to vote appear those who have and don't have the power of decision making, material well-being, information, knowledge, technology, connections, experience, influence.

Is [Student Union] now an organization or a network of autonomous organizations:

Are people who are in the Executive Board of [Student Union] carrying out their will or the will of the people they represent? . . . Do members of [Student] Union generally have their own will and vision or do they only listen to recommendations (read: directives) from the center?

The article ran on for several pages. The critique struck right at the heart of the new modes of knowledge production that Student Union leadership had identified as necessary to its continued relevance in changing political contexts. Playing on long-standing tensions in the organization between the importance of local chapters' knowledge and experiences and the expertise of a nationally and internationally circulating central leadership, the article crystallized some of the most uncomfortable and tense debates of the time. That the critique centered on distribution of knowledge and ideas was no surprise, given that developing technologies of knowledge had been critical to the changing face of student activism. The Student Union of the Faculty of Philosophy (Studentska Unija Filozofskog Fakulteta, or SUFF) was a local branch of Student Union. It was considered more left wing than Student Union as a whole, and many of its members were self-proclaimed anarchists. No one was really surprised that such a critique would come from SUFF. But the vehemence of the reaction to the article indicated that it had hit a deep nerve within the organization. The national-level leadership was particularly upset, because they were in fact concerned about the dwindling activity and initiative of the local union branches. Rumor of the article spread like wildfire, and the black-and-white photocopied publication was quickly pulled out of distribution. While some members of Student Union I spoke with agreed with the thrust of the article, they were nonetheless angry and betrayed by the public airing of organizational dirty laundry. Many among the national leadership believed that the faculty union should have gone through internal mechanisms within the larger organization to complain. Few seemed to pick up on the irony of this suggestion and the way it reproduced the authority and centralized power of the groups' national leadership to determine what was and was not appropriate action and expression. In the absence of a clear path for censure, SUFF was at first reprimanded for using the Student Union photocopier for the publication without permission.

"From Network to Organization"

Why was the reaction so forceful? What was really at stake in the crackdown on SUFF? Student Union began with the founding of the first faculty union in 1992.[15] Throughout the 1990s, new faculty unions sprung up, developing into a loose network of highly independent groups that sometimes coordinated actions. More often than not, local unions targeted issues of educational reform and state intervention in educational policy at the department level. This network of department-level organizations gained more organizational coherence following the 1996–97 student protests: three months of daily street protests organized both by student activists and opposition parties. A new kind of student movement emerged from the protests with an organized leadership experienced in mobilizing large numbers of students in highly visible protest for an extended period of time. In the wake of the protests, membership in local faculty organizations swelled. The loose and informal network began to take the shape of a coordinated national movement.

With crackdowns on university autonomy in 1998 and the three-month NATO bombing of 1999, organizing became more difficult. Student groups had to develop new ways to be resilient, flexible, and effective. While Otpor developed a strategy of a seemingly spontaneous and informal network with no clear leadership to avoid government repression and violence, Student Union followed a different tack. Leading activists of local faculty unions began to reach out to a larger, international student movement. Student Union formed a nationally organized network in 1998 (Student Union of Serbia) and joined the National Unions of Students in Europe (ESIB) in 1999. ESIB was Europe's largest network of student organizations and was highly influential, particularly in matters of European higher education reforms. One of the conditions for ESIB membership

was that a national-level organization coordinate branches of that organization at lower levels. A Student Union leadership emerged at the national level, although the autonomy of local faculties remained critical to
Student Union's organizational identity, mandate, and sense of democratic
legitimacy.

After the October 5 revolution, Student Union activists struggled to
reinvent the organization. The group had always been rooted in faculty-
level activism, including protecting students' rights and encouraging reform of the most egregious problems in the university. It was in some sense
natural to turn back to university reform after October 5 and to focus the
group's organizational network and expertise on wide-scale institutional
change. By 2002, Student Union was a member of ESIB and a recognized
partner in civil society circles. It received funding for projects from foreign
and local donors. As Student Union extended its network of contacts and
partners with Serbian and international nongovernmental organizations,
donors, and the ESIB, it became clear that a stronger central organization was needed to maintain the group's professionalism and coordination.
Systems for managing and distributing grant money called for more central oversight, as did implementation of specific, sometimes donor-driven,
programs. As the group's organizational structure had grown increasingly
complex to accommodate expanding membership and initiatives, the tensions between Student Union as a democratic, locally directed network
and a democratic national organization were beginning to tear the group
apart at the seams.

By 2003, when SUFF launched its critique, Student Union had a
national-level office with an executive board composed of representatives
from university-level branches in the four main university towns in Serbia
(Novi Sad, Belgrade, Niš, and Kragujevac). In turn, those university-level
branches were coordinated with local unions at individual faculties. In theory, each faculty union was an autonomous organization coordinated in a
network that stretched across universities and the country. The various levels of Student Union had names that indicated the level at which they supposedly operated: Student Union of Serbia, Student Union of Novi Sad,
Student Union of the Philosophy Faculty or of the Political Science Faculty.
The Student Union branches at the department level (*fakulteti*) were most
often referred to as "the locals" in shorthand (*lokali*, or *lokalna unija*).

With the focus on university reform and adoption of the Bologna
Process, it became more important for the national organization to

coordinate local unions in pursuing the goal of reform. This meant that student leaders needed to become fluent in key policy issues and the technical nitty-gritty of European higher education reform. For example, Bologna Process reforms included policies such as the introduction of standardized credits (*bodovi*, in Serbian) that would assign specific values to certain courses on the basis of workload. The introduction of standardized credits would allow for a Europe-wide system of educational mobility and exchange, enabled by the commensurability of knowledge units across disparate university systems. Even understanding the complex formula for standardizing classes and credits required tremendous time and expertise.

These shifts were not only technical and administrative. As I've discussed throughout this chapter, a number of students leaders felt that their ties to ESIB and their extensive knowledge of reform processes made Student Union a far more effective and influential group. In mobilizing this expertise, student leaders, especially in Student Union, could claim to represent the real long-term interests of students. Student leaders argued that Serbia's official membership in the European Higher Education Area created by the Bologna Process would help students with issues of educational standards, employment, and personal mobility. It would also help Serbia integrate back into Europe, overcoming the long shadow of its violence and nationalist legacies. To this extent, student activists within Student Union of Serbia were able to articulate uncomfortable or even unacceptable issues to the broader student body as more technical and seemingly apolitical questions of education reform and improving student standards.

In contrast, as an organization promoting Serbian democracy, it was important to Student Union's legitimacy within its membership and with the student body in general that it function as a fully democratic organization. This translated into policies for transparent and inclusive membership and decision making, including internal elections and general electoral competition with other student organizations. Top leadership passed from local-level unions to university and then national administrative bodies like the executive board (*izvršni odbor*). Decisions were still affirmed in the semiannual student assembly (*skupština*), where representatives from the local, university, and national unions discussed and voted on key initiatives and elected new members to administrative bodies. However, assembly initiatives came from the national leadership as often as they came from locals. The executive board also was overrepresented by Belgrade and Novi

Sad, leaving Niš and especially Kragujevac at the margins of power. I heard people within local unions speak disparagingly about the supposed importance of the local unions, even as national-level representatives clung to the local unions as the site of democratic legitimacy for the organization. Thus, the terms *local* (*fakultet*), *university*, and *national* coded not only different kinds of knowledge and levels of expertise within Student Union; the relations between these levels began to be expressed in terms of a center and its peripheries.

Structurally, faculty-level unions were autonomous and localized. The existence of weak, undirected faculty unions increasingly became a problem as Student Union began to compete with other organizations for student votes and membership. The elections determined which groups were represented on the administrative bodies that set educational and administrative policies for the faculty. Having strong, visible faculty-level unions in this context was extremely important for mobilizing votes and successfully competing in elections. Rival student groups, such as Student Alliance, focused on increasing membership at the faculty level and promoted themselves as serving the needs of local constituents, in contrast to Student Union. They often did much better than Student Union at faculty elections.

In response to this increasing centralization and the pressure of faculty-based elections, Student Union's national leadership developed several new ways to better coordinate the organization and strengthen the local branches. They initiated university-level unions to facilitate contact between local unions and the national organization. In 2002 they introduced a national training team to provide training and expertise for faculty union activists to improve their organizational, advocacy, and public relations skills (see chapter 3). While the national training team was meant to empower local unions, it was also meant to streamline their programming and public relations, thus making them more effective and more in concert with Student Union of Serbia's goals as a whole. In conjunction with these training efforts, the executive board of the organization proposed a massive reorganization of the group to strengthen the local representation and participation and to invest resources in local development.[16] For Student Union to become a recognizable and desirable brand in student life and student elections required a degree of homogeneity in the way the locals represented their goals and achievements. Student Union, always highly skilled in the aesthetic side of representation, also coordinated public relations materials for elections, using its recognizable orange and black color scheme, promotional materials, T-shirts, lighters, and pens.

The Assembly's Decision: Making Public and Private

It was in this context that that the zine *Bogeyman of Freedom* launched its critique, resisting the newly dominant models of knowledge production and representation within the larger national organization. After heated debate, the national leadership decided to hold a hearing on the matter at its biannual national assembly in December 2003. The Ninth Student Union of Serbia Assembly (Skupština) took place in November 2003 at the mountain resort of Zlatibor. After a long bus ride begun at six-thirty on a chilly, gray morning, I arrived with the Niš delegation in time to check in to the hotel and make the three-o'clock opening of the event. The assembly took place in a large meeting room with a podium and raised dais at the front, and two sets of enormous doors flanking the back. The heavy wood paneling and yellowing rugs felt like complete throwbacks to an earlier era—one could have easily imagined the Communist Party meetings and workers councils and junkets that had taken place in the space for years before students appropriated it for their newly configured democratic congress.

The event opened with roll call and confirmation that each delegate held the papers that proved he or she was a voting representative of his or her local organization. Those assembled were then asked to reshuffle where they were sitting according to delegations, and the room buzzed while students got up, moved across the room, and found their seats. After the meeting was called to order, the group held several initial votes on procedural matters. One such matter was whether to close some of the issues on the agenda to the public. The points in question concerned membership, the financial report, and the question of the status of Student Union of the Philosophy Faculty, given the critical article in *Bauk Slobode*. While the question of closing the meeting during discussion of finances was less contested, the hearing on the status of SUFF caused quite a stir, although the group voted overwhelmingly to close those parts of the session to the public (in this case, guests, including myself, the ESIB members who had come as observers, and nondelegate members of Student Union of Serbia). I was told it was the first time that any part of the Skupština had ever been closed.

The decision to close the formerly public proceedings of the assembly turned out to be an issue that defined much of the meeting for that day. In the process, members and nonmembers began to construct and enact a new understanding of what was rightfully public and private knowledge within the organization. When the proceedings turned to the question of membership, the facilitators asked nonmembers to leave. I rose and left the room along with others. One of those asked to leave was Bojan, a former member of Student Union Belgrade, who had attended the assembly out of loyalty to the organization and to see old friends. He had been a member for years until he transferred to a private university, and he was absolutely fuming. Student Union is and always has been a public organization, he declared, and this had never happened before. Bojan was the most vocal of those of us who formed a tight knot just outside the floor-to-ceiling doors that had suddenly become a very real barrier between those who were in and those who were out.

Several people who were not allowed to be in the hearing milled outside and eventually wandered off as time passed. I stayed in the foyer in front of the meeting room, waiting to go back in. After awhile some of the other "excluded" guests came back up to the area outside of the meeting room. Bojan had gotten ahold of a copy of the Student Union statute. He was waving it around, showing everyone who passed the article that stated that the work of Student Union was public and that all sittings should be open to the public. The decision to shut the meeting was in violation of the statute, he told anyone in earshot. Bojan was most upset by this statutory violation. The sudden shift in policy has left him excluded from an organization of which he had long been a part. Indeed, the group seemed to be redefining itself, before our very eyes, on the basis of that exclusion. If the statute had at one point codified publicity as a feature of the organization, then that was no longer the case. In physically circulating the document and creating publicity around the statute, Bojan seemed to be attempting to counteract the process. His small act of circulating the document was a symbolic enactment of what should have been the free flow and movement of knowledge.

The events that unfolded at the assembly in Zlatibor were a microcosm of processes within the organization more broadly. As with the example of the unwitting student who opened this chapter, student activists were establishing insider and outsider status through access to knowledge. What's more, knowledge also mediated a process of making spaces public and private within organizations themselves. Those who were experts could mobilize gatekeeping levels of secondary knowledge that mediated access to core sites of knowledge production, like the assembly debate. In addition, those "in the know" also became agents who enacted and policed the emerging boundary of public and private, much like full-member students policed the doors that sealed off the assembly room. As I stood with the excluded folks outside the doors, I watched a new discourse develop, in part serious and in part quite playful. Those of us on the outside performed a kind of confusion, as we asked one another and those full members who wandered in and out, "Are we allowed in? Is it still closed?" There was, no doubt, a certain pleasure in this performance, as we threw up our hands in confusion, trying to establish just how hard and fast the boundaries were. The joking frustration established a kind of solidarity among the excluded, and it pointed both humorously and uncomfortably to new power dynamics between insiders and outsiders. The very knowledge of whether we were allowed in or not was itself a new kind of knowledge, created (and made relevant) in the moment of exclusion that would have been unthinkable without the public-private division being acted out on both sides of the doors.

In framing and reframing space as public and private, people were negotiating a variety of issues, from what constituted legitimate forms of political and moral action within the organization to what kinds of representations of the organization were authoritative and appropriate. Susan Gal and Gail Kligman (2000, 41) have termed this process *fractal recursivity*, in which "everyday public and private distinctions—whether of activities, spaces, or social groups—are subject to reframings and subdivisions in which some part of the public is redefined as private, and vice-versa." This initial framing of public and private thus became the basis for a reorganization of relations within the organization itself.

Such negotiations were happening in the name of democracy: to protect the image of the organization so that it might be able to carry out its work of representing and appealing to a broader student constituency. At stake was also the reputation of the organization for yet another imagined public. The potential audience for both the *Bauk Slobode* critique was also a potential voting student body. In addition to worrying about which kinds of information ought to be public within the group, the censure of SUFF was also about managing the circulation of information outside of the organization itself. Ironically, Bojan was not particularly sympathetic to the plight of SUFF. In fact, he was angry at the organization for having "muddied" (*blatiti*) the reputation of Student Union. His response to the actual question of SUFF's membership echoed that of the leadership and others who had voted to close the session. When debating in the opening session whether to close the assembly to the public, one of the leaders of Student Union had argued that SUFF's actions and any information about those actions could only hurt the reputation of Student Union. Others told me that they objected not to the complaints in *Bauk Slobode* but to their public nature.

One student leader from Novi Sad complained that SUFF had been disrespectful (*bezobrazan*), using a word that one might invoke to scold naughty children and that implies a loss of honor or self-respect. "We have institutional methods, and they didn't use them," he told me. If you have "goodwill," he went on to say, then the problem should have been resolved "internally." The problem was not the critique per se but that it publically embarrassed the organization and bypassed institutionally established methods for internal resolution of conflict. The private disciplining of SUFF would restore the internal logic of conflict management and at the same time privatize knowledge about Student Union that, if in public circulation, could hurt its reputation. By the end of the assembly, the entire organization had voted to revoke SUFF's full membership, stripping them of their right to vote in the assembly.

In addition to creating new hierarchies within the organization, the controversy around SUFF produced new configurations of public and private, internal and external, and inclusion and exclusion by establishing which kinds of knowledge should and should not circulate. Again, following Gal and Kligman, once these lines of public and private were made to seem natural or taken for granted, they became the basis for further divisions of social and political space. In redrawing lines between public and private spaces within the assembly proceedings, student activists were able to redefine the meaning and significance of knowledge anchored to those newly emerging distinctions. Knowledge that emerged in closed proceedings was private. It was not appropriate for circulation outside particular networks of people who were both designated and constituted as insiders by their relationship to redefined knowledge practices.

This production of a new public-private distinction in the organization then became the basis for a secondary distinction between public and private knowledge about the organization. Particular kinds of visibility in one domain required other kinds of silencing, including of public dissent. No longer concerned with open access to information, a policy, as Bojan pointed out, that had defined an earlier, activist iteration of the group, Student Union of Serbia became a political entity concerned with managing reputation and image in particular ways. In turn, student leaders and participants in the vote to censure SUFF redefined the kind of talk that could and should circulate publically.

The closing of the session was thus an enactment of new practices of knowledge production that enabled the organization to create, maintain, and control a public persona—as a coherent group of experts who could both understand and represent student interests. Many students had objected to the zine article because it publicly and embarrassingly undermined Student Union's presentation of itself in other public spaces. The article questioned the very possibility of representation in a centralized organization with a strong national leadership by countering with a vision of a direct, unmediated, and locally specific form of democratic practice. Controlling critique necessitated turning into private spaces those spheres of the organization that had previously been open and available to the public. Of course, this process was not merely abstract. As it unfolded, real friendships and intimacies in the group were also reconfigured, as people like Bojan and the SUFF delegate who had written the original article in *Bauk Slobode*, found themselves suddenly on the outside.

Managing Publicity and Managing Knowledge

The attempt to privatize controversy around *Bauk Slobode* demonstrates the ways that new democratic publics in Serbia have relied on nested forms of public and private. People collectively negotiate new ways of being citizens when they debate where and how forms of public talk ought to take place (Eliasoph 1998). Such "distinctions between public and private simultaneously create a context for interaction and a relationship to the wider world" (Eliasoph 1998, 16). Yet here, in an ironic twist on Nina Eliasoph's (1998, 16) observation that "speaking public-spiritedly creates the public sphere," these student activists rely on the privatization of talk to secure space and authority under changing conditions of publicity. Feminist political theorists have long argued that democratic publics rely on the split between public and private (and the consequent erasure of the gendered private sphere from public life) (Phillips 1991). Here we see that the dichotomy of public and private is reworked and remapped within the putatively "public" sphere of activism.

Safeguarding the boundary of public and private becomes critical in contexts in which processes of representation are tied to processes of branding (Manning 2010). As in the case here, even activist groups must manage and safeguard their image as part of the representative process. This emphasis on branding is perhaps not surprising, given the increasing importance of consumer forms of citizenship in which "consumption becomes the dominant means for defining personal and collective identities" (Foster 2002, 4). Indeed, the incredible importance of marketing and image have accompanied the rise of mass-mediated electoral politics. This is particularly relevant when the performance of electoral stability is tied to peripheral nations' ability to attract foreign investment and international recognition (Graan 2010; Bishara 2008).

What the case of student activists demonstrates is that these dynamics are linked, but not wholly reducible, to the interpenetration of logics of capital and consumption with those of democratic citizenship. When some students mobilize ideas of brands or marketing and others emphasize the importance of seemingly noncirculating forms of discourse, they are getting at more fundamental contradictions of democratic representation. How does one make representation visible? What constitutes evidence that representation has taken place? What is the role of those being represented versus those who might claim to represent them? And what does it mean for democracy if democratic representatives (like socialist vanguards before them) know the interests of "the people" before "the people" even do?

5

"We Have to Be Politicians"
Proceduralism and the Depoliticization of Politics

Eastern Europeans identify politics with fraud, with something that's no business of theirs.

—György Konrád, *Antipolitics*

THE LAST PLACE YOU'D EXPECT to find a student with an intense disdain for politics is behind an imposing desk in a well-appointed corner office in a university administration building. It was therefore odd to find Ivana, a student activist deeply frustrated by the politicization of student life in Serbia, in just such an office. She had recently been elected by the faculty at the University of Belgrade to be the student vice dean. Ivana exemplified student activists' uneasy relationship with politics in postrevolutionary Serbia. She was willing—indeed, she felt compelled—to take up the mantle of (limited) power in a formally elected position. And yet she eschewed politics and its impact on the life of students in Serbia.

Ivana and I chatted in her office one day in May 2003, shortly after her election to the position. A longtime and very active member of Savez Studenata (Student Alliance) in Belgrade, she described the juggling act she was facing. She had to meet the many demands of student constituents and maintain good relations with faculty, who were often suspicious of student groups. She was bound by the institutional rules and constraints of her position, but she was supposed to represent students who often bucked at those constraints. Sitting in her office overlooking the plaza in front of the Faculty of Philosophy—the storied site of student resistance in Yugoslavia and Serbia—Ivana struggled to bridge very different kinds of student activism, from protest to democratic institution building. This was bound to produce not only disappointment but also accusations of being "political," which so often accompanied those who juggle impossibly contradictory roles.

Ivana's nonconfrontational demeanor, combined with her obvious intelligence and academic track record, made her the ideal candidate for the faculty-elected student vice dean (*student prorektor*). Yet despite her qualifications, she was ambivalent about her new role and her different responsibilities. When I asked her what she thought the ideal role of student groups should be, she responded:

It's through, I don't know, some center for career or scientific work, for sports, for uh, I don't know . . . parties and concerts. We are not living in very happy times so I really . . . I would really like that students [do not have to be] busy about reform and all that stuff. That they don't have to be worried about what is going to [happen] with them tomorrow, whether they are going to find some job or something. And that all their problems would be how to have a party. It's not possible right now. We have to be little politicians, I think, right now and to do some big stuff. To fight with big beasts [*zveri*].

Ivana and I had just had a long conversation about how to effectively deal with professors, students, and administrators. It was telling, then, that she would suddenly present this strategic engagement as a necessary evil— a heroic, if undesired, fight against "beasts." I was struck by her framing of her student activist work as a kind of compulsion. The image of the student forced to fight for reform in unhappy times worked as a narrative strategy of student activists as necessary victims and heroes of democracy. Politics was an unwanted but compulsory obligation at odds with Ivana's other commitments and desires.

This language of compulsion was just one discursive strategy by which people in Serbia negotiated a major dilemma: how to justify being politically engaged when politics was viewed as corrupting, dirty, and self-interested. "We have to be politicians" was an example of how activists could "portray themselves as subject to external control" (Hull 2003, 303) in order to justify their involvement in the messy world of politics. The language of compulsion was a genre of activist talk that also included appeals to proceduralism, expertise, youth innocence, or altruism. In focusing on talk such as proceduralism or expertise, we can see how seemingly depoliticizing moves are paradoxically crucial to the production of new political publics as people negotiate the "etiquette for political participation" (Eliasoph 1998, 17).[1]

Indeed, in my field research with student groups, I quickly discovered that there was no worse accusation than being political. The idea that that politics is dirty has given rise to alternative citizen practices outside formal political institutions in places as diverse as the United States, Latin America, and formerly socialist Eastern Europe (Forment 2007; Gutmann 2002; Fox 2004). Framing social engagement as not political can paradoxically create room for activism in such contexts. Here I show how students mobilized a language of proceduralism, which, while seemingly apolitical, was an attempt to manage complicated relations of power and politics. Such cases challenge the distinction between technocratic domains of governance and more authentic democratic politics that eschews administrative forms of rule (Comaroff and Comaroff 1997). In Serbia, genres of apolitics were rhetorical techniques and ethical strategies for remaining socially engaged in contexts in which such engagement is deeply suspect. Increasingly, it is necessary to look in antipolitical spaces to understand sites where postsocialist democratic activism is taking place.

Student groups in Serbia after 2000 walked this fine line between being socially engaged and not political. They highlighted continuities between student protest in the 1990s and student organizing after the 2000 revolution. In doing so, they drew on long-standing associations of youth as innocent and altruistic. However, after 2000, the mechanisms for creating and signaling innocence began to change. Students began to advocate for procedural and legal frameworks to safeguard student groups from political manipulation or the moral taint of self-interest. Like the discourse of university reform or expertise, appeals to procedure seemed antithetical to the spontaneous, collective politics of revolutionary and protest movements. For students, this disavowal of politics became a site for reconfiguring political agency by wedding social action to technocratic and procedural ethics. If they were compelled by legal frameworks and administrative procedures, how could they be acting out of personal motivation or gain? By regimenting their actions to such frameworks, they could effect a purification of politics.

The Problem with Politics

The idea that formal politics and state power are corrupting has long-standing resonance in socialist and postsocialist Eastern Europe. In this context, people often negotiate their uncertainty about a changing world by talking about the gap between appearances and realities, whether pertaining to the value of currency (Lemon 1998) or the motivations of intimates (Pesman 2000). In the Serbian case the suspicion of inauthenticity was most present when people were talking about politics. Such associations were intensified in the wake of Yugoslavia's violent breakup. As several anthropologists studying the former Yugoslavia have demonstrated, people in the region frequently drew the distinction between dirty politics and a morally valorized apolitical world. This framework was often mobilized to make sense of wartime violence and the dissolution of everyday forms of sociality and community (Grandits 2007; Helms 2007; Kolind 2007; see also Neofostis 2009).[2]

Narratives of distrust in formal politics often took the form of tragic tales of Serbia's descent into nationalism and violence. In both everyday conversation and scholarly discourse, people in Serbia attributed the country's nationalist path, Milošević's decadelong rule, and violence in the region to the manipulation of political and economic elites (Greenberg 2006b; Lazić 2000; Goati 1997).[3] Tropes of self-serving, power-hungry elites and victimized ordinary folk go back to much earlier socialist-era discourses in Yugoslavia and Eastern European communist countries (Cohen 1989).[4]

But the critique of politics did not only implicate the world of official political power. The taint of politics was part of a larger set of cultural cosmologies surrounding the breakdown of everyday social relations. Indeed, many people I spoke with assumed not only that formal politics was corrupt but also that the problem was endemic to Serbia, a society "without values." Sometimes these narratives of Serbian "mentality" (*mentalitet*) were vague and shadowy, peopled by deceitful and immoral characters. Being a foreigner, I was particularly privy to the mundane ways that such distrust permeated everyday life. I was frequently offered unsolicited advice, despite the fact that I rarely, if ever, was taken advantage of as an outsider. But to hear people tell it, navigating everyday life entailed wading through a moral morass and hidden agendas, dealing with everyone from untrustworthy taxi drivers to student activists who were trying to pull the wool over my eyes.

Indeed, so prevalent was this suspicion of hidden motives that I even encountered young people who didn't really trust themselves. The link between politics and personal gain meant that even student activists felt the need to disavow their own engagement in student organizations. For example, for Saša, a leading member of a student group in Niš, the threat of his own self-interest was so problematic it became a carefully managed secret.[5] The afternoon I met with him, Saša hung back after having had a lively conversation with members of his group in which he had held forth loudly and frequently. Given his strong advocacy for his student group during the meeting, it was particularly surprising that he would undercut that narrative in our private conversation. As the two of us continued to talk, I asked an innocuous background question about his reasons for getting involved in student organizing. He fixed me with a serious look and asked me to stop taping. With the tape recorder off, he confided to me: "Anyone who didn't admit to being involved in student groups partly out of personal interest [*lični interes*] was lying." And then, as if taken aback by the severity of such an accusation, he hesitated and added that it didn't all come down to personal interest, but it was definitely a factor.

This admission was more banal than Saša imagined. But the secrecy and taboo surrounding it spoke volumes. When I asked him what "personal interest" meant, he described everyday practices that might emerge organically for any engaged student. He told me that when he went to sit for an exam, a professor might know him better than another student, which might be beneficial to him. He also cited professional benefits, such as having access to people in city government. In another example, he noted that if there were a problem at the faculty, he could go in and talk to a professor to resolve it. What's more, he added, because of previous interactions through his student organization work, that interaction with a professor could be casual to the point of joking around (*zezanje*). It was particularly ironic that he saw such a relationship as tainted by self-interest. Indeed, oftentimes student constituents relied on their representatives to mobilize precisely such connections on their behalf. But the line between the skills and relationships needed to be a good representative and those that could be considered self-interested and political was impossibly thin. Formal representation could easily bleed into personal joking around. Crossing that boundary was deemed to be "personal interest."

The disjuncture between Saša's enthusiasm in talking about the work of his organization and his embarrassed confession of potential personal gain revealed just how difficult it was for a socially engaged young person to justify actions—even to themselves—that might be seen as political. What's more, the work of being a good student leader inevitably implicated people in webs of social relations that made it hard to distinguish the professional from the personal. So deeply interwoven was personal interest or professional advancement with politics that the idea of students balancing their own interests with those of whom they represented was unthinkable.

The stakes for convincing oneself and others that one was not political were high. For Saša, his moral authenticity was on the line. In turn, moral duplicity threw into question the possibility of democratic action. What Saša was confessing was not merely that he might stand to gain from his involvement in a student organization. His admission struck at the very core of whether it was possible to be democratically representative at all. How, given that politics was seen as corrupting and dirty and that personal gain lurked behind every action, could people prove that they were really democratic actors? Indeed, establishing the sanctity of the representative relationship—the assurance that an individual could authentically speak *for* a collective without hidden motivation—was both the essence of becoming democratic and the site of collective anxiety. The question was not only, how could one be socially engaged in a context in which politics was immoral? But also, how could one be democratically authentic in a context in which authenticity was impossible? Democracy as a set of procedural techniques that established the authenticity of one's intentions was a response to the problem of politics-as-(im)morality.[6] A good deal of student activism that I observed was rooted in creating discourses and practices of proceduralism that would make democratic representation more authentic.

Antipolitics and the Problem of Authenticity as a Problem of Communication

Linkages between politics and inauthenticity were built into widely circulating definitions of politics across many formerly state-socialist contexts. These genealogies help us understand why discourses of procedure and even rule of law found such fertile ground in Serbia as a postsocialist and postconflict, context. Perhaps the most prominent and influential theory of politics and authenticity emerged from socialist dissident writings beginning in the 1970s. Antipolitical dissident writings are relevant to the analysis of contemporary Serbian ideas about politics for four key reasons. First, earlier critiques of state-socialist party politics are resonant with contemporary views on the corrupting nature of power. Second, antipolitical dissident writers demonstrate the ways in which the antipolitics-politics distinction rests on a particular understanding of language in relationship to truth and ideology. These writers see politics as antithetical to transparent, truthful human communication. This problematic—how do you know that people mean what they say?—remains at the heart of the problem of politics. Third, the tradition of antipolitics has direct ties to early protests in Yugoslavia, and in particular, to the emergence of youth as a mode of authorizing social engagement and critique. As in other socialist contexts, antipolitics in Yugoslavia entailed a world-making form of social engagement premised on the rejection of power in favor of more democratic forms of governance and communication. This is exemplified by Yugoslavia's Praxis school of Marxist-humanist critique. This approach to democratizing socialism emerged after 1968 as a way to ensure more authentic democratic engagement in existing state-socialist relations.

Finally, as Paul Stubbs (2012) has argued, the tradition of antipolitics found its way directly into the reconfiguration of civil society based on nongovernmental organizations (NGOs) in the former Yugoslavia beginning in the early 1990s. The emergence of "technopolitics" was part of a broader process of "NGOization" across the region, in which earlier networks of antiwar and feminist organizing were "squeezed" into the framework of technical NGOs (Stubbs 2012; see also Bagić 2004). However, at the same time, depoliticized politics was not (only) an imposition of an NGO-style, "project society" from the outside (Sampson 1996). It was also a culturally resonant response to long-standing debates about the possibility of political authenticity.

Antipolitical thinkers often framed the problem of politics and authenticity in terms of language and communication. Not unlike the challenge articulated by Ivana and Saša earlier in this chapter, the concern of antipolitical dissidents was to create authentic democratic action despite the total politicization of everyday life. Antipolitical writers thematized the tricky nature of communication within this struggle. Given this emphasis on language, David Ost has argued that the antipolitical tradition is squarely within the realm of Enlightenment thought. In speaking of Solidarity, the Polish Union resistance movement, among other post-1968 "anti-political third road" groups, he argues, "If these movements fetishize anything, it is the value of free and undistorted communication, a belief that links them with the Enlightenment's view of a world based on reason as well as with Habermas's cautious utopia of communicative competences" (Ost 1990, 31). In the antipolitical scheme, social transformation and moral capacity lie in the ability to transparently represent an authentic self in the world. Anything that obfuscates that self, lurks within and behind it, splits it, manipulates it, or mystifies it is politics.

György Konrád's highly influential book *Antipolitics* was a critique of the socialist state and society that linked moral and social corruption to Socialist Party politics. It was also is a scathing indictment of political power and state repression in communist Eastern Europe. Konrád argued that everyday life under state socialism had been saturated with forms of ideological domination, which led to the breakdown of human solidarity necessary to produce civil society. Konrád (1984, 16) saw politics as fundamentally corrupt and corrupting, because it is tied to the pursuit of power and self-interest: "Statesmen, by reason of their occupation, are necessarily more interested in political power than in metaphysics or ethics, aesthetics or scientific knowledge. The medium of politics is power over people—power backed up by weapons." Here politics is coterminous with the state and state institutions, in particular the party. Konrád sees state power as backed by ideological manipulation (often masked as moralizing discourse) and military might. In the context of Cold War realpolitik, the specter of war, potential nuclear annihilation, and imperial occupation, how could politicians be anything but cynical and self-serving? These warmongers pursued power through institutions that were fundamentally corrupt and corrupting.

Ultimately, *Antipolitics* was also a new vision of democratic politics and sociality in which people would have control over the decisions that affected their lives and well-being. Konrád (1984, 35) proposed an alternative to state-centered politics in the form of a "permanently open democracy." Antipolitics would combat a drive for power as the all-consuming force of politics because it "strives to put politics in its place and make sure it stays there, never overstepping its proper office of defending and refining the rules of the game of civil society" (Konrád 1984, 92). Konrád's critique of politics was that it obscured authentic expressions of the self. Given the corruption of communist state and society, how could expression be anything other than obfuscation? As such, *Antipolitics* was fundamentally a theory of how human communication was corrupted by those in power. Konrád attempted to open up the possibility for authentic human communication, decontaminated from the obscuring effects of ideology and the drive for political power and personal gain.

From this perspective, theorists and practitioners of antipolitics exemplify a widespread language ideology at work in many socialist and postsocialist contexts. By "language ideology" I mean a set of beliefs about the ties among language, social identities, and political and moral competencies (Irvine and Gal 2000; Woolard 1998). The nature of this language ideology is particularly clear in Václav Havel's famous 1985 essay "The Power of the Powerless," which was also written in the antipolitical tradition. For Havel, the possibility of a moral and authentic subject was grounded in a one-to-one correspondence between an interior self and the truthful representation of that self, uncorrupted by ideological forms of language and semiotic representation. Communist state power colonized and corrupted the possibility of an authentic self. The instrument of power at work there was a "flexible ideology" that rendered "the centre of power . . . identical with the centre of truth" (Havel 1985, 25). The work of dissent entailed fixing or stabilizing the relationship between semiotic representation and an absolute and authentic truth.[7]

For Havel, the posttotalitarian state was enabled by the gap between representation and reality produced through semiotically mediated ideological misrepresentation and mystification. Thus, "there is nothing to prevent ideology from becoming more and more removed from reality, gradually turning into what it has already become in the post-totalitarian system: a world of appearances, a mere ritual, a formalized language deprived of semantic contact with reality and transformed into a system of ritual signs that replace reality with pseudo-reality" (Havel 1985, 32). Implicit in this analysis is a linguistic ideology in which an authentic interior self can be realized only through acts of transparent communication. At the heart of Havel's version of antipolitics is a communicative capacity to speak a truth to the world, to articulate the workings of power in order to transform them. Truth for Havel (1985, 41), like democracy for Konrád, enables control over representation of one's authentic self and links addresser and addressee through models of direct talk: "It is from this sphere that life lived openly in the truth grows; it is to this sphere that it speaks, and in it that it finds understanding. This is the where the potential for communication exists."

As Alexei Yurchak (2003) has argued, such approaches to language are problematic for their simplistic understanding of agency and resistance and their unitary vision of personhood. As people on both sides of the Cold War divide struggled to know and interpret the intentions of others, the slippages between knowledge and representation grew increasingly politicized. Indeed, the ideological battles of the mid- to late twentieth century were fundamentally configured through the impossibility of knowing (or empathizing) with the Cold War "other" (Lemon 2009). However problematic such representations of language, morality, and authenticity might be, they nonetheless shaped people's understanding of political engagement in the years leading up to and after the fall of the Berlin Wall. Cold War ideologies of self and other were not only operations of geopolitical power at a distance. They have become powerful conditions for shaping post–Cold War democratic politics both East and West. Contemporary models of civic democracy—grounded in Eastern European antipolitics as much as in Western European liberal democracy—have shaped contemporary struggles over the nature of democratic representation and the possibility of political authenticity. The struggles that student activists face as they try to practice democracy shed light on the slippery and contradictory nature of Euro-Atlantic democracy as a form of communicative practice.

I call the phenomenon in which the slipperiness of language is taken to be evidence of the inauthenticity of the speaking subject the "metapragmatics of distrust." Language ideologies act as frames by which people make sense of specific contextual features of language in an ongoing interaction. In the context of some language ideologies, the ambiguity of the speaking self is neither a moral problem nor a challenge to authenticity. This may be especially true in explicitly ritual contexts, or when social actors are playing with normative cultural scripts (Kulick 1998). Contradictory stances are not always interpreted as signs of disingenuousness (Gal 1993). However, the metapragmatic frames at work in antipolitical language ideologies allow for the interpretation of multivalence as evidence of inauthenticity. It is the nature of the pragmatic, or context-dependent, features of language to be multivalenced, shifting according to culturally meaningful frames for action and interaction (Silverstein 1976). These pragmatic features of language come to be seen as the limits of democratic communication.

The metapragmatics of distrust made it difficult for student activists in Serbia to produce evidence of their moral authenticity and youthful innocence in real-time interaction. As students struggled to represent their intentions and actions as authentic (and authentically democratic), they reached for ways to anchor the meaning of their words in a stabilizing semiotic order.

From Antipolitics to Depoliticization: The Purification of Politics Through Procedures

How, then, could student activists counteract suspicion of hidden motives and interests? How might they provide evidence of their moral authenticity? In this regard, appeals to law and procedure were compelling for activists for several reasons. Young people in Serbia often framed their experience of life in Serbia through narratives of chaos, in which everyday life was both hyperpoliticized and unpredictable. For many students, moral corruption and political chaos were tied to the absence of the rule of law. Many saw the passage and implementation of laws and administrative procedures as the only hope for purging corruption, political nepotism, and abuses of power. The need for such procedures extended to safeguarding student organizations from political manipulation. In addition, statutes, laws, and regulations would provide reliable sources of information and appeal, especially when no one's word could really be trusted. Indeed, one student leader told me that the problem with politics was that it was "all talk." Instead, the codification of procedures would ensure that talk was backed up by something real.

In part, students were dealing with a widespread sense among young people that adults could not be trusted. After all, as I detail in Chapter 1, those who came of age during Yugoslavia's breakup saw their parents' generation as guilty of all manner of betrayals and selfishness. This sense of adults (and political figures) as unreliable extended to interactions within student organizations. Chief among students' complaints was that people in charge were inconsistent and unreliable. Faculty and administrators could be compelled to act only if made to do so by an authority superior to them. Unless something was in writing, professors or administrators could not be expected to follow through on their promises or obligations.

At the same time, proceduralism was an effective response to others' distrust of student intentions and claims to be representative. Laws and procedures codified students' "innocence." As students became more and more embedded in institutional relations of power, they shifted the problem of authenticity from expression of a true self into frameworks of legal compulsion. Pegging their actions and intentions to laws and procedures became a way to purify politics. Students would act in the best interest of others because they had to. At the same time, such laws would establish students as a particular class of citizens, separate from civic groups that were enmeshed in "actual" politics. What better way to protect student groups as beyond and outside of politics than to regulate them through a supposedly objective legislative framework?

The purification of politics and the work of democracy were thus fundamentally tied to establishing one's authenticity as a (non)political subject by anchoring action, intentionality, and communication. But how could activists establish authenticity in a context so fraught that people couldn't even trust themselves? Student activists not only had to prove their good intentions to others but also had to put systems in place to prevent their own possible political corruption. Anything else, students argued, would lead to chaos and political corruption, recalling the Milošević period.

The significance of law and procedure was particularly evident in a heated interaction between activists from Student Union and the deputy minister of higher education. The scene of the dispute—a 2004 press conference about all that Student Union had accomplished—was ironic. If anyone was looking for evidence that students were enmeshed in relations of politics and power, they needed to look no further than an audience that included ministry officials, university administrators, and even members of the diplomatic community. The press conference was held in Belgrade's Student Cultural Center (Studentski Kulturni Centar, or SKC)—an aging but grand yellow-brick building emblematic of the mythic position of students and young people in Yugoslavia. By holding the event at the SKC, it was clear that student activists were also trying to link themselves to a long history of student activism.

The exchange between the deputy minister and the student leaders focused on whether the Serbian parliament ought to pass a specific law on student organizing. The deputy minister thought a specific law for student organizations was unnecessary and cumbersome, and she had previously made her position clear to the same group of activists. While students argued that they were a special class of social actors, she argued that they were regular civil society organizations and did not need their own legal framework. Students resisted this classification by pointing to the continuity of their work with earlier youth activism. As youth organizations, they deserved special status and protections. Despite being "nongovernmental," NGOs were viewed as highly politicized in Serbia and in other postsocialist contexts (Wedel 2001). For the students, such an association would directly undercut their claims of innocence.

It may seem paradoxical that students who claimed to be outside of politics were demanding parliamentary intervention to regulate their activities. But as the following exchange shows, many activists invested tremendous power in the law as a means to depoliticize student civic engagement. These activists saw the law as a way to establish students as a special class of actors, outside the fray of politics. They argued that only a formal law could protect democratic student institutions from being co-opted by renegade student groups or manipulated by shadowy outside political interests. They framed themselves as a special group of citizens in need of protection from a corrupting world of politics so that they could continue to be the bearers of a pure democracy. In this interaction students invoked not only texts such as legal codes and statutes. Students also used appeals to recent political history and culturally recognizable social roles of "innocent" youth and students. These dual approaches—legal regulation and a history of altruistic youth activism—best positioned young people as the bearers of an authentic postsocialist democracy.

As the question-and-answer portion of the press conference opened, the deputy minister wasted no time in challenging the students' demand for a law, asking why students needed their own particular law (*zakon*) to regulate student organizing. In challenging the necessity of the law, she also challenged student activists' central argument that students were a separate group of citizens in need of special protection. Andrijana, a member of Student Union, and one of two student representatives on the ministry's official working group tasked with drafting new legislation for higher education in Serbia, immediately countered by trying to establish the unique nature of student organizations. She argued:

It's important that the status of student organizations as such is also defined. Student organizations in Serbia . . . are currently registered as citizens' associations [*udruženje građana*] for the simple reason that there is no legal possibility to be registered as a student organization. . . . [W]e want to be registered as student organization . . . [because] it means that the state accepts the fact that student pluralism is very important. . . . Pluralism of student organizations, on the other hand, doesn't mean that there will be chaos, which . . . currently exists within the student scene. . . . The other important thing is a law that should protect the pluralism of student organizations, and what's more important, their independence. . . . [E]ven last year . . . we had certain political parties in Serbia that wanted to create, indirectly or directly, . . . their own powerful influence [*svoj veoma veliki uticaj*] influence on student parliament. We can't dare let what happened during the during the 1990s, [when] the official student organization was under the total control of the regime, happen again.

Andrijana's response is exemplary of how student activists tried to distinguish themselves from other kinds of citizen groups. While she acknowledges that some student groups were in fact registered as citizen groups, she notes that this is an unfortunate historical accident that urgently needed to be corrected. She appealed to "the state" to acknowledge the position and status of student groups, and to the law as the mechanism through which the state could protect those groups. Andrijana uses the notion of pluralism to reframe the debate about student groups as part of larger social transformations toward democratic pluralism and procedure. In arguing for pluralism, protected by the law, Andrijana appeals to tropes of democracy, which would be compelling to the deputy minister as a strong prodemocracy (and former anti-Milošević) activist in her own right. In addition, Andrijana juxtaposes the scenario of chaos to one of order, playing on fears of students who are out of control and unmanageable—it is a dystopian vision of student organizations. She posits such chaos as the opposite of (managed) pluralism. In so doing, she positions student groups as a possible (and unique) engine for democratization in Serbia, if they are properly managed.

The second term Andrijana invokes is *independence*, playing on concerns about the role of political parties' manipulation of student organizations. Here she refers to the role of the Milošević regime in using a major student group, Student Alliance, to consolidate power in the 1990s. This is a clear warning about the intersection of two spheres that should be kept separate: politics and students. Ironically, Andrijana is co-opting critiques of student activists that they are easily manipulated by outsiders. By voicing this critique, which often comes from state officials, administrators, faculty, and other students, she mobilizes the threat of politicization. She draws on popular narratives of students as easily manipulated as evidence for her claim that an objective, legal framework is necessary. In this scenario, law is the neutral field that separates the realms of politics from that of nonpolitics and ensures student organizations' protection. Her language here echoes that of Ivana at the beginning of this chapter. "We can't dare" is itself a rhetoric of compulsion, born of altruistic motives to protect students as an innocent group that is necessarily (and selflessly) treading in murky political waters.

The deputy minister's response is to blur Andrijana's distinctions by simply refusing to acknowledge the line between students and other kinds of groups. By continuing to class student groups as NGOs, she refuses to acknowledge their special vulnerability and the urgency of the appeal for a law, posing the question "Do you then think that it would be necessary to pass a law for every NGO with regard to its activity? In other words, [why should this be so for] student organizations, which are nongovernmental organizations?" In asking this, the deputy minister directly challenges

Andrijana's distinction between students and other activists. In addition, she questions the efficacy of the law at all. Why have a law for students and not for every other group that considers itself unique? In contrast to Andrijana's vision of a legally managed pluralism, the deputy minister invokes a slippery-slope argument that makes the application of law to all kinds of organizations appear ridiculous. While Andrijana presents the law as a way to order chaos and create clarity, the deputy minister suggests an unnecessary proliferation of legal regimes will have the opposite effect.

In response, Andrijana continues to insist on the unique position of student groups. She argues that youth organizations are vulnerable to manipulation by different political interest groups: "It's because of that, that we think that a separate law would protect first the independence and the pluralism [of student groups] because of that particular role that they have." Indeed, Andrijana then implies that the deputy minister's refusal to distinguish NGOs and student groups is extremely dangerous. It opens up borders between students and others that led to the political manipulation of the past and could lead to the potential politicization of groups in the future. Her narrative of the history of student manipulation and the corrupting force of political interests at the university is calculated to appeal to the deputy minister, herself a member of the academic and NGO community who directly suffered in the 1990s under the Milošević regime and its university policies. In this way, even as Andrijana insists on the unique position of students in Serbia, she also appeals to the common history and experiences of political repression faced by both student opposition groups and members of civil society.

At this point, another Student Union of Serbia leader, Boban, picks up Andrijana's thread about the dangers of unregulated and unprotected student organizations, and appeals to solidarity with the deputy minister. He first mobilizes a rhetoric of altruism and then provides an example of what is at stake, which are the potential abuses that might take place if parliament is not carefully monitored and regulated:

I would like also to reply to Professor Marija [calling her by her first name, here a pseudonym] in the same vein. . . . I think that here [we are doing] something from which future generations will benefit much more [than we will,] . . . meaning education reform. Surely, all who are now at the university won't experience what the student parliament does. . . . And I also think that we had abuse at the University of Novi Sad, where article 64 of the university law was used to create a student parliament, and

the current leader of that student parliament—quasi parliament [*kvazi-parlament*]—
[is someone for whom] students didn't vote. . . . In reference to that, when there is no
law, there's no control.

It is worth noting Boban's peculiar form of address to the deputy
minister—Professor Marija. He uses her academic title (and when addressing her directly, the formal second-person plural form of address, *vi*) and
her first name. Such a move is emblematic of the ambivalent relationship
of formality and intimacy, opposition and alliance, that the students have
with the deputy minister and others in positions of political power whom
they know from their common activist work and history. They must negotiate their interactions with the deputy minister both as individuals and
as an institutional authority. The deputy minister is both their advocate
and their partner in reform, and yet she also in a position of authority as
a professor and a representative of the state. It is precisely this interplay of
institutional power, legal and state authority, and individual relationships
that puts students in the position of managing "interest" and politics in
almost every interaction they have. Students must simultaneously negotiate their role as individuals with personal history and relations and their
role as interchangeable representatives in a supposedly neutral institutional
framework.

Boban invokes another set of concerns that both distinguishes students as a different category of active citizens and plays on fears about
student manipulation and political influence at the university. First, he
invokes the altruism of student activists in the present. They won't get to
experience the rights they are fighting for (but they fight anyway). This
rhetoric of self-sacrifice is resonant with themes from an earlier era: innocence and goodwill toward their fellow citizens and the students' link
in an unbroken chain of future young citizens. This narrative also links
the student parliament to a longer history of student action, including the
student parliaments held during the period of anti-Milošević protest in
the 1990s.

Boban references an incident intended to demonstrate the dark side
of an unregulated student parliament in which there is no accountability
to constituents, the university, or the state. Echoing Andrijana, he invokes
the specter of chaos and unregulated student control at the university. In
this case, a group of students at the University of Novi Sad started their
own student parliament through what Boban felt was an inadequate and
unrepresentative process: they didn't have proper elections. He hints at

undemocratic practices within this "quasi parliament" and argues that such uncontrolled institutions and financial misconduct would flourish if student activity were not regulated.

The irony of his intervention is that he notes that this false parliament was actually created under article 64, probably a clause in the university statute. In this sense, Boban rejects the authority of this particular text and calls for another, more powerful text: a national law. As I discuss later, this attempt to authoritatively fix one text as the final arbiter of other lesser texts is what Silverstein and Urban (1996) have identified as the essence of politics—the metadiscursive struggle in and through which people attempt to fix authority.

The students throughout this interaction continue to tack back and forth between visions of uncontrolled and chaotic student politics and the need to protect the innocence of student activism from external control. They emphasize the importance of having a law, noting that it should be on a higher level than that of the faculty and shouldn't be simply a regulation or some low "legal act." They also mobilize a language of regulation, as when Andrijana argues, "It's important to us that the way student organizations be protected is regulated [*pravno uređeno*]." Fixing institutional relations through legal mechanisms is also a way to fix the very problem of political interest itself. Manipulation, self-interest, and inauthenticity can be "regulated" through formal procedures.

The deputy minister continues to reject the urgency of the students' demands, taking on the tone of a frustrated parent to a recalcitrant child. She insists, "I simply have the feeling that you—for reasons you are not aware of—that Student Union of Serbia, like other student organizations, is a part of the NGO scene." Here the deputy minister is positioning herself in a slightly different role from that of before, as an adult with a longer-term perspective and wisdom. She references knowledge that she has about student life that students themselves "are not aware of." She also plays on her own foundational role in the NGO scene in Serbia, a role that predates the involvement of the students whom she is addressing. She thus refuses the students' attempts to construct a historical narrative that makes the law seem a necessary and logical response to past grievances and dangers.

In an almost scolding tone, she continues:

And at least many of these organizations, for a long time, have [had] more serious problems because of the previous regime than Student Union of Serbia or other student organizations [have had]. Accordingly, this problem isn't unique for students; [it]

is the problem of all organizations. . . . [T]he basic problem of the law [on NGOs] is . . . management of finances and property. . . . For some reason, the first version of that law on NGOs [didn't go through], and then an association of these organizations [NGOs] was formed. As far as I know, SUS [Student Union of Serbia] is a member of the organization—I have that feeling, or I read it in the newspaper—which in fact should push through that law about NGOs. A version of the law acceptable for everyone was created and has been before parliament since spring 2002.

Whereas Boban and Andrijana have linked Student Union to a genealogy of the student movement and youth in Serbia, the deputy minister offers a counternarrative that puts them squarely in the history of NGO development, of which she herself is a central part. She references Student Union's membership in an NGO association (that it had then just joined) as proof and mentions that she saw this fact in the newspapers. What seems like an offhanded reference to the media is in fact a biting critique. Student Union's media presence, particularly in connection with this group, bolsters the deputy minister's point that it operates like, and is seen to be, a professionalized and high-profile organization, much more like an NGO than a motley crew of altruistic innocents. In this case, what has left SUS open to the deputy minister's critique is precisely its own attempts to manipulate the lines between student and nonstudent, including both the group's presence on the NGO scene and its recent involvement in a new network of NGOs in Belgrade. The deputy minister further situates SUS as an NGO by arguing that its problems are simply the same as, or even less serious than, those of other NGOs.

The deputy minister goes on to advise them: "What I'm trying to ask [is] why are you insisting on one particular law? . . . There is no specificity to your [concerns]." Students simply aren't special, she argues. Furthermore, a law would only hurt them rather than help them. She tells the students:

An acceptable solution to us, in the Ministry of Education and Sport, is that Student Parliament can establish Student Parliament, without passing a law about student organizations. Therefore, you can create something [a regulative framework] lower, [but] necessarily regulated by law [*pravno uređen*]. . . . Now, you explain to me . . . why do you want to kick this whole process ahead a year and not just begin it in a month. That's what I singularly do not understand.

Here the deputy minister is channeling her authority as a government representative, refusing the calls to solidarity and appeals for sympathy based on her more personal relationship with students as "Professor Marija." She undermines the crisis-level language the students have been using to describe the situation of an unregulated student parliament. The scenarios they have described—lack of responsibility, financial misconduct, undemocratic practices—seem far less serious and easily resolved. In the end, she makes a point she has made many times before in response to the students' attempt to bind lower regulatory texts with a law: the students are making this process far more complicated than it needs to be. Organizations and parliament, she argues, function perfectly well with statutory authority. In fact, the students' push for a law will only delay their ability to found a student parliament. Finally, she also points out that their demands not only affect students but also are holding up the work of the ministry (herself, for example) and the actual Serbian parliament. To this extent, her annoyance at the students' rigidity, which she sees as a waste of everyone's time, smacks more of an annoyed parent scolding spoiled children.

If the deputy minister tries to shut down the argument by claiming students are simply wasting time and energy by insisting on formal legal mechanisms, Vlada, then president of Student Union of Serbia, has the last word. His response reflects the fact that he has thought extensively about the relationship of law, institutions, and democracy. As a student of politics and political theory, he is both aware of and committed to philosophies and practices of democracy. For Vlada, as for other students in Student Union, proper procedure is also a question of ensuring properly functioning democratic institutions. His argument draws on a larger discourse of democratic transition in Serbia and all the urgency and importance that such a process implies:

If we are supposed to have a student parliament for September or October and [around the time of] the usual fuss about tuition, quotas, [and so on,] . . . then it's necessary to consider the time [frame]. We can't have student parliament, meaning elections, in June, during the June exam period, and we can't have [them] during summer because students aren't at the university. We would have chaos, . . . and I think that's really problematic.

Vlada begins by challenging the deputy minister on her own technical grounds: her proposed time frame for creating a student parliament without passage of an official law. By complicating the process of student elections, he challenges the deputy minister's claim of how easy it would be to simply found a student parliament outside a formal legal framework.

Next, Vlada responds directly to the deputy minister's attempt to lump Student Union in with all other NGOs (thus making it subject to laws on NGOs rather than to specific laws on student organizations). In fact, he insists, Student Union is part of the youth scene:

Student parliament and student organizations are part of youth politics [*omladinska politika*. . . . Maybe not youth politics—*politics* is a word with an ugly connotation in this country—but the whole youth scene [*omladinska scena*], the whole of that youth scene began at the beginning of the 1990s and was built through some student youth protest, first in 1991 . . . then 1996–97—and 2000. I believe that it's necessary to respect these things. . . . [B]ecause of that we need a law. It doesn't have to be a particular law. . . . I don't want [it to be the case] that student organizations are so important that they receive their own law.

What is evident in this particular part of the discussion is how unstable the line is between student and nonstudent status. Vlada even catches himself when he has crossed the line, replacing *youth politics* with the vaguer *youth scene*. However, having done this, he invokes the genealogy of student protests in Serbia as proof both of student organizations' uniqueness and of the specificity of the student and youth scene from that of NGOs in Serbia. It is out of respect for that history, he argues, that a specific law for students, as students, is necessary. At the same time, like Ivana at the beginning of this chapter, he closes by saying he doesn't *want* a situation in which students need their own law. He'd rather that NGOs and students could be lumped together, all free of political manipulation. Here Vlada takes on a language of compulsion ("I don't want it to be the case . . . but it is"), as evidence of the purity of his motivations.

As he just argued that student organizations are part of a nonpolitical youth scene in Serbia, Vlada's next comments may seem odd. He introduces democracy and responsibility—in the financial and legal sense—toward the state. This seems to contradict his attempts to place student organizations outside the sphere of politics. However, in this case, *democracy* refers to the larger political-philosophical idea. Democracy is reduced to procedures for ensuring abstract principles: a level playing field, accountability, and responsibility.

Finally, when introducing his example from the faculty, Vlada directly and comically refers to his own institutional "authority" as a counterweight to that of the deputy minister. He positions himself as head of the government at his faculty:

I'll give you a concrete example. At the faculty of political science—excuse me, that's my authority, I'm the president of the government [said tongue in cheek—*izvini to je moj autoritet, ja sam predsednik vlasti*]—there was an attempt to call elections. We have five student organizations, one registered as an official organization . . . the second as an NGO, the third was created and financed by the faculty, the third is actually a faculty organization, the fourth founded and funded by faculty [and] the fifth is some kind of interfaculty hybrid organization. These five organizations aren't equal. They don't have the same responsibility [*odgovornost*] toward the state, in a legal, political, and financial sense. The point of democracy is that we are equal when we enter the race with somebody else [*poenta demokratije jeste da budemo jednaki kad ulazimo sa nekim u trku*]. I fear . . . we will have chaos.

In this comment, Vlada mocks both the pretensions and power of official authorities and the legalistic language of students who play at formal politics and take on institutional roles and titles that mimic government institutions (e.g., parliament, president). The deputy minister has positioned herself as both a representative of state power and an adult (who knows better than students), thereby distancing herself from the students' attempts to construct a common historical narrative that ties their fate to hers. Vlada mocks that distancing by referring to himself as an authority as well. This is both funny—a student or kid playing at formal political titles—and quite serious. Vlada does have authority within his faculty, and he does represent students on the basis of the same principles and the same processes as the deputy minister: democratic elections that brought her party to power. The implication is that if her claims to channel democratic authority should be taken seriously, so should his. Students may not be political, but they are democratic.

This interaction demonstrates the subtle ways in which students negotiated space for themselves as political agents by insisting on particular features of student organizations that were paradoxically depoliticizing. By pointing out the specificity of students' needs (as opposed to those of civil society organizations) and their vulnerability to outside manipulation, they hoped to convince politicians to architect formal mechanisms to protect and preserve student innocence. The law would also need to be authoritative enough to protect them from the influence of corrupt outside forces, politicians, and those pursuing outside interests. At heart was the ability not only to keep "politics" out of student organizations but also to manage perceptions and representations of student activism.

In contrast, the deputy minister seemed to be operating according to a very different model of establishing authoritative frameworks for action in the world. She focused on practice and precedent rather than textual authority. While she acknowledged that textual authority could be important—after all, she indicated, students could simply join the effort for a law regulating NGOs—she was frustrated with students' desire to ground their actions in law. This was both a needless waste of time and an abuse of textual and legal regulations. Her advice to them was to use their own practice, and eventually institutional precedent, to establish a student parliament. Why wait, she asked, when you can simply pull a parliament together yourselves? Perhaps her own experience embedded in the bureaucracy of the ministry, as well as her own persecution at the hands of Milošević's many legal regulations governing the university, gave her far less faith in the ability of a legal framework to fix or finalize any social or political process. Or perhaps her experiences in moving seamlessly between government positions, the NGO world, and education made such distinctions seem specious.

In the interaction discussed here, the deputy minister responded to students by refusing to acknowledge that they were entitled to fix or frame interactions through legal frameworks. She challenged the validity of their efforts to propose new laws by questioning whether students qua students are unique and worthy political subjects. In other words, she challenged both their tropes of youth as a special category and their insistence on legal frameworks to protect students per se. Instead, the deputy minister used two (seemingly contradictory) logics to argue that students did not deserve their own law. On the one hand, she argued they were not legitimate bearers of law because they were not unique kinds of citizens. On the other hand, in invoking her status not only as a minister but also as an adult (referring to things that students were not aware of), she implied that students are unique as youth. It is their youthful inexperience that means that law is better left to adults.

Fixing Authority: The Significance of the Law

In the interaction discussed above, proceduralism was a response to the particular metapragmatics of distrust at work in many of the interactions among student activists and their interlocutors. If the heart of the problem is the gap between appearances and reality, then proceduralism becomes a mechanism to stitch the two back together. In this sense, students in this interaction drew on what they believed to be authoritative discourses in order to put in place other sources of "neutral" textual authority (i.e., law) that they would then be able to appeal to in the future. For these students, the stakes of law and codified legal procedure were clearly high. These stakes are tied to their fears of chaos, political manipulation, and antidemocratic and fraudulent quasi parliaments. Students invoked a common fear that political parties manipulated youth to argue for legal regulations to protect students. Using these worst-case scenarios, students put the value of law at the center of the debate. In so doing, they focus on establishing rules of the game, a framework in and through which they can create a neutral political playing field and a legal regime that will grant them authority and efficacy across different interactions.

The debate between the students and the deputy minister was also a conversation about how student negotiations should be structured, as well as about who was able and entitled to enact and draw on law and legal authority, who had the authority to demand and mobilize law. Students used appeals to recent political history and culturally recognizable social roles of "innocent" youth and students to make their appeals for greater institutional intervention and legal regulation seem urgent and important. These appeals attempted to argue that students per se were best poised to impose an externally mediated link between truth and action.

By invoking their history of innocence and selflessness, as well as their status as victims, rather than agents, of political corruption, students positioned themselves as already innocent. Thus, if they were protected through law, students would be best poised to wield and be agents of neutral legal discourse, without interference from other, negative influence. From this perspective, because students have a history of altruism, they are better positioned to use the law well in the present moment. Thus, law is significant not only in its own right but also when mobilized by young people in particular. I had many conversations with students who argued that they could not trust adults because, in their experience, adults had a history of masking other intentions and meanings in their speech. The breakdown of the chain of meaning in adult speech—from words to intentions to action—is in fact what many people perceive as the problem of politics: the corruption, lack of trustworthiness, and slipperiness attributed to language. In managing perceptions of who is or is not political, students tried to pin the problem of multivalent language onto certain types of people: untrustworthy adults, shadowy interested political parties out to manipulate innocent youth. Of course, given their own social standing, they could not do this simply by uttering their intentions. Those utterances needed to be backed by the power of something that they believed to supersede even untrustworthy adults—the law. In this way, student activists appealed to institutions to fix meaning when communication itself was suspect.[8] Laws would regulate not only behavior but also the relationship between intention and action, between words and deed.

Proceduralism and European Belonging

In addition to more localized histories, the proceduralization of student politics in Serbia was part of a larger trend of student organizing in Europe (Manning 2007). The rise of powerful networks of student groups like the Federation of National Unions of Students in Europe (known as ESIB) meant that student representatives were increasingly present in high-level negotiations about the Bologna Process, a series of ministerial meetings and agreements among European countries that resulted in the creation of a European Higher Education Area through the standardization of country-level university systems. In the context of these supranational sites of politics and governance, student representatives found themselves subject to scrutiny. As were students in Serbia, student activists more generally were being called on to establish that they democratically and transparently represented their student constituents in these high-level negotiations. Groups like the ESIB produced models for authenticating themselves as democratic actors. Students in Serbia drew on ESIB organizational models and procedures to develop new interactional scripts in their domestic activism (Gal 2003).

For example, as the largest independent student organization in Serbia, Student Union was an active member of ESIB. Student Union went to great lengths to integrate ESIB recommendations for procedure and policy. They drew on textual sources and practices generated by ESIB to ensure Student Union's democratic transparency. In doing so, activists in Student Union tried to establish themselves as part of a recognizably democratic organization, in line with "European" standards.

Proceduralism seemed to circulate translocally among student groups as both a trope and a set of specific practices. The uptake of these forms was especially evident when students from different organizations across Europe came together to share experiences and observe one another's activities. One such reunion took place at a Student Union event in December 2003. Kristina from Sweden, Ana from Croatia, and Dragana from Serbia were sitting together on a bank of couches in a rare moment of calm during Student Union's semiannual congress. The three women had an easy rapport, due to many previous meetings and chat sessions at various student events held across Europe. They talked with me in the fluent, vaguely accented English that was the common parlance of the international student movement.

Befitting the setting, the hour-long conversation turned to the importance of procedure in European student organizations. When I asked why procedure was so important for ESIB, Ana responded curtly, "Legitimacy." Kristina went on to add that this legitimacy came from having guaranteed mechanisms for ensuring that ESIB policies were not only representative but also seen by outsiders as such. She noted that in the face of intense scrutiny—"a lot of organizations are looking at us, because they are seeing that we are getting greater and greater power," she said—it was critical to establish a "completely transparent process." She told me, "If, for instance, we would put a policy out on the table, and somebody would find out that, hey, this is just something we got together and wrote one evening over a bottle of wine, I mean. . . . And also, in a traditional sort of sense, if you want to be a legitimate NGO, you have to have these procedures, as much as you might laugh about them . . . There should never, ever be a doubt where someone can go in and not have a clear understanding of how a decision was taken."

Here Kristina cites both an external and an internal legitimacy deriving from consistency and transparency in decision-making processes. The idea that a policy might come from just a handful of individuals making decisions informally (over a bottle of wine) would undercut ESIB's central claims to be democratically transparent and representative. Democratic policies must come from an open and deliberative process that separates the personal from the organizational. This is especially important for an organization that represents so many constituents and also consists of a suspect group of political subjects—young students, who are not always trusted to behave in a responsible manner. In addition, ensuring that everyone has access to and understands policies and decisions within the organization also required sets of formal procedures and rules.

In this case, certain types of procedure provided an architecture for making organizational practices democratic. Although formal systems of representation might seem at odds with popular images of political participation among students in Europe, ESIB understood proceduralism as central to democratic representation. Procedures safeguarded decision making from personal interest and allowed the group to "prove" its democratic credentials in a wide range of interactions. Given the fraught relationship between self-interest and politics of students' milieu, no wonder such mechanisms resonated with student activists from Serbia.

Ana went on to explain the importance of external legitimacy. Her comments are particularly interesting because she stages a conversation within our conversation to demonstrate students' hyperawareness about the trope of their untrustworthiness or intransparency. Here we can see how she mobilizes ESIB's rhetoric as a response to those imagined critics, thus wedding national contexts and translocal discursive strategies:

When you stand in front of all these people who are from their governments, or from the commission, or from whatever institution, and then they just ask you, like, Why are you saying this? And who is behind you? Then you have a straight answer to tell them. This is how we reached this policy, this is how our members think, this is not my own opinion. This is like an ESIB point of view, which is your National Union of Students [point of view].

Ana described the way that the transparency of procedure would allow any one student representative to invoke the entire weight of the organization, and all its members, when presenting a policy. This would then allow any individual to embody the authority of the larger organization. The representativeness of the policy and the speaker were both constituted and mobilized in the process. In further talking about the importance of such procedure, Dragana noted that procedures bound the organization together, thus preventing a diverse group of individual unions from simply not following the rules:

Procedures, in my opinion, are extremely important, internally, because we are such a diverse group of unions, and this is the rules that we set up for ourselves, like, all together. So this is what we all follow to feel, like, equally involved. And in that sense, this is why we have been stressing over the years here in the Student Unions of Serbia, as well, statutes and standing orders are important. You can't just say, like, "Oh, let's just disobey this because it doesn't apply to this specific issue we're discussing." And people have been . . . increasingly aware of the importance of procedures, because these are the rules that we set up for ourselves. And we are together, as a group of sixty-five local unions, and we have to obey them, because . . . you cannot just say, "Oh, I'm not, the other sixty-four will just comply with this and I won't because it doesn't suit me." It doesn't go this way.

Procedures not only regiment the meaning of policies, statutes, and regulations but also perform a disciplinary function within an organization. The rules of the organization derive from the group, but they also supersede any individual interest or action—you can't just disobey them because they don't suit you. In this way, the production of rules and procedures becomes an essential *democratic* act that constitutes the representative authority of a group of individuals. In a strange—because banal—echo of theorists of democratic sovereignty, rule making is the site for the production of democratic will. An antipolitics entails something of a paradox: it requires constant acts of mediation and translation to produce something like political sincerity, authenticity, or solidarity.

Cosmologies of Truth Making: Proceduralism as Power

Student activists understood the law as a form of compulsion that would force democratic behavior by creating consistency between intentions and deeds. The irony was that many older people with whom the student activists interacted saw student activists' focus on procedure as itself overly politicized. Many of the students' interlocutors understood appeals to legalistic language itself as an operation of power. In other words, students' appeals to rule of law and procedure unfolded in a culture of "procedure talk" in Serbia. Proposing or invoking new regulations and laws had been long-standing ways to circumvent the existing hierarchies of power and knowledge that were constantly in play in official meetings and negotiations at the university and elsewhere. References to statutes, laws, and other procedural documents were thus locally relevant and historically resonant ways to establish one's position as authoritative through appeals to an outside (and all-powerful) set of institutions. I witnessed many meetings in which establishing "correct procedure" became a proxy space for micro-level negotiation over power and authority. Here students were caught between their understandings of proceduralism as particularly European and democratic and a history of procedure talk that was enmeshed in localized practices of authorizing discourse. Student activists' attempts to establish themselves as innocent through legal regulation were thus paradoxically read as part of a highly politicized field of procedure talk.

Jelena, a professor of English in her early forties who worked at the University of Novi Sad, advised me to think about procedure talk in terms of a strong oral tradition in Serbia. I had been complaining to her about the difficulty of pinning down accurate information about a bevy of newly proposed or recently passed university laws and statutes. She told me an anecdote in which a colleague at the faculty had given her a piece of administrative information. When Jelena challenged the woman, she was told, "It's in the statute." Jelena bothered to go and track down the statute, only to find that the relevant information was not there. As she told me, the woman she was dealing with simply didn't think that Jelena would check; it was more important that the woman had said it was there. Such chains of oral authority may refer to statutes and regulations. But power is grounded less in formal administrative codes than in the act of asserting that something appears in an original source. Authority is thus produced as much in talk about procedural codification as in the act of codification itself.

In one meeting of the faculty council at the University of Niš I attended with a student representative, it was especially clear that talk about procedure, laws, and information was a highly politicized site for negotiating power relations in a changing university system. At stake was the readjustment of pay scales, which had been increased at the beginning of the year. After a ministry audit found that the increases were not in accordance with the law, the council was tasked with bringing the pay scales into harmony with the new requirements. In effect, this meant keeping the pay increase for professors and lowering or eliminating the increase for nonteaching staff (including service people, librarians, teaching assistants, and people working in student services). Although the topic of the meeting was salary, the most contentious parts of the meeting did not focus on the fairness of shifts in wage structures. Rather, people debated whether information about the new law had been fairly distributed and transparently represented. Indeed, as the meeting unfolded, faculty and staff were most concerned with establishing a chain of reliable information about what the new regulations actually entailed and who was responsible for their implementation. Complaints about the murkiness and confusion surrounding the procedural and legal issues at hand were in effect ways to undercut the authority of the law (and those channeling it) as neutral and transparent.

Like Ivana at the beginning of this chapter, the faculty dean who was chairing the meeting appealed to law as a form of compulsion that shifted responsibility from individuals to an institutionalized authority beyond anyone's control. He apologized to the group for the new pay structure, as if it were an unfortunate accident over which he had no control. Indeed, he told them, the article that governed his actions was unpleasantly clear (*član je neprijatno jasan*), and his hands were tied—"What other [choice is there]?" (*Šta drugo? Nema drugo*). The appeal to authority of the law bound his actions and exonerated him from responsibility for individual interpretation and implementation.

In response, others in the room questioned this picture of external legal obligation, thus muddying the dean's disavowal of either power or responsibility for the law and its interpretation. "To jeste pitanje odgovornosti" (it's a question of responsibility), one English professor known to be an advocate of staff and teaching assistants proclaimed angrily. She continued on, pointing out that even establishing information about laws and new regulations, or figuring out where directives were coming from, could be impossible. One day there was one piece of information and another day something different (*danas jedna informacija, a sutra druga*). In introducing the notion of responsibility, the professor attempted to force the dean to admit that he might have control over the interpretation and implementation of the law, thus undercutting his attempt to establish himself as a merely neutral vessel of an external authority. Indeed, she tried to lay bare that the authority of legal regimes was as much in their deployment and control over as in the fact of the law. The librarian of the philosophy faculty, who stood to also lose from this shift in pay scale, noted that it was unclear whether something had actually changed in the law (governing pay coefficients) or in the dean's reading of the law. In an attempt to figure out whether the power play was at the level of the Ministry of Education or the dean, she complained that she had heard countless definitive positions (*Ja sam čula bezbroj definitivnih stavova*) and was totally confused. As in Jelena's previous anecdote, there was no guarantee that appeals to supposedly neutral metatexts like statutes would create transparency among faculty, students, administrators, and anyone else involved.

The invocation of "countless definitive positions" seems like a contradiction in terms. How could something be countless (unspecifiable) and definitive? In pointing out the ways in which seemingly fixed texts like laws can in fact produce endless interpretations, the librarian attempted to undercut the dean's legalistic language. Although the dean told those assembled that the administrative order about pay scales was in compliance with the law, not something of his own doing, others pointed out that such assertions were not convincing when clearly the law was open to interpretation at any number of points along the chain of authority.

Complaints about the murkiness and inconsistency of policies and procedures were common in many of the contentious contexts in which student representatives found themselves. Yet instead of being suspicious of proceduralism, many student activists felt that if only the regulatory frames could be made clear and authoritative, they could achieve some kind of democratic transparency. At the same time, being aligned with such legal frameworks was a way for students to manage perceptions of themselves as political and self-interested. In this way, proceduralism was a form of pragmatic politics, an attempt to create spaces for active and activist engagement while negotiating the everyday contradictions, frustrations, and suspicions that haunted new democratic practices.

Yet as the brief example of the faculty meeting shows, appeals to procedure and discourses of law had their own social lives and histories, which sometimes had the opposite effect. Many people recognized that laws and procedures—and their invocation in interactions—could always be deployed to make authority and counterauthority. Indeed, faculty and administrators often expressed annoyance at how hung up student activists were on such issues. The deputy minister in the previously mentioned exchange was in no way convinced (as the student activists were) that a law on student organizing would fix the problems of student organizations. Indeed, for her, as for the English professor I discussed earlier, the language of procedure is itself potentially suspect, a space of opacity and negotiation of power.

The discrepancy here may well be generational, and it may mark different cosmologies of truth making that emerged in the immediately postsocialist context. Indeed, as the interview with members of the ESIB demonstrated, student investment in procedure operates as a kind of transparency regime: the potentially murky processes of democratic representation and decision making can be pegged to specific people, places, and outcomes. This is one particular relationship among democracy, regulatory regimes, and truth making—grounded both in liberal democratic and antipolitical understandings of language and politics.

However, under state socialism, the relationships among interest, procedures, and outcomes were quite different. In discussing Western policy approaches to making and regulating capitalism in the postsocialist world, Katherine Verdery (2003, 26) argues that policy makers failed to understand the profoundly different relationship between procedure and outcome in the socialist context:

> The assumption behind [Western policy makers'] social engineering was that by establishing the rules that enable playing the game in some sort of concert, institutions help to create the predictability within which actors can strategize and act. Notably, this assumption rests on another: that the normal state of society is for rules and procedures to be clear, although outcomes may be uncertain. But this is only one way of organizing power in society, a way that sees organization and predictability as "good" power at work. What, however, if people at the top do not want rules and predictability but opacity, to keep others off balance? . . . Valerie Bunce and Maria Csanadi pose the matter slightly differently; for them, in capitalist democracies rules and procedures are certain and outcomes are uncertain, whereas in socialism it was the other way around—outcomes were certain, and the rules and procedures were not.

Here the relationship between procedure and outcome is reversed from the democratic order. While socialist states invoked procedure and law on an official level, the ambiguity and differential applications of procedures (and rules for distribution of resources) were critical sources of the socialist state's power. Elizabeth Dunn (2004, 129), building on the work of Burawoy and Lukacs, has noted that "a wide gap between what socialist ideology promised and what socialist reality delivered made power visible." The gaps between socialist reality and ideology, then, were not merely exceptional to state power but also constitutive of it. Indeed, in Milošević's socialist-postsocialist Serbia of the 1990s, rule by procedure, democratic elections, and the law alternated with random acts of naked state power. State power was thus rooted, at least in part, in unpredictability. This phenomenon bridges peoples' experiences of socialist and postsocialist state formations, something Anna Fournier (2012) has pointed to in a recent ethnography of Ukraine. Fournier (2012, 105) notes that "the state becomes difficult to pin down (but equally difficult to evade)."

In this sense, state regulatory power in Yugoslavia and in Milošević's Serbia was important not only because of its visibility but also because the state staged the presence *and* the absence of the law: state power emerged in the performance of certain aspects of democratic process and procedure, and in the violation of those aspects, thus proving that the state could transcend the very limits it had set for itself (Wedeen 2003).

The reversal of means and outcomes produced a distinct relationship between forms of state power and everyday life under socialism.[9] Procedure was intrinsic, not extrinsic, to a sense of confusion, frustration, and randomness. Law did not manage and solve the unpredictability of everyday life; it produced that unpredictability. It is in this context that the Serbian idea of politics as fundamentally corrupt provides a framework for interpreting power that procedures and legal frameworks cannot. If law was unpredictable, one could at least read the arbitrariness of state power through the logics of the self-interest of politicians and elites. In liberal democratic contexts, self-interest may corrupt democratic processes, but it remains exceptional to procedure and law (and thus can be managed through legal and political institutions). In the socialist context, procedure itself is tied up with a history of perceived manipulation and opacity. Self-interest, power, politics, and procedure were inextricably bound together.

The attempt of young student activists to mobilize laws and procedure as the tools for management of self-interest thus strikes at the heart of how the arbitrariness of state power was explained in the socialist context. Here procedure did not depoliticize; it embedded the individual in politics even more firmly. The use of procedure to create a space outside of politics, a contemporary depoliticized politics rooted in law, thus raises the specter of the very self-interest that students were trying to disassociate themselves from. Even as students attempted to manage others' disappointment in them (as political, as self-interested), the discursive tools they reached for only served to cast greater suspicion on them. No wonder, then, that they did not want to be politicians, even when they felt that they had to be.

Conclusion
Democracy and Revolution After the Cold War

THE GRAFFITO IN FIGURE 1 adorned an aging, dirty-gray building in the heart of Belgrade in the summer of 2005. The red text, in messy, all-caps Cyrillic, demanded that passersby contend with one simple question: why is there no more Otpor? (*Zašto nema Otpora!*) Otpor most likely refers to the eponymous student and people's group that stood for the anti-Milošević movement and the October 5 revolution. But one could just as easily read the message as, why isn't there any resistance? In this sense, Otpor is not a group of people but a state of being, the exclamation mark a call to arms.

If we were to meet the author of this provocation, we might ask him or her, Whose resistance? Where? For or against what? Indeed, the poignancy of the message lies not only in a nostalgia for resistance; it rests in a longing for the clarity of a political field that makes resistance thinkable and possible. That longing for clarity is not surprising given the state of things in Serbia only five years after the revolution. The opposition and resistance-leaders-turned-politicians came to represent a political system that produced high unemployment, a fractious and messy political field, the assassination of a beloved leader, and continued nationalist revanchism. As in other newly democratic contexts—particularly postrevolutionary and postsocialist ones—neither the domain of politics nor the object of resistance was clear cut (Snajder 2008).

This graffito, like the ethnographic encounters throughout this book, challenges us to ask how people configure political action and agency in the face of such ambiguity and in the shadow of idealized moments of

FIGURE 1. Translation: Why is there no Otpor/resistance? Belgrade, Serbia, 2005

social transformation. In Serbia, student activists combined the familiar and the novel to produce a new form of youth revolution. This framework, combined with the clear goal of toppling Milošević and a general commitment to democracy, allowed young activists to sidestep the hegemonic frameworks of nationalism and ethnic politics. But after the revolution, the conditions that made these framings and practices particularly resonant and powerful did not always pertain. Where once youth protesters were a revolutionary vanguard that stood in for all citizens against the regime, student organizations became merely one of many citizen groups vying for dwindling entitlements in a fiscally strapped state. No longer the darlings of alternative media outlets and international news agencies, students jostled for room on newspaper pages crowded with tales of discontent. Under Milošević, taking to the streets was a powerful act against the state and an assertion of citizen power when formal electoral processes had been co-opted by the regime. After his ouster in 2000, activists struggled to articulate the relevance of their protest politics. Was anyone listening? Did what they had to say still matter?

In framing the revolution as fundamentally about youth-driven social and political transformation, youth activists opened themselves up to particular kinds of critiques when their post-2000 political engagements departed from those earlier framings. As activists began to engage in the messy practices of constructing democracy within institutions, they inevitably made compromises and pursued contradictory agendas. Such behavior called to mind darker narratives of youth politics from the socialist past, narratives that had been powerful tools in controlling and limiting student dissent during the socialist period. The multivalent meanings of youth politics both made youth as a category a productive discursive resource and opened students up to interpretations of their actions that they could not fully control.

Yet many among the first generation of Serbian student activists after 2000 tried to push past this interplay of expectations and disappointments by embracing the complexity and messiness of politics in the present. Whereas many observers of student activism drew a line of before and after Milošević, many students saw continuity with their past experiences. Their post-2000 engagement was a new phase that grew naturally from earlier periods of activism. At the same time, post-2000 activists mobilized images of youth vanguardism and innocence in their interactions with professors, administrators, and the media, because this was a resonant and effective way to authorize student politics. In other words, students struggled to construct a politics of the present, even as they got caught up in the expectations, and disappointments, of the past.

Through this politics of the present, activists focused on the negotiated processes of democracy across multiple social and political domains, if in small and partial ways. In the face of expectations of how they ought to behave, student activists took on multiple roles and mobilized a wide range of strategies that, on the face of it, seem highly contradictory. But it was precisely the ability to negotiate these contradictions as a feature of political engagement, and not as a failure external to it, that allowed student activists to produce creative interpretations of democratic action. This is not to say that student activists operated without normative frameworks or did not orient their actions toward possible futures. Many did work with categories like "Europe" or mobilized modernizing civilizational tropes in authorizing their action. However, in playing with normative categories, from nation to democracy, they created spaces in which they tried to figure out what those categories might mean in practice—often with unintended consequences.

To apprehend the spirit of democratic (as opposed to revolutionary) activism, I have shown not only narratives of disappointment but also the fact of action and activism in their wake. A politics of disappointment embraces contingency and failed sovereignty; it is an emergent set of practices structured by the fundamentally contradictory experiences of actually lived democracy. In other words, disappointment in Serbia was not a failure of political modernity but a central feature of it.

Utopia and Disappointment in the Post–Cold War World

Disappointment provides a way to think about the gap between utopia and political practice not only in Serbia but also in a context that many scholars have defined in terms of the death of grand narratives. The fall of the European state-socialist project combined with the rise of post-Fordist economic restructuring has challenged visions of progress that defined twentieth-century modernity (Harvey 1990). In addition, the rise of poststructuralist epistemological projects over the past thirty years has challenged taken-for-granted assumptions by which scholars and others measure progress and change. Indeed, "utopia and progress both became concrete in the twentieth century, but neither survived intact" (Trouillot 2003, 13). It is necessary in this new millennium to ask whether, and how, transformative political action is possible without the horizon of a utopian vision for change (Gutmann 2002). In other words, has the utopian vision of modernist revolution hindered political engagement as much as it has enabled it?

The struggle over politics following the death of grand narratives was never just an epistemological problem for anthropologists and other scholars at the close of the Cold War.[1] The postsocialist democratic reorientation of politics toward a pragmatic present was in part a reaction to the utopian imaginaries of both socialism and the civic frame of the revolutions that swept Europe in 1989. When democratization became a global export industry in the 1990s, many newly democratic states faced economic and political pressure to comply with a liberal, normative ideal that carried specific visions of teleological human progress. This normative, Western, democratic framework is historically specific and in many ways idiosyncratic (Nugent 2002, 2008). Yet at the same time, citizens and leaders of newly democratic states found themselves judged as "poor imitations" of the democratic West by everyone from the European Union and NATO to international investors and donors (Creed 2010, 215). One vision of teleological and totalizing political transformation thus came to be wedded to another, combining to shape post–Cold War politics. The efforts of student activists in Serbia demonstrate the ways in which defining politics in the wake of state socialism—and outside the framework of modernist and liberal democratic progress—was an actually lived social, political, and epistemological problem.

The disappointment that emerged in relation to these future-oriented visions of change was not a sign of failed democratic transition. Instead, it was a form of historicity that emerged from the rubble of twentieth-century visions of revolution, state, and nation and the logics of liberal progress architected in their wake. An anthropology of disappointment might take into account this movement, as well as the uptake of normative political concepts and modernist theologies of progress and the alternative and contingent spaces that these frameworks open up in a political present. It might also provide new analytic purchase on democracy as a lived experience of the open ended and the contingent. This method of disappointment is indebted to Hirokazu Miyazaki's (2004) "method of hope." Miyazaki argues for hope as a method that aligns the anthropologist with the producers of knowledge at the present time of action. Hope is thus a particular stance toward the present that opens up a space for future action, without committing that present to the burdens of necessity.[2] By focusing on the time frame of ongoing, real-time interactions, I have tried to show how new forms of democracy, however necessarily imperfect, are made in practice, in ways that are always contingent and shifting. Such acts always entail both possibility and foreclosure as the fundamental condition for the practice of meaning. Or, in the words of Charles Saunders Peirce, the present is a "Nascent State between the Determinate and Indeterminate" (Peirce 1960, 459, quoted in Miyazaki 2004, 20). If judged against a teleology of progress, this "nascent state between" is sure to look like failure. But if viewed from the present of action, it seems less inevitably so.

From Utopian Revolution to Political Present

How does a focus on disappointment help us reconsider revolution as either an analytic concept or a social phenomenon? The pressure to conceptualize the wholly and radically new, and to be a "self-generating" subject of history (Marx 1932/1998, 59), leaves practitioners and theorists with an impossible task. However, there are ways to approach revolution as a political practice of the present not bound by the burdens of teleological inevitability. For Antonio Gramsci (1971, 175n75), the utopian is problematic insofar as it applies to "specific wills which are incapable of relating means to end, and hence are not even wills, but idle whims, dreams, longings, etc." Utopia as an idealized version of longed-for futures rather than a program for the transformation of the concrete present stifles political action. For real change, "it is necessary to direct one's attention violently towards the present as it is" (Gramsci 1971, 175n)—Gramsci thus released the idea of transformation from a necessary telos. Instead, the "ought to be" of revolutionary politics was a "concrete" set of practices, subject to negotiation, historical, and social conditions, and yet open to multiple possible futures (Gramsci 1971). Politics was transformative only insofar as it embraced both impossibility and necessity, passion and pragmatism, as the basis of real and specific change. The conditions of revolution, "the perishable nature of all ideological systems," existed alongside the limits of change, the "historical validity" and necessity of those systems (Gramsci 1971, 138). Like a "politics of disappointment," this approach is rooted in an awareness of the limits of coherent revolutionary change and yet creates a space for action nonetheless. It represents a "pessimism of the intelligence [and an] optimism of the will" (Gramsci 1971, 175n75).

Coming from a different philosophical tradition, Hannah Arendt was no less concerned with how abstract revolutionary ideals stifled rather than enabled politics. Arendt (1963/2006, 32–42), in her concern for the sustainability of postrevolutionary institutions, directly addressed revolution as a normative frame that sets up unrealistic expectations. Arendt challenged the idea of revolution as a transformative politics that brings about the totally new. Instead, she critiques the modernist temporalities built into the frame of revolutionary politics in the wake of the French Revolution. Judging revolutionary action against the time line of history not only produces a limiting model of revolution but also turns action into spectatorship. Insofar as revolution provides a framework for authorizing and interpreting political action, it forecloses both self-understanding and self-actualization of political agents. The model of revolution elides the indeterminacy and open-endedness of action as it unfolds in real time.

For both Arendt and Gramsci, utopian ideals run counter to transformative politics. It is through this analytic frame, derived from two central, if very different, theorists of politics, that I approach revolution as a messy social process that nonetheless generates powerful expectations. In starting from this point, I have approached student activists' practices, both before and after 2000, as contingent, complex, and often contradictory attempts to define and enact a political present, sometimes through and sometimes despite the teleological logics of revolutionary time. Conventional narratives of revolution sever postrevolutionary practice from prerevolutionary protest, even though shared experiences, relationships, and institutional forms shape political discourse and social meaning making for years to come. Revolutionary mass protests, like revolutions themselves, are as much processes as they are events (Sewell 1996). And revolutions produce their own ideological forms, which makes it essential to trace the ways in which those forms affect the interpretation of and scripts for future political action. We might consider revolution, like democracy, from the perspective of the varieties of disappointment in the present as well as the hopes that animated them.

Making Sense of the Political

In the past two decades we have witnessed the emergence of a new vocabulary for post–Cold War political transformation. Political and social movements are increasingly shifting away from Cold War models of revolution to a language of democratization or democratic revolution (Bunce and Wolchik 2011; Goodwin 2001; McAdam, Tarrow, and Tilly 2001). Yet the meaning of democracy is highly varied. From the direct democracy of the Occupy movement (Nugent 2012; Razsa and Kurnik 2012; Juris 2012) to the popular nature of the 2011 protests at the Wisconsin capital (Collins 2011), in the streets of Spanish cities (Sánchez Cedillo 2012), and in the Arab Spring (Abul-Magd 2012), democracy is often defined in popular and populist terms. At the same time, democracy has been a rallying cry that has justified neoliberal policies of economic restructuring through tropes of choice and practices of violence—the consumer-citizen (Foster 2002) and military intervention (Klein 2008). Democracy is the name of the game, but what that means is entirely up for grabs (Paley 2008).

The rallying cry of democracy as a shared, but often highly varied, site of political mobilization means that assessing the meanings of democracy in situ is all the more urgent. Why does democracy play out in any given context in the way that it does? What is the relationship between on-the-ground struggles and the normative concepts and expectations against which people judge their own and others' practice? Indeed, judging the nature of political practice has become increasingly complicated in an era in which texts, scripts for action, and shibboleths of political belonging are made to circulate across disparate contexts. It is the irony of the contemporary political moment that student activists may take up concepts and categories essential to the project of neoliberal education reform in Europe, and yet deploy them in a democratic project to expand citizen entitlements at the state university or to combat entrenched nationalist interests. In Serbia, rule of law had roots in both neoliberalizing forms of governance and popular responses to authoritarian rule. Tropes of civilization and European belonging were simultaneously responses to long-standing nationalist rhetoric and sites of new, classed elitisms. Thus, students could be committed to democratic representation and participation while perpetuating technocratic and elitist forms of rule, and even protest. Such moves may seem contradictory at one scale and entirely sensible at another.

If a revolutionary-cum-democratic project may be radical in one context and shore up status quo relations of power and social distinction in another, how do we assess and judge the nature and meaning of politics? To answer such a question, it is increasingly necessary to consider democratic practice not only in multiple sites but also at multiple scales of action and meaning. Given the proliferation of meanings, and the slippage of Cold War political certainties, we will do well to make sense of post–Cold War meanings of politics with a range of interlocutors: nongovernmental organization activists and university reformers, old-school politicians and new-school technocrats, the radical and the apathetic, the decidedly progressive and the seemingly conservative. Such wide-ranging and comparative perspectives are necessary because it has become increasingly difficult to make sense of Cold War categories of Left and Right, capitalist and communist, democratic and authoritarian, populist and progressive.[3]

It is, then, fair to say that the conditions of post–Cold War politics mean, among other things, that there is no pure politics for any of us. There is no project or ideal that is not contradictory at some intersecting scale of action—a fact made clear by the mass mediation of political movements, the seeming circulation of ideas and platforms of action across various borders and boundaries, and the intensified self-reflexivity that such processes produce. It is not merely that we must understand horizons of the political as always both local and global. Rather, politics itself is mediated by that conjuncture. In this context, like the student activists in Serbia, we are all disappointed political subjects contending with frustrated expectations and the zombie life of our dreams and desires (Comaroff and Comaroff 1999).[4]

This is not to abandon the possibility of practicing or analyzing politics, only the investment in the stability of political meaning. Anthropologists bring to this project a sense of action as they move across time and space, the shaping and reshaping of intended goals, ethical commitments, and the unintended consequences of the complex movement of political form. This is fundamentally a project of comparative politics—not case study against case study but comparison animated by the knowledge that there is no political project that is not imbricated in multiple contexts simultaneously at all times. Such a project entails an admission that our politics, like those of the activists that we study, are subject to constant reinterpretation, reframing, uptake, and co-optation, in ways that can make the work of assessing politics incredibly destabilizing and deeply frustrating. It is at this point that disappointment becomes the beginning and not the end of politics. It is at this point that the question "Why is there no resistance?" becomes an invitation to a more programmatic—though not unhopeful—set of questions: Whose resistance? Where? For or against what?

Reference Matter

Notes

Introduction

1. Yugoslavia was a member of the Non-Aligned Movement, a network of nations that fell outside the Western European–American and Soviet spheres of influence during the Cold War. Tito's leadership of the Non-Aligned Movement contributed greatly to Yugoslavia's international status and its ability to negotiate an alternative position in the Cold War world. Tito broke with the Soviet Union in 1948, ensuring financial support from the West that enabled two decades of rising living standards for many citizens of Yugoslavia.

2. The segment of the speech quoted here can be viewed in the documentary *Ako Srbija Stane*, YouTube video, 9:26, posted by "Novosadjan," November 25, 2006, http://www.youtube.com/watch?v=OWWH3kCGNFM.

3. "5. oktobar—12 godina razočaranja," b92.net, October 5, 2012, http://www.b92.net/info/vesti/index.php?yyyy=2012&mm=10&dd=05&nav_id=648804.

4. Slobodan Milošević came to power as a Communist Party functionary in the late 1980s and was elected president of Serbia in the first wave of democratic elections across socialist Yugoslavia in 1990. He ruled Serbia from 1990 to 2000, maintaining his regime through corruption and cronyism, crackdowns on dissidents, and an atmosphere of fear and intense nationalism. As Yugoslavia disintegrated in a violent civil war, Milošević promoted military action across the former Yugoslavia, including state support for paramilitary groups involved in acts of genocide and ethnic cleansing. Meanwhile, back at home in Serbia, Milošević presided over a rapidly impoverished population, including waves of refugees and a declining urban middle class. In 1999, after Milošević refused to withdraw troops from the province of Kosovo (an Albanian-majority province fighting for independence from Serbia), the North Atlantic Treaty Organization (NATO) bombed the country for three months straight, destroying civilian as well as military targets, public infrastructure, and much of Serbia's remaining industrial base.

Milošević's rule did not go uncontested throughout this time. Although many people who lived through the 1990s in Serbia remember it as a time of poverty, fear, isolation, and war, many others recall the sense of political possibility, best expressed in the protests that occurred throughout the decade. These were led over the course of the decade by students, opposition politicians, longtime antiwar activists, and members of Serbia's flourishing civil society and NGO scene. As frustration with Milošević's rule increased, the ranks of protesters grew, bolstered by ordinary citizens from across the political spectrum. Many were frustrated with plummeting standards of living, control over the media, and egregious violations of electoral procedures. Ironically, side by side with those who advocated democracy were the discontented of Milošević's own base, for whom his promises of military victory and Greater Serbia rang hollow or seemed less compelling in the face of unemployment and hunger.

In September 2000, Milošević called for elections, hoping to tap into widespread anger about the NATO bombing campaign and to consolidate power. He underestimated the popular sentiment against him, as well as the improved organization and unity of the opposition. Milošević was defeated at the polls by the constitutional lawyer Vojislav Koštunica, who had been the rare consensus candidate among a fractured opposition. The student movement had played a decisive role both in getting out the vote and in the electoral victory. Milošević refused to honor the election results for almost two weeks, until finally, on October 5, hundreds of thousands of citizens from all parts of Serbia marched in Belgrade. They stormed the Serbian parliament and the headquarters of the state-controlled media, Radio and Television Serbia. Instead of firing into the crowds, Milošević's massive police force stood quietly aside. By the end of the day, Milošević had conceded the election and stepped down.

5. James Siegel (1998, 47), writing about this phenomenon in the context of postrevolutionary Indonesia, notes that criminality may be an "effect of acting like a revolutionary after the revolution."

6. It has been extremely difficult to characterize Serbia during this period. Technically, Milošević's Serbia was a multiparty system, but in reality he ruled through a combination of threats and intimidation of opposition groups and capture of key state institutions either by the ruling party or by elites loyal to the regime. This is not to say that there weren't many people who continued to vote for Milošević in elections. However, at key points, including in the municipal elections of 1996, there was strong evidence of electoral fraud.

7. I also met with members of the group in Belgrade in 2001 and in Croatia in 1998.

8. The category of "student activist," with its associations with urbanity and Yugoslav modernism, provided an important counternarrative to that of national and ethnic belonging. At the same time, student activists and opposition leaders embraced idealized notions of democracy, often focusing on procedures like elections and freedom of the press, without addressing contentious issues like increasing economic inequality or Serbia's responsibility for war crimes during the 1990s. Youth politics also explicitly challenged discourses of nationalist mobilization in the 1990s, even as individual youth groups and opposition politicians continued to make implicit appeals on the basis of national belonging.

9. As Thomas Blom Hanson (1999, 18) has argued in his analysis of middle-class and conservative social movements in India, "Politics . . . denotes a generative and destructive process, questioning hierarchies and certitudes, while producing undecidability, as it reveals that every institutionalized and ostensibly naturalized practice is founded on acts of power and decision."

10. In his ethnography of the Chinese student movement in Tiananmen Square, Craig Calhoun (1997, 159) notes that common "rhetorical tropes" for student action, such as spontaneity or fatalism, may mask the more complex interplay of structure, agency, and chance in shaping mass protest movements.

11. Here I contrast the notion of disappointment to recent writing on hope in anthropology. A focus on hope often runs the risk of reinscribing a binary of hope and hopelessness in which loss and absence define the "negative" affective experience (Appadurai 2007). Thus boredom (Mains 2011), shame (Jeffrey 2010), despair (Oushakine 2009), and disconnectedness (Allison 2009) are understood in terms of stalled temporalities and unrealized hopes. Such states are mapped along the progressive space of a life cycle (Johnson-Hanks 2002) that intersects with broader geopolitical configurations of development and modernity (Ferguson 1999; Koselleck 2004). In response, many see a return to hope as an animating horizon for new and globalizing forms of protest, what Hardt and Negri (2011) have called a "cycle of struggles." Here I argue that disappointment is no less important in understanding the practice of politics over time.

12. It is fair to ask whether October 5 was a revolution at all, as scholars and public intellectuals in Serbia have (Popović 2010; Spasić and Subotić 2001). Of course, whether or not October 5 was a revolution depends largely on the operational definition of *revolution* that one is using. But more important, to take a definitive stance on the "fact" of revolution would reproduce precisely the kinds of problematics that I am trying to move beyond in this book. Revolution has emerged in Serbia as a terrain for debate and contestation about the meaning of the political present. There has been an ample literature in the social sciences that attempts to parse the meaning and definitions of revolution (for an excellent review, see Goodwin 2001).

13. This is especially true in formerly state-socialist contexts in which revolutionary conceptions of political time were central in shaping institutional forms and cultures (Hanson 1997). Indeed, from an absolutist Marxist perspective, true revolutions ought to sweep aside previous social, economic, and political relations until "a situation has been created which makes all turning back impossible" (Marx 1852/1994, 19).

14. Yugoslav politics had in many ways been configured around particularly twentieth-century, modernist understandings of time and political progress. As in many other countries that experienced rapid modernization within a socialist or developmentalist framework, expectations among citizens were often bound to particular visions of the good life—work, travel, consumption—and confidence in a government that both participated in world affairs and was respected as a member of the global community (Winegar 2006; Ferguson 1999). In many ways, the experience of uneven temporalities and the comparative frameworks and judgments they invited had been heightened by Serbia's rapid decline (in

contrast to Yugoslavia's more successful global image). This dynamic of moving backward in the context of comparative global frameworks of progress is central to understanding the disappointments of citizens in the former Yugoslav space in the 1990s.

15. The use of "the past" to frame and authorize social movements in the present has broad resonance. See, for example, Abelmann (1996).

16. Such mutually imbricated life worlds and ideological mirroring have prompted Sharad Chari and Katherine Verdery (2009) to talk about post–Cold War contexts rather than distinct socialist and nonsocialist spheres.

17. The shift to models of democratic transition, civil society, and the electoral revolution has profoundly challenged Cold War typologies of political transformation, such as those documented in classic analyses of twentieth-century revolution and protest (Goodwin 2001; McAdam, Tarrow, and Tilly 2001; Skocpol 1979). This is not to say that there is one necessary model for the relationship between revolution and democracy, or even transformative politics (see, for example, Hardt and Negri 2005; Holloway 2002). In the past twenty-five years, transformative political movements have produced everything from progressive participatory practices, new socialist regimes based on economic populism, and liberal and neoliberal democracies premised on state withdrawal and new modes of governmentality.

18. The rubric of civic revolution that I discuss here became a powerful and widely circulating trope because it combined local responses with growing transnational trends in the late–Cold War world. Civil society was also a powerful framework for political and moral critiques of a socialist state that many dissidents viewed as at best ideologically incoherent and at worst morally corrupt and corrupting (Hann and Dunn 1996; Havel 1985). The idea of a civic space that would prevent incursions of state power into citizens' everyday lives was critical to a progressive vision of socialist and democratic form in Eastern Europe. On the ground, the language of civil society was also an emerging response to the threat of nationalist populism, a form of politics that always existed in uneasy tension with the state-socialist project that both drew on nationalist rhetoric and officially decried it (Verdery 1991). Conflict between a rising class of new party elites and the rank and file of the socialist masses was a central tension in many socialist contexts, despite the official rhetoric of proletarian revolution (Cohen 1989; Konrád and Szeléyni 1979; Ðilas 1957).

19. The analysis of contemporary democratization models might similarly reveal the manifold ways in which socialist and capitalist worlds have long been embedded in the same discursive and social field (Bockman 2011; Greenberg 2010; Rogers 2010; Gal 2003; Burawoy 1985).

20. The ramifications of these experiments can be seen in the US model of democratization that has wedded the language of democratization to that of military intervention, using "shock" to create the tabula rasa on which liberal democracy can be built (Friedman 2007; Klein 2008).

21. This was particularly true in Yugoslavia in 1968, when mass student protests challenged the authority of Tito's rule, if only briefly. These protests generated important precedents and scripts for student protest as an important part of political life in socialist

Yugoslavia, although many involved, including faculty, ultimately suffered crackdowns (Arsić and Marković 1988; Pervan 1978; Popov 1978).

Student interventions were important because the university had long been a key institution in Yugoslav ideological and state-building projects. From the founding of the Socialist Federal Republic of Yugoslavia in 1945, socialist ideologies of progress and modernization hinged on the massive and rapid industrialization and urbanization of a largely rural and uneducated population.

Policies of equal access to education were put into place after the war, even if they didn't always translate into real access. By the 1960s, the university system had exploded, partly because of new federalist policies by which republics and regions attempted to establish increased economic, social, and political autonomy from Yugoslav state structures. Massive postwar expansion of the education system also served several ideological and practical goals: to create a legitimate state site for the production of a new socialist subjects, to keep young people out of an overburdened labor market, and to break with the past system of education that was seen as reproducing privilege. The University of Belgrade has its origins in nineteenth-century Serbia but was officially founded in 1905. State-run universities were later founded in Novi Sad (1960), Niš (1965), Priština, (1970), and Kragujevac (1976).

22. For analysis of how students framed their interventions in the 1990s, see Lazić (1999).

23. For an analysis of these social geographies of politics in the 1990s, see Gordy (1999) and Gagnon (2004).

24. Otpor's efforts combined tactics that stemmed from reflections on earlier protests, as well as new ideas about nonviolent revolution, based on the writings of Gene Sharp, a theorist and practitioner of nonviolent resistance.

25. Individuals' names have been changed to protect anonymity.

26. By 2000, Serbia was no stranger to international media attention, and to political and economic sanctions during Yugoslavia's bloody wars of secession. Slobodan Milošević's role in supporting paramilitary groups in Bosnia, and in covering up acts of genocide and crimes against humanity, earned him the reputation as the "Butcher of the Balkans." At the same time, the student and opposition activism, and the eventual overthrow of Milošević in a peaceful revolution on October 5, 2000, put Serbia on the map as a new model for nonviolent, democratic revolution. These dual legacies of reviled nationalism and internationally acclaimed democratic achievement mean that democracy in Serbia has also been an experiment in political mediation of Serbia's image within nested transnational contexts.

27. All translations in this text are my own. Interviews were conducted in both Serbian and English (or a mix) over the course of more than two years of fieldwork. The decision as to interview language depended on the context of the interaction and the preference and comfort of the person being interviewed. Where interviews have been translated, I have inserted key terms or phrases in the original Serbian in parentheses.

28. Practically speaking, I spent the majority of my time with students from Student Union. In each city, Student Union had a centrally located office, which made it easier

to drop by to find out about events and programs. The organization produced a great deal of promotional material, from glossy compendiums of their most important documents to posters, flyers, and policy papers laying out their positions on key issues. The national-level group also had a relatively systemized schedule of board meetings and informational sessions. Student Union's commitment to a broader range of issues and its desire to weigh in on issues affecting civil society also meant that it had a wider range of events I could attend. By contrast, I had greater trouble gaining access to the events or meetings of Student Alliance. I conducted interviews with members of Student Alliance in Novi Sad and Belgrade. I also attended some planning meetings in Belgrade. Initial inroads into these events were cut short by a shake-up in the organization's leadership in 2003 and the eventual ouster of members I had developed relationships with. Student Alliance also had fewer public events, and so I relied more heavily on accounts of events from individuals with whom I formed relationships. My relationship with Student Association in Niš fell somewhere in between. The Student Association had two main offices where I knew I could find various members of the group and group leadership. While hanging out, we talked at length about Student Association, their mission, and their activities. However, the association did not seem to have a number of well-publicized events that I could attend.

Chapter 1

1. Several of these issues, like the outdated exam system, were the legacy of the socialist system of education, from when Serbia had been one of six federal republics in the Socialist Federal Republic of Yugoslavia. But many of the other issues emerged with the violent breakup of Yugoslavia in 1991. Under Milošević, the university was subject to a combination of economic disinvestment, overcrowding (students flocked to the university to avoid being drafted into the military, or they stayed in the university as a strategy to deal with rising unemployment), administrative restructuring, and purges that were part of the regime's effort to consolidate political control.

2. More recent data have shown that youth unemployment in Serbia continues to be high. A 2012 study indicates that for young people age fifteen to twenty-four, the unemployment rate was 50.9 percent, and for those age twenty-five to thirty-four it was 33.2 percent (Mojić 2012, 116).

3. Many others have written about the prevalence of the victim narratives that so dominated Serbian public discourse in the 1990s with a range of powerful and widely circulating tropes, such as lament, cynicism, and conspiracy theory (Živković 2011; see also Jansen 2005; Van de Port 1998; Dragović-Soso 2002). Such tropes were themselves ways of making sense of and acting in the present, but they often operated in lieu of, rather than in conjunction with, more specifically programmatic ways of talking about the possibility for political change and transformation.

4. I have talked elsewhere about the sense of being out of control of one's fate as a particular feature of Serbian ideologies of agency in the period after 2000, as well as the ways in which discourses of normalcy, travel, and a desire for certain kinds of consumption were about the loss and possible restoration of this historically specific linkage between Yugoslav cosmopolitanism and individuals' ability to control their own agentive capacities

(Greenberg 2011). I have also talked about the generationally marked trope of being "post-cynical" (Greenberg 2006c).

5. As a quote from the presidium of the Belgrade city assembly makes clear, the critique of the "radicals" and "extremists" was that they could not speak for any interests but their own: "We consider that nobody can claim the right arbitrarily to declare himself the champion of social progress, and that usurpation of such a right by any groups represents and attack on democracy. Who can claim the right to declare himself a member of the ideological vanguard without the consent of those whose interests he allegedly represents" (quoted in Pervan 1978, 25).

6. It is worthwhile contrasting 1968 to another set of famous student protests in Yugoslavia's history, those of Kosovar Albanian students in 1981, shortly after Tito's death. The protests in Priština also began as a response to the failures of the state to make good on promises to university students. As in 1968, officials attempted to manage the impact of the protests through charges of hostile and antirevolutionary elements among students. However, the extreme violence of the state's response, and other tensions within Kosovo and Yugoslavia, made the 1968 appeal to a greater social good an impossible rhetorical move. In the case of 1968, a clear dichotomy between "us," the socialist people, and "them," antisocialist, foreign, and self-interested elements, was rigidly maintained in the discourse on student politics and protest. In 1981, the collectivity was being called into question as the socialist nation began to fracture into regional and ethnic forms of belonging. It is possible that in 1981, following Tito's death, questions surrounding Kosovo and the very future of Yugoslavia made a collective Yugoslav interest less conceivable or appealing. In turn, it was harder to imagine the unified collective for whom the students could be seen as selflessly fighting. Whereas in 1968 Tito could frame good and bad students as for or against the interests of the socialist collectivity, by 1981 this was no longer possible, especially in the context of Kosovo. In the case of the Kosovo protests, the party leadership was unable or unwilling to co-opt student demands by framing them as a call for the greater "social good" or for the reinforcement of a notion of larger community. The results were a tragic series of events that shook the loyalties of even Communist Party officials, forcing people to choose between Kosovo and the Yugoslav state (Von Kohl and Libal 1997, 65).

7. Thanks to Fabio Mattioli for helping me articulate this link.

8. *Sevdah* is derived from the Turkish word for the humor "black gall." It is largely associated with a genre of Bosnian folk music, *sevdalinke*, which is characterized by rich songs full of loss and melancholy. The beauty and pathos of the songs gives the listener a sense of both pain and joy.

9. In his analysis of education and social distinction in France, Bourdieu (1984) demonstrates just such a process, as young people longed for a "good life," promised to them by the institutions and practices of their parents' generation, while facing increasingly difficult conditions for class and social reproduction.

10. For a wonderful depiction of Yugoslavia as a fantasy, see *Cinema Komunisto*, a 2010 documentary written and directed by Mila Turajlić and produced by Dribbling Pictures, 3K Productions, and Intermedia Network. Information about the film (available on DVD) can be found at http://www.cinemakomunisto.com.

11. For a more detailed analysis of tropes of moral breakdown, see Greenberg (2011).

12. Thanks to Michael Herzfeld for pushing me to think about disappointment as a rhetorical frame.

13. Such discourses certainly have strong ties to neoliberal formations of state, economy, and society, and the rise of technocratic politics has narrowed the domains of political activism (Mitchell 2002; Comaroff and Comaroff 1997, 1999a, 1999b; Ferguson 1994). However, as I show in chapter 3, their origins and impetus cannot be reduced to the imposition of neoliberal political transformations in Serbia or elsewhere. Rather, the emergence of these terms also has roots in the particular experience of student activists struggling to rethink political possibility in a postrevolutionary way.

Chapter 2

1. The question of what kind of politics is "appropriate" for a democracy, especially when former protesters are elected to office, can also be used to undercut the democratic authority and legitimacy of more unruly forms of politics (see Paley 2001). The complexity of the situation increases when it involves students who may be considered a crucial source of protest energy in one period and unruly, impertinent, and even dangerous in another. As Dipesh Chakrabarty (2007) argues with respect to Jawaharlal Nehru's changing relationship to student protest before and after India's independence, what is considered revolutionary political action against an oppressive regime can appear quite different when turned against a newly formed independent or democratic state.

2. State-directed urbanization policies followed suit, such that "urbanization was no longer a spontaneous, slow drift to the towns, but a deliberately stimulated transfer of population away from the perceived backwardness of peasant society" (Allcock 2000, 164).

3. For example, Yugoslav state officials explicitly modeled and promoted the policy of nonalignment through architectural projects, including the Palace of Federation, which was opened specifically to host the first summit of the Non-Aligned Movement in 1961 (Erić 2009, 136).

4. Protest, within limits, remained part of a repertoire of citizen action in socialist Yugoslavia. The historian Nebojša Vladisavljević (2008) has challenged the widespread scholarly and policy assumption that the rise in mass protest in the 1980s and early 1990s was elite manipulated and top down. According to Vladisavljević, the emergent grassroots forms of mass mobilization ushered in an era of state-sanctioned popular and populist protest as a viable model for citizen participation in late-socialist Yugoslavia. The protests of this period combined grassroots mobilization around issues of national identity and economic populism with forms of appeal sanctioned by the communist state. The wave of mass protest in Serbia in the late 1980s, the so-called antibureaucratic revolution, began as a grassroots initiative to hold party officials accountable for their own legislative frameworks and ideological promises. The protests also mobilized a broad base of citizens, particularly industrial workers, who were dissatisfied with the worsening economic conditions across the country. Once again, the regime largely tolerated protests that called for reforms of the socialist state without challenging the essential authority of the socialist system.

5. Practices of spatially and bureaucratically controlling resistant citizens are most evident in Milošević's policies of militarization. Wartime meant closed borders, a more dangerous political climate for open public protest, and forced movements of refugees across borders.

6. Lenard Cohen (2001, 135) argues that "the 'heroization' of mafia activity in Serbia made a mockery of the regime's claim to be upholding the rule of law and transformed the climate in Milošević's soft dictatorship into a disorderly and dangerous environment in which wild and arbitrary justice became increasingly routine."

7. The first major anti-Milošević protest of the decade began on March 9, 1991, in response to increased state control over the media. Students joined opposition leaders in Republic Square (Trg Republike) in the center of Belgrade, eventually marching on the Serbian parliament building. The demonstrations were met with military force, arrests, beatings, and national media coverage lambasting the demonstrators as unruly, violent traitors. State police demonstrated that they would meet public displays of citizens' discontent with violent crackdowns, thus literalizing state control over public, urban space in a battle over the regime's legitimacy (Gordy 1999, 37–43; Popov 2000).

In June and July 1992, student protests in Belgrade began in response to opposition calls for greater democracy in the country. Again, students mobilized through the university, calling for the disbanding of parliament, Milošević's resignation, and elections. Fueled by the introduction of international sanctions, student protests broke out at the University of Belgrade, the University of Niš, and the University of Novi Sad. In addition to the demands listed already, students also protested the university's decreasing autonomy (Popov 2000, 323). Despite a universitywide petition, the so-called University Act was passed shortly thereafter. The law increased the state's control of the university by increasing government representation in university bodies and government control in electing rectors and deans.

The years 1991 and 1992 established mass public protest as a counterresponse to Milošević's increasing consolidation of power through institutions of state, including state-controlled media, parliament, and the university. While the first two protests focused on laws and policies through which Milošević and his cronies consolidated power, the student and civic protests in 1996 and 1997 responded to a direct instance of electoral fraud. The protests lasted every day from November 17, 1996, through March 20, 1997. At various peak points, the protesters numbered between two hundred thousand and five hundred thousand. The most famous images from this period are of columns of people walking through Belgrade and other cities. The demonstrations were organized when the government annulled local election results in which the opposition coalition Zajedno (Together) defeated the ruling Socialist Party of Serbia by significant margins in most urban centers. The protesters mainly represented the urban middle class, galvanized by dwindling economic opportunity and the government's refusal to restructure the failing economy (Lazić 1999). The government's blatant fraud only added to the opposition's urban support base, particularly among students. The opposition-led part of the protests ended in mid-February, when the government conceded Zajedno's victories. However, students continued to demonstrate until key demands relating to university administration were met. In part because of the

NATO bombings in 1999, the marches of 1996 and 1997 were the last large-scale public protests before the October 5 revolution.

8. The fate of the gay pride parade is a particularly clear example of this process. After the violence and bloodshed of the first parade in 2001, it took nine years for activists to again move forward with a similar public event in 2010, which was also met with violence from nationalist groups. Police were heavily criticized for not being able (or willing) to protect protesters. In 2011 the state refused to let the parade go forward, citing public safety. State officials and police declared that it was for the protesters own good, since, they argued, they could not guarantee the safety of protesters. Pro-pride supporters largely saw such declarations as tacit admission of the state's unwillingness or inability to mobilize resources to protect one group of citizens from the violence of another.

9. Student protests continued in the years after I left Serbia, but, interestingly, they increasingly adapted to changing conditions. As Bačević (2010) has shown, by 2006 student demands took up an explicit critique of neoliberal policies (a discourse that was virtually absent when I had been in Serbia only a few years earlier). Protests were directed at a more complex field of power than stand-alone state institutions.

10. In her analysis of changing forms of youth and student citizenship in Kerala, India, Ritty Lukose (2009) has demonstrated how students enact their visions for an ideal relationship between state and citizens through different gendered practices and uses of public space. These vary widely, including new ideologies of consumer citizenship and civic publics, as well as older forms of political publics, which are defined through open, mass protest and the shutting down of public space such as streets and universities. She argues that a "'logic of representation' centers on the right of groups and individuals to make their desires and needs known, to represent themselves to others and to the state—even if through struggle—as legitimate claimants to public considerations. Such a logic requires the acceptance of a (near) universal and positive right of representation. Yet, as with any other right, such a right cannot be guaranteed in the abstract—rather, it is something always to struggle toward. In this struggle, the development of a space for representation, a place in which groups and individuals can make themselves visible is crucial. . . . The logic of representation demands the construction—or, better, the social production—of certain . . . kinds of public space" (Lukose 2009, 33). The specific use of public space can thus be constitutive of different forms of citizenship and rights, and as such it is highly contested (see also Mitchell 2003).

11. Such distinctions were tenuous and had to be carefully maintained. For example, two of the Novi Sad Student Union leaders made a show of annoyance, bordering on indignation, in informing me that Student Alliance had not bothered to show up. I didn't comment that in the two weeks leading up to the protest I had heard Student Union's organizing team telling group members to keep quiet about the event because they didn't want Alliance to hear about it and take up the idea.

12. This included riots in 2004 in response to violent clashes in Kosovo. Rioters set fire to mosques in Belgrade and Niš. Mass protests and riots in Belgrade also broke out in response to Kosovo's declaration of independence in February 2008. Rioters set fire to the US, Slovenian, and Croatian embassies and damaged property across Belgrade.

13. The first Exit festival was organized by Student Union in Novi Sad and was a hundred-day festival on the banks of the Danube that featured music, parties, information sessions, and an active get-out-the-vote campaign. It combined the political goals of the anti-Milošević movement with the cultural associations of urbane rock music and global youth culture. While Exit continued to retain some social-activist programming and themes, at least through the one I attended in 2003, the festival became more of a cultural phenomenon designed to attract tourism and put Serbia on the map of a global youth festival scene. Its lineup tended toward local and regional rock bands associated with Yugoslav and post-Yugoslav urbanity, as well as international rock, punk, hip-hop, and other groups of increasing prominence as the years went on.

However, Exit changed in significant ways after 2000. The festival moved to the Petrovaradin Fortress in Novi Sad, in an attempt to repackage the city's existing tourist sites as an appealing and hip destination for Europe's youth. The small core of organizers who had started in Student Union of Novi Sad broke off into their own organization, which caused some crisis in the group among those who wanted to pursue only the festival and those who were committed to maintaining a focus on university reform and other kinds of advocacy. The direction of Exit was indicative of the way different student-led groups began to articulate claims in and on public space differently after 2000. As the festival gained more commercial appeal, students affiliated with Student Union had less and less to do with it, other than to go as attendees. In one conversation I had in 2003, a student activist and member of the Novi Sad group that had initially launched Exit dismissed the festival as a commercial venture, interested only in making money rather than in the concerns of young people. It was a particularly revealing comment, because it called out a highly popular, massive cultural and social manifestation as not in the interests of young people. At the time she made the comment, this student had been working intensively on developing and promoting a youth policy platform for Novi Sad, and she had been frustrated by low turnout at a recent press conference.

14. This is not to say it is impossible. For example, on the emergence of direct democracy activists in Slovenia with roots in the anticorporate globalization movement, see Razsa and Kurnik (2012). In addition, many students had their own critique of the effects of neoliberal restructuring in Serbia. Some in Student Union supported the National Unions of Students in Europe's platform on the commodification of education and the right of students to free or affordable higher education. But the association of a politics grounded in such issues had a dangerous resonance with populist and nationalist calls for state subsidies, which often targeted populations like pensioners who were most reliant on the state.

15. Indeed, although the rector worked closely with students, she could also be critical of them. She once confessed to me some irritation that students always expected to be included in every decision, the implication being that they were overstepping their bounds. She told me, "It's self-management; they get it from their parents," thus linking their sense of entitlement to socialist legacies in which all employees and citizens participated in self-managing councils through which firm-, municipality-, and even neighborhood-level decisions were meant to be reached by consensus. This was yet another legacy and meaning of

participation in the democratic context that students might not have necessarily realized they were invoking in how they framed their demands.

Chapter 3

1. The effects have been particularly devastating in England, as universities slashed academic programs according to their economic viability and usefulness. On the implications of the Bologna Process for US higher education, see Greenwood (2009); Washburn (2006).

2. For earlier attempts to systematically analyze the structural logics and conditions of educational institutions, see Willis (1977); Bourdieu (1984). On student activism in relationship to institutional contradictions, see Burawoy (1976).

3. The Serbian version of the document was originally accessed on the Student Union website in 2004, at http://www.sus.org.rs. An English version can still be found at the website of the South East European Educational Cooperation Network, at http://www.see-educoop.net/portal/id_serbia.htm.

4. For more on this particular vision of agency as it relates to normalcy, see Greenberg (2011).

5. These dual tasks are particularly interesting in the European context, because from early on, EU strategies for economic expansion and dealing with social inequity and redistribution hinged on the production of citizens as knowledge workers.

6. With Tito's break from Stalin in 1948 and the creation of self-management socialism in response to the perceived failures of the Soviet model, Yugoslavia forged its own approach to the communist goal of the withering away of the state. The tensions of this process most often manifested in debates about decentralization of political and economic power, the role of the party as vanguard in relation to the rank and file, and the relationship between experts and administrators and a system of worker control (Gagnon 2004; Cohen 1989; Carter 1982). In addition, such high-level debates often manifested in specific bureaucratic and social polices intended to encourage citizens to be simultaneously self-directed and ideologically in line.

7. As Pervan (1978) demonstrates in his analysis of the 1968 protests, in the years leading up to the protest, the Union of Students, the official socialist student organization, came under fire for failing to mobilize larger numbers of students at the universities. The response to the lack of mobilization or general interest in the Union of Students was to shift the blame to the organizational leadership for being too self-interested and careerist. In addition, critique of the Union of Students also followed the antibureaucratic line that became so important after Yugoslavia's 1948 break from Stalin (Cohen 1989). Student leaders were blamed for being more concerned with bureaucratic hierarchy than with the interests and needs of their members. The programmatic response was to encourage a freer, more democratic approach that emphasized full participation of the rank-and-file membership, a move paralleling political and economic reforms in the country more generally (Carter 1982; Gagnon 2004).

8. According to the official EU website "About the Bologna Process," the main goals of the European Higher Education Area are to "facilitate mobility of students, graduates and

higher education staff; prepare students for their future careers and for life as active citizens in democratic societies, and support their personal development; and offer broad access to high-quality higher education, based on democratic principles and academic freedom" (http://www.ond.vlaanderen.be/hogeronderwijs/bologna/about/index.htm).

9. Level of support tended to vary from university to university. The University of Novi Sad had already begun making connections with foreign students and faculty and developing courses and programming in European studies. Many at the University of Belgrade were more resistant to reform, given that the university was considered the most prestigious and had longer-standing traditions.

10. This is not to say that everyone who was critical of the Bologna Process on these grounds automatically held a nationalist position on other issues. Rather, student activists and others could differentiate themselves in subtle ways through a language of tradition that had implications and social weight when mobilized in other arenas of debate and talk.

11. With low salaries for professors, it was relatively easy to arrange to pay for passing grades. Students could also pay other students to take exams for them. Such opportunities don't come cheaply. I was told that a student could charge around 250 euros to take an exam. In a country in which the average salary at the time was 150 euros a month, the best testament to students' frustration and hopelessness is that they would pay so much simply to pass an exam.

12. For a summary of the June 16, 2003, report, "A Note on University Autonomy and the New Law on Higher Education in Serbia," see the website of the University of Novi Sad, at http://www.uns.ac.rs/sr/novosti_dogadjaji/magnaCharta/RepSerbiaVisit190503.pdf.

13. He had not been at the morning session, and indeed, Student Union had not known the meeting was going on. I had told Petar about the event during the lunch break.

Chapter 4

1. The importance of "expert" talk is certainly part and parcel of this process, particularly in relationship to the increased emphasis coming from the European Union on higher education reform as primarily an administrative and technical-managerial exercise rather than a total overhaul of the political and social mandate of the university (see chapter 3).

2. As Julia Paley (2001) has argued in her ethnography of changing democratic practice in postdictatorship Chile, activists with experience in local community organizing often face the challenge of reframing their knowledge as professionalized and expert in liberal and neoliberalizing democratic contexts. Not only are new forms of technocratic knowledge and political practice valorized in emerging democracies, but also alternative ways of representing collective concerns and interests are often denigrated as irrelevant or inappropriate in contexts of formal political participation.

3. For more on these debates, particularly the role of the vanguard party in relationship to the rank and file, see Cohen (1989).

4. The party has since changed its name to United Regions of Serbia.

5. Expertise was also used to bypass or manage extremely contentious and complex social and political issues. For example, as Victor Friedman (1996) has shown, the census has

been one such form of statistical measurement that international and national policy makers have presented as a "neutral" apparatus for managing postconflict conditions, despite the incredibly politicized nature of both the process and the instrument.

6. She told me, "With regards to marketing [*što se marketinga tiče*] we should look to be more acceptable to students . . . to impact and target them in a certain way. However, when it comes to public relations, I worked on public relations for a year. I didn't only work in contact with the media, but also with rectors, deans, with specific certain stake holders [*sa izvesnim certain stake holderima*], with other student organizations, other youth organizations. Simply to work on the image (*na imidžu organizacije*) of the organization."

7. This slogan sounds awkward in Serbian and English but is a play on a slang phrase, "Čemu ovo služi [a uz to i ne radi]," which roughly means, "What does this do, and by the way it doesn't work." It can be used, for example, to refer to random or confusing junk that one might find in a cheap shop or the market. It's origins are reported to stem from translations of old Disney cartoons.

8. Many thanks to Susan Gal and Alejandro Paz for their insights into the idea of circulation as it is formulated here.

9. For example, around the time I was leaving the field, the Belgrade office was also drafting a student survey to better assess how much students knew about Student Union. The goal, in part, was both to see what kind of reputation Student Union had and to determine which types of students the organization was attracting. This production of knowledge both about Student Union as a group—how it was perceived, how it circulated—also created typologies of the student body, which would then further determine types of intervention, appeals, and marketing.

10. Interestingly, branding of the university was also going on at the time, a process about which student activists in the groups I discuss here were very much aware. Such branding also entailed a process of making the university intelligible and visible, something that students as well as faculty and administrators were engaging in, in anticipation of Serbia's universities competing for European students and funding within the Bologna European Higher Education Area. For example, the rector of the University of Novi Sad was the most active and engaged in Bologna Process reforms during my time in the field. As part of this process, she did a good deal to rebrand the university as a particularly European space, emphasizing both the region's long-standing ties to Central European traditions and cultures and the specific institutional organization of the university as more reflective of the kinds of administrative regulations that Bologna would require (e.g., a more centralized rectorate). For example, in May 2003, she hosted the first university *info-sajam* (information fair), designed to recruit high school students to the university. During this event, the rector promoted the idea of university education and the University of Novi Sad in particular. Like Student Union's attempts to develop a coherent image, she also relied on particular artifacts and images to give the university a sense of identity. For example, she drew attention to the idea of the University of Novi Sad as a campus-based institution that was more than the sum of its parts. Indeed, out of all the Serbian universities, it has coherent campus space, including a large, green quad ringed with university buildings, which backs onto the Danube River. The universities of Belgrade and Niš, for example, consist

Notes to Chapters 4 and 5

of buildings scattered through the city, although Belgrade does boast the small Students' Square (Studentski Trg), ringed by a cluster of faculties, the main administrative building, and the famous coffeehouse and bookshop Plato—the unofficial gathering place for students across the city.

11. This may well have been a reference to a common Serbian saying that wishes death to a neighbor's cow (*da komšiji crkne krava*). This saying signals a belief that Serbs lack solidarity even with their intimates (figured as neighbors) and that this resentment is born of jealousy and long-held grievances. It is also a saying associated with the Serbian notion of *inat*, associated with self-defeating actions taken out of spite.

12. From the Student Union website, accessed March 10, 2004, at http://www.sus.org .yu/dokumenta/ugs-sus.doc.

13. As Dominic Boyer (2005) has argued, notions of expertise often assume and reproduce distinctions between the body and the mind, erasing the fundamental corporeality of knowledge practices from assessments and evaluations of what is and what is not legitimate knowledge production. Although this distinction has a long history in Western intellectual and philosophical tradition, it becomes particularly salient at moments in which certain specifically embodied practices, often grounded in socially mediated hierarchies of value and difference, condition the performance of expertise while simultaneously being erased and denied. If the erasure of the corporeal as a site of specific and local kinds of knowledge is a condition of expertise, then this is no less true for the textually mediated artifacts of expertise.

14. The appearance of this article and the resulting controversy were sensitive issues within the group at the time. As such, I have not written publically about the episode until now. A decade has passed, and the students involved in this controversy have graduated or moved on to other organizations and activities. Given this, and the fact that I saw it as a pivotal moment in struggles to redefine the meaning of democratic practice for the group, I am including it here. I hope to show that this wasn't an episode about controlling knowledge or antidemocratic trends in the group. It was a genuine and often very personal struggle with the demands of organizational accountability and democratic representation. Both sides held ethical positions but drew on very different understandings of the issue at hand. That said, there were other administrative and budgetary issues that the group wished to discuss behind closed doors that I do not detail here.

15. According to the official history on its website, the first Student Union branch was founded at the Law Faculty in Belgrade, although there are different origins stories, depending on who you talk to (see http://www.sus.org.rs/istorija-sus-a).

16. At the time of a follow-up visit to Serbia, in 2005, the reorganization team had not yet been successfully constituted. It was clear from several follow-up conversations that the tensions between local and national levels within the organization had not yet been resolved.

Chapter 5

1. As Nina Eliasoph (1998) argued in her ethnography of US-based civic action, the particular form that political conversation takes is critical to the kinds of sociopolitical imaginaries that people collectively forge. For Eliasoph (1998, 15), the creation of publics is

tied to "a process of giving voice to a wide circle of concern—a public spirited *way of talking*, not a topic ('politics')."

2. For example, Torsten Kolind (2007) has shown how "politics" and "decent folk" are categories used in postwar Bosnia to make moral distinctions and to negotiate social connections. Such distinctions are shifting and flexible resources that people can use to narratively make sense of their world. Politics is frequently figured through gendered distinctions that pit a dirty, corrupting sphere (alternately figured as virile and masculine or dishonorable and shameful, like a "whore") against a purer realm of family (Helms 2007). In the postwar context, politics was seen as antithetical to moral life in Serbia as well. Young men and women in Serbia have established a moral distance from the violence in the 1990s and the debates about Serbian responsibility for war crimes and genocide by arguing that they had no control over political decision making (Greenberg 2010). Such distinctions between politics and the nonpolitical world has become an important way to manage people's senses of guilt, responsibility, and betrayal during Yugoslavia's bloody history.

3. There is a great deal of historical and sociological evidence for the central role of political elites in the promulgation of violence and nationalism throughout the former Yugoslavia (Gagnon 2004). However, what is important here is the cultural and tropic power of the idea of politics as a sphere of elite, self-serving politicians (Bracewell 2000).

4. One evening, sitting over a beer with a student activist from Niš, I was shocked to hear her describe herself as not political. By then a good friend, she was one of the most dedicated activists I had met, a woman who not only involved herself in student and rights organizations but also lived out her principles. But for her, like many others in Serbia, the realm of politics meant formal political systems and was a corrupt and corrupting set of institutions. At the heart of this sense of politics as dirty was a belief that politicians were interested only in their own needs and careers.

5. Because of what one interviewee felt was the sensitive nature of our exchange, I have eliminated any more specific reference to the group he belonged to or the faculty in which he studied. Like other names in this text, the name used here is a pseudonym.

6. It is worth noting that I use *politics* here in two ways. First, it designates a relationship between strategic, organized social action and people's aspirations to transform the institutional and social environment in which they live. Although the students with whom I worked were reluctant to use the language of politics, what made their interventions political in this sense were their attempts to redefine the parameters for legitimate social action. I also use the notion of the political as a key ethnographic category in the Serbian context. Here *political* connotes self-interest, and often corruption, and it is irreconcilable with claims of representation and selflessness that many student leaders made.

7. Consider Havel's (1985, 27) widely cited example of the manager of a fruit and vegetable shop who places a sign in his window that reads "Workers of the World Unite." Havel goes on to diagnose the sign, whose message may or may not mean anything to the greengrocer, as a communicative act that makes the shopkeeper complicit with the ideological deception that underpins power in the posttotalitarian state. The sign is merely one node in a system of power that obscures reality through a semiotics of obedience.

The manipulation of the "day-to-day existence of all citizens" (Havel 1985, 26) takes place through an obfuscation of power that relies on such gaps between reality and its representation. Hence, "life in the system is so thoroughly permeated with hypocrisy and lies: . . . the complete degradation of the individual is presented as his or her ultimate liberation; depriving people of information is called making it available; the use of power to manipulate is called the public control of power, and the arbitrary abuse of power is called observing the legal code" (Havel 1985, 30).

8. As Judith Irvine (1996) has argued, drawing on Goffman and Bakhtin, the layering and distinctions in the category of "speaker" mean that an instance of speech or discourse can produce multiple subject positions, as well as multiple levels of responsibility and ownership in relationship to what is actually said. By differently inhabiting speech forms, one can speak but not be the author or agent of the meaning conveyed. There are a multitude of layering and positions with utterances and discursive frameworks in which people can position themselves or others (Goffman 1983, 144). This distinction in the notion of the speaker is critical to understanding why law and procedure were so important to students. In the context of the "problem of interest," students were attempting to fix and purge multivocality through use of authorizing discourses of law. Given the problem of self-interest in politics, which haunts students' attempts to argue that they are in fact not self-interested, and that they are not manipulated by some outside power, such fixing is critical. In invoking laws and regulations, students can take on the authority and meaning of that speech. By drawing attention to the ways in which students are inhabited by legal discourse, students attempt to purge the multiple voices and intentionalities (e.g., foreign or political interests) that they are commonly seen as channeling. The emphasis on fixed law and codified procedure is, then, an attempt to create an authorizing framework for viewing students merely as animators (Goffman 1983).

9. One could not predict the particular nature of delays and breakdowns in achieving the most basic of goals, only that there would be delays and breakdowns. Katherine Verdery (1996, 48–49) has captured the qualities of a life uncertain but for uncertainty in her notion of etatization. The central appropriation of planning and initiative was furthered by a monopoly over knowledge that might have allowed people to use their time "rationally," that is, otherwise. Not knowing when the bus might come, when cars might be allowed to circulate again, when the exam for medical specializations would be given, or when food would appear in stores, bodies were transfixed, suspended in a void that obviated all projects and plans but the most flexible and spontaneous ones.

Conclusion: Democracy and Revolution After the Cold War

1. This alternative framing of Cold War and post–Cold War owes much to Sharad Chari and Katherine Verdery (2009). Understanding socialism as part of a larger modernist project that encompassed Cold War boundaries of East and West helps us to both draw on and move beyond the implicit social geographies that continue to haunt postsocialism as a scholarly category (see Creed 2010; see also Rogers 2010). Analyzing broader geographies of democratic triumphalism also help us draw out key links between Cold War and

post–Cold War visions of politics. A contemporary anthropology of democracy in and of the postsocialist world thus reveals the interconnectedness of geopolitical worlds that are often treated as distinct, as well as the powerful impact of discursive and ideological frames about that distinction on everyday political and social practice. It also highlights practices of mirroring and uptake that have long defined broader European publics across national borders and even common language areas (Gal 2006).

2. See also Gilbert et al. (2008). In this sense, disappointment as a method echoes what Hannah Pitkin has called dialectical thinking. Dialectical thinking is an epistemological frame that allows one to move back and forth between the abstract and the concrete, to both push the limits of existing assumptions and play out new critical modes of thinking against a range of possible actions. It is thus a fundamentally open-ended and contingent mode of engagement that fuses praxis and analysis. Pitkin notes that "the value of heavenly abstractions, seen dialectically, is that they loosen the grip of existing assumptions on our thinking, but the early practicalities, however reconceptualized, remain the test of what counts as political possibility" (Pitkin 2000, 248).

3. Similarly, in a post-Marxist context, how do we assess the project of political trans-formation? As I mentioned in the introduction, many people feel the lack of a post-Marxist vocabulary for social justice or redistribution in formerly socialist Europe. This is true across Eastern Europe, with the discrediting of Marxian frameworks in light of the abuses of the socialist state. It is even truer in the former Yugoslavia, and Serbia in particular, where socialist populist rhetoric often went hand in hand with nationalist populist agendas. This is not to say that commitments to the redistributive principles of the socialist or welfare state have been completely abandoned. But more often than not, the Marxist vocabulary is weighted with the political associations of the past.

4. Perhaps it is not a coincidence that at the time of this writing there has been a re-newed interest (including reported sightings) of vampires in Serbia: like zombies, they are the undead monsters of past tradition, aggrieved dead, and repressed pasts returning to haunt a dissatisfied present. On the cultural and political significance of Serbia as a vampire nation, see Longinović (2011).

Works Cited

Abelmann, Nancy. 1996. *Echoes of the Past, Epics of Dissent: A South Korean Social Movement.* Berkeley: University of California Press.

Abul-Magd, Zeinab. 2012. "Occupying Tahrir Square: The Myths and the Realities of the Egyptian Revolution." *South Atlantic Quarterly* 111 (3): 565–72.

Agha, Asif. 2005. "Voice, Footing, Enregisterment." *Journal of Linguistic Anthropology* 15 (1): 38–59.

Allcock, John. 2000. *Explaining Yugoslavia.* New York: Columbia University Press.

Allison, Anne. 2009. "The Cool Brand, Affective Activism and Japanese Youth." *Theory, Culture and Society* 26 (2–3): 89–111.

Alvarez, Sonia. 1997. "Reweaving the Fabric of Collective Action: Social Movements and Challenges to 'Actually Existing Democracy' in Brazil." In *Between Resistance and Revolution*, ed. Richard Fox and Orin Starn, 83–117. New Brunswick, NJ: Rutgers University Press.

Anderson, Benedict. 1972. *Java in a Time of Revolution, Occupation and Resistance, 1944–1946.* Ithaca, NY: Cornell University Press.

Appadurai, Arjun. 2007. "Hope and Democracy." *Public Culture* 19 (1): 29–34.

Arendt, Hannah. (1963) 2006. *On Revolution.* New York: Penguin.

Arsić, Mirko, and Dragan R. Marković. 1988. *'68: Studentski bunt i društvo.* Belgrade: Istraživački Centar SSO Srbije.

Bačević, Jana. 2010. "Masters or Servants? Power and Discourse in Serbian Higher Education Reform." *Social Anthropology* 18 (1): 43–56.

Bagić, Aida. 2004. "Talking About Donors." In *Ethnographies of Aid: Exploring Development Texts and Encounters*, ed. Jeremy Gould and Henrik Secher Marcussen, 119–226. Roskilde, Denmark: Institute for Development Studies, Roskilde University.

Bakhtin, Mikhail. 1981. *The Dialogic Imagination.* Ed. and trans. Michael Holquist and Caryl Emerson. Austin: University of Texas Press.

Bakić-Hayden, Milica, and Robert Hayden. 1992. "Orientalist Variations on the Theme 'Balkans': Symbolic Geography in Recent Yugoslav Cultural Politics." *Slavic Review* 51 (1): 1–15.

Benjamin, Walter. 1968. *Illuminations*. New York: Houghton Mifflin Harcourt.

Berdahl, Daphne. 2001. "Go Trabi Go: Reflection on a Car and Its Symbolization over Time." *Anthropology and Humanism* 25 (2): 131–41.

Berman, Marshall. 1988. *All That Is Solid Melts into Air*. New York: Penguin Books.

Binnendijk, Anika Locke, and Ivan Marović. 2006. "Power and Persuasion: Nonviolent Strategies to Influence State Security Forces in Serbia (2000) and Ukraine (2004)." *Communist and Post-Communist Studies* 39: 411–29.

Bishara, Amahl. 2008. "Watching U.S. Television from the Palestinian Street: Representational Contests of the Palestinian Authority, the U.S. Media, and the Palestinian Public." *Cultural Anthropology* 23 (3): 488–530.

Bitter, Sabine, Jeff Derksen, and Helmut Weber, eds. 2009. *Autogestion, or Henri Lefebvre in New Belgrade*. Berlin: Sternberg Press.

Blagojević, Ljiljana. 2009. "The Problematic of the 'New Urban': The Right to New Belgrade." In *Autogestion, or Henri Lefebvre in New Belgrade*, ed. Sabine Bitter, Jeff Derksen, and Helmut Weber, 119–34. Berlin: Sternberg Press.

Blom Hansen, Thomas. 1999. *The Saffron Wave: Democracy and Hindu Nationalism in Modern India*. Princeton, NJ: Princeton University Press.

Bockman, Johanna. 2011. *Markets in the Name of Socialism: The Left-Wing Origins of Neoliberalism*. Stanford, CA: Stanford University Press.

Bourdieu, Pierre. 1984. *Distinction*. Cambridge, MA: Harvard University Press.

Boyer, Dominic. 2005. "The Corporeality of Expertise." *Ethnos* 70 (2): 243–66.

———. 2006. "Ostalgie and the Politics of the Future in Eastern Germany." *Public Culture* 18 (2): 361–81.

———. 2010. "What Is Driving University Reform in the Age of Globalization?" *Social Anthropology* 18 (1): 74–82.

Bracewell, Wendy. 2000. "Rape in Kosovo: Masculinity and Serbian Nationalism." *Nations and Nationalism* 6 (4): 563–90.

Bringa, Tone. 2004. "The Peaceful Death of Tito and the Violent End of Yugoslavia." In *Death of the Father: An Anthropology of the End in Political Authority*, ed. John Borneman, 148–200. New York: Berghahn Books.

Brown, Keith. 2006. *Transacting Transition: The Micropolitics of Democracy Assistance in the Former Yugoslavia*. Bloomfield, CT: Kumarian Press.

Bucholtz, Mary. 2002. "Youth and Cultural Practice." *Annual Review of Anthropology* 31: 525–52.

Bunce, Valerie J., and Sharon L. Wolchik. 2006. "Youth and Electoral Revolutions in Slovakia, Serbia and Georgia." *SAIS Review of International Affairs* 26 (2): 55–65.

———. 2011. *Defeating Authoritarian Leaders in Post-Communist Countries*. Cambridge: Cambridge University Press.

Burawoy, Michael. 1976. "Consciousness and Contradiction: A Study of Student Protest in Zambia." *British Journal of Sociology* 27 (1): 78–98.

———. 1985. *The Politics of Production: Factory Regimes Under Capitalism and Socialism.* New York: Verso Press.

Caldeira, Teresa. 2001. *City of Walls: Crime, Segregation, and Citizenship in São Paulo.* Berkeley: University of California Press.

Calhoun, Craig. 1997. *Neither Gods nor Emperors.* Berkeley: University of California Press.

Carothers, Thomas. 2004. *Critical Mission: Essays on Democracy Promotion.* Washington, DC: Carnegie Endowment for International Peace.

Carr, Summerson. 2010. "Enactments of Expertise." *Annual Review of Anthropology* 39: 17–32.

Carter, April. 1982. *Democratic Reform in Yugoslavia: The Changing Role of the Party.* Princeton, NJ: Princeton University Press.

Chakrabarty, Dipesh. 2007. "'In the Name of Politics': Democracy and the Power of the Multitude in India." *Public Culture* 19 (1): 35–58.

Chari, Sharad, and Katherine Verdery. 2009. "Thinking Between the Posts: Postcolonialism, Postsocialism, and Ethnography after the Cold War." *Comparative Studies in Society and History* 51: 6–34.

Cody, Francis. 2009. "Daily Wires and Daily Blossoms: Cultivating Regimes of Circulation in Tamil India's Newspaper Revolution." *Journal of Linguistic Anthropology* 19 (2): 286–309.

Cohen, Lenard J. 1989. *The Socialist Pyramid: Elites and Power in Yugoslavia.* New York: Mosaic Press.

———. 2001. *Serpent in the Bosom: The Rise and Fall of Slobodan Milošević.* Boulder, CO: Westview Press.

Cole, Jennifer, and Deborah Durham. 2007. Introduction to *Generations and Globalization: Youth, Age, and the Family in the New World Economy,* 1–28. Edited by Jennifer Cole and Deborah Durham. Bloomington, IN: Indiana University Press.

Coles, Kimberly. 2007. *Democratic Designs: International Intervention and Electoral Practices in Postwar Bosnia-Herzegovina.* Ann Arbor: University of Michigan Press.

Collin, Matthew. 2004. *This Is Serbia Calling: Rock-n-Roll Radio and Belgrade's Underground Resistance.* London: Serpents Tail Press.

Collins, Jane. 2011. "Theorizing Wisconsin's 2011 Protests: Community-Based Unionism Confronts Accumulation by Dispossession." *American Ethnologist* 39 (1): 6–20.

Čolović, Ivan. 2002. *Politics of Identity in Serbia.* New York: New York University Press.

Comaroff, John L., and Jean Comaroff. 1997. "Postcolonial Politics and Discourses of Democracy in Southern Africa: An Anthropological Reflection on African Political Modernities." *Journal of Anthropological Research* 53 (2): 123–46.

———. 1999a. *Civil Society and the Political Imagination in Africa: Critical Perspectives.* Chicago: University of Chicago Press.

———. 1999b. "Occult Economies and the Violence of Abstraction: Notes from the South African Postcolony." *American Ethnologist* 26 (2): 279–303.

———. 2005. "Children and Youth in a Global Era." In *Makers and Breakers: Children and Youth in Postcolonial Africa,* ed. Alcina Honwana and Filip De Boeck, 19–28. Oxford, UK: James Currey.

Coronil, Fernando. 1997. *The Magical State: Nature, Money and Modernity in Venezuela.* Chicago: University of Chicago Press.

Council of Europe and the International Labor Organization. 2007. *Employment Policy Review: Serbia*. Strasbourg, France: Council of Europe.

Creed, Gerald. 2010. *Postsocialism: Ritual and Cultural Dispossession in Bulgaria*. Bloomington: Indiana University Press.

Dave, Naisargi. 2012. *Queer Activism in India: A Story in the Anthropology of Ethics*. Durham, NC: Duke University Press.

Dick, Hilary Parsons. 2010. "Imagined Lives and Modernist Chronotopes in Mexican Nonmigrant Discourse." *American Ethnologist* 37 (2): 275–90.

Đilas, Milovan. 1957. *The New Class: An Analysis of the Communist System*. New York: Harcourt Brace.

Donham, Donald. 1999. *Marxist Modern: An Ethnographic History of the Ethiopian Revolution*. Berkeley: University of California Press.

Dragović-Soso, Jasna. 2002. *"Saviours of the Nation": Serbia's Intellectual Opposition and the Revival of Nationalism*. Montreal: McGill-Queen's University Press.

Dunn, Elizabeth. 2004. *Privatizing Poland: Baby Food, Big Business and the Remaking of Labor*. Ithaca, NY: Cornell University Press.

Dunn, Elizabeth, and Chris Hann, eds. 1996. *Civil Society: Challenging Western Models*. London: Routledge.

Durham, Deborah. 2008 "Apathy and Agency: The Romance of Agency and Youth in Botswana." In *Figuring the Future: Globalization and the Temporalities of Children and Youth*, ed. Deborah Durham and Jennifer Cole. Santa Fe, NM: School of Advanced Research Press.

Eliasoph, Nina. 1998. *Avoiding Politics: How Americans Produce Apathy in Everyday Life*. Cambridge: Cambridge University Press.

Erdei, Ildiko. 2006. "'The Happy Child' as an Icon of Socialist Transformation: Yugoslavia's Pioneer Organization." In *Ideologies and National Identities: The Case of Twentieth-Century Southeastern Europe*, ed. John Lampe and Mark Mazower, 154–79. Budapest: Central European University Press.

———. 2010. "Migrants of the Future: Serbian Youth Between Imaginary and Real Migration." *Ethnologia Balkanica* 10: 109–28.

Erić, Zoran. 2009."The Third Way: The Experiment of Workers' Self-Management in Socialist Yugoslavia." In *Autogestion, or Henri Lefebvre in New Belgrade*, ed. Sabine Bitter, Jeff Derksen, and Helmut Weber, 135–50. Berlin: Sternberg Press.

Fehervary, Krisztina. 2011. "The Materiality of the New Family House in Hungary: Postsocialist Fad or Middle-Class Ideal?" *City and Society* 23 (1): 18–41.

Ferguson, James 1994. *The Anti-Politics Machine*. Minneapolis: University of Minnesota Press.

———. 1999. *Expectations of Modernity: Myths and Meanings of Urban Life on the Zambian Copperbelt*. Berkeley: University of California Press.

Ferguson, James, and Akhil Gupta. 2002. "Spatializing States: Toward an Ethnography of Neoliberal Governmentality." *American Ethnologist* 29 (4): 981–1002.

Fikes, Kesha. 2009. *Managing African Portugal*. Durham, NC: Duke University Press.

Forment, Carlos A. 2007. "The Democratic Dribbler: Football Clubs, Neoliberal Globalization, and Buenos Aires' Municipal Election of 2003." *Public Culture* 19 (1): 85–116.

Foster, Robert J. 2002. *Materializing the Nation: Commodities, Consumption, and Media in Papua New Guinea*. Bloomington: Indiana University Press.

Foucault, Michel. 1995. *Discipline and Punish*. New York: Vintage Press.

Fournier, Anna. 2012. *Forging Rights in a New Democracy: Ukrainian Students Between Freedom and Justice*. Philadelphia: University of Pennsylvania Press.

Fox, Jon E. 2004. "Missing the Mark: Nationalist Politics and Student Apathy." *East European Politics and Societies* 18 (3): 363–93.

Fridman, Orli. 2006. "Alternative Voices in Public Urban Space: Serbia's Women in Black." *Ethnologia Balkanica* 10: 291–304.

Friedman, Jack. 2007. "Shock and Subjectivity in the Age of Globalization: Marginalization, Exclusion, and the Problem of Resistance." *Anthropological Theory* 7: 421–48.

Friedman, Victor. 1996. "Observing the Observers: Language, Ethnicity, and Power in the 1994 Macedonian Census and Beyond." In *Toward Comprehensive Peace in Southeast Europe*, ed. Barnett Rubin, 81–105. New York: Twentieth Century Fund Press.

Gagnon, V. P. 2004. *The Myth of Ethnic War: Serbia and Croatia in the 1990s*. Ithaca, NY: Cornell University Press.

Gal, Susan. 1993. "Diversity and Contestation in Linguistic Ideologies." *Language in Society* 22 (3): 337–60.

———. 2003. "Movements of Feminism: The Circulation of Discourses about Women." In *Recognition Struggles and Social Movements*, ed. Barbara Hobson, 93–118. Cambridge: Cambridge University Press.

———. 2006. "Contradictions of Standard Language in Europe: Implications for the Study of Practices and Publics." *Social Anthropology* 14 (2): 163–81.

Gal, Susan, and Gail Kligman. 2000. *The Politics of Gender after Socialism*. Princeton, NJ: Princeton University Press.

Gaonkar, Dilip, ed. 2007. "Cultures of Democracy." *Public Culture* 19 (1): 1–22.

Gilbert, Andrew, Jessica Greenberg, Elissa Helms, and Stef Jansen. 2008. "Reconsidering Postsocialism from the Margins of Europe: Hope, Time and Normalcy in Post-Yugoslav Societies." *Anthropology News*, November, 10–11.

Gitlin, Todd. 1993. *The Sixties: Years of Hope, Days of Rage*. New York: Bantam Press.

Goati, Vladimir. 1997. "The Disintegration of Yugoslavia: The Role of Political Elites." *Nationalities Papers* 25 (3): 455–67.

Goffman, Erving. 1979. "Footing." *Semiotica* 25 (1–2): 1–29.

———. 1983. "The Interaction Order." *American Sociological Review* 48 (1): 1–17.

Goldstein, Daniel. 2004. *The Spectacular City: Violence and Performance in Urban Bolivia*. Durham, NC: Duke University Press.

Goodwin, Jeff. 2001. *No Other Way Out: States and Revolutionary Movements, 1945–1991*. Cambridge: Cambridge University Press.

Gordy, Eric. 1999. *The Culture of Power in Serbia.* University Park: Pennsylvania State University Press.

Gorsuch, Anne. 2000. *Youth in Revolutionary Russia.* Bloomington: Indiana University Press.

Graan, Andrew. 2010. "On the Politics of Imidž: European Integration and the Trials of Recognition in Post-Conflict Macedonia." *Slavic Review* 69 (4): 835–58.

———. 2012. "Nema Rabota: Korzo and Youth Unemployment in Skopje, Macedonia." *Balkanistica* 25 (2): 173–84.

———. 2013. "Counterfeiting the Nation? Skopje 2014 and the Politics of Nation Branding in Macedonia." *Cultural Anthropology* 28 (1): 161–79.

Graeber, David. 2004. *Fragments of an Anarchist Anthropology.* Chicago: Prickly Paradigm Press.

———. 2007. *Possibilities: Essays on Hierarchy, Rebellion and Desire.* Edinburgh, UK: AK.

Gramsci, Antonio. 1971. *Selections from the Prison Notebooks.* New York: International Publishers.

Grandits, Hannes. 2007. "The Power of 'Armchair Politicians': Ethnic Loyalty and Political Factionalism Among Herzegovinian Croats." In *The New Bosnian Mosaic*, ed. Xavier Bougarel, Elissa Helms, and Ger Duijzings, 102–22. Burlington, VT: Ashgate.

Green, Sarah. 2005. *Notes from the Balkans.* Princeton, NJ: Princeton University Press.

Greenberg, Jessica. 2006a. "'Goodbye Serbian Kennedy': Zoran Đinđić and the New Democratic Masculinity." *East European Politics and Societies* 20 (1): 126–51.

———. 2006b. "Nationalism, Masculinity and Multicultural Citizenship in Serbia." *Nationalities Papers* 34 (3): 321–41.

———. 2006c. "Noć Reklamožsdera: Democracy, Consumption, and the Contradictions of Representation in Post-Socialist Serbia." *Political and Legal Anthropology Review* 29 (2): 181–207.

———. 2010. "'There's Nothing Anyone Can Do about It': Participation, Apathy and 'Successful' Democratic Transition in Postsocialist Serbia." *Slavic Review* 69 (1): 41–64.

———. 2011. "On the Road to Normal: Negotiating Agency and State Sovereignty in Postsocialist Serbia." *American Anthropologist* 113 (1): 88–100.

———. 2012. "Gaming the System: Semiotic Indeterminacy and Political Circulation in the New Age of Revolution." *Language and Communication* 32 (4): 372–85.

Greenberg, Jessica, and Andrea Muehlebach. 2007. "The Old World and Its New Economy: Notes on the Third Age in Western Europe Today." In *Generations and Globalization: Youth, Age, and Family in the New World Economy*, ed. Jennifer Cole and Debra Durham, 165–90. Bloomington: Indiana University Press.

Greenwood, Davydd J. 2009. "Bologna in America: The Spellings Commission and Neo-Liberal Higher Education Policy." *Learning and Teaching* 2 (1): 1–38.

Guilhot, Nicolas. 2005. *The Democracy Makers: Human Rights and the Politics of Global Order.* New York: Columbia University Press.

Gupta, Akhil. 2008. "Literacy, Bureaucratic Domination, and Democracy." In *Democracy: Anthropological Approaches*, ed. Julia Paley, 167–92. Santa Fe, NM: School of American Research Press.

Gutmann, Matthew. 2002. *The Romance of Democracy*. Berkeley: University of California Press.

Hancox, Dan. 2011. *Kettled Youth*. N.p.: Vintage Digital.

Haney, Lynn. 2002. *Inventing the Needy: Gender and the Politics of Welfare in Hungary*. Berkeley: University of California Press.

Hann, Cris, and Elizabeth Dunn. 1996. *Civil Society: Challenging Western Models*. London: Routledge.

Hanson, Stephen. 1997. *Time and Revolution: Marxism and the Design of Soviet Institutions*. Chapel Hill: University of North Carolina Press.

Hardt, Michael, and Antonio Negri. 2005. *Multitude: War and Democracy in the Age of Empire*. New York: Penguin Press.

———. 2011. "The Fight for 'Real Democracy' at the Heart of Occupy Wall Street: The Encampment in Lower Manhattan Speaks to a Failure of Representation." *Foreign Affairs*, October 11. http://www.foreignaffairs.com/articles/136399/michael-hardt-and-antonio-negri/the-fight-for-real-democracy-at-the-heart-of-occupy-wall-street.

Harper, Krista. 2006. *Wild Capitalism: Environmental Activism and Postsocialist Political Ecology in Hungary*. East European Monographs. New York: Columbia University Press.

Harvey, David. 1990. *The Condition of Postmodernity*. Oxford, UK: Blackwell.

Havel, Václav. 1985. "The Power of the Powerless." In *The Power of the Powerless: Citizens against the State in Central-Eastern Europe*, ed. John Keane, 23–96. London: Hutchinson.

Helms, Elissa. 2007. "'Politics Is a Whore': Women, Morality and Victimhood in Post-War Bosnia-Herzegovina." In *The New Bosnian Mosaic*, ed. Xavier Bougarel, Elissa Helms, and Ger Duijzings, 235–54. Burlington, VT: Ashgate.

Helms, Elissa, and Stef Jansen. 2009. "The White Plague: National-Demographic Rhetoric and Its Gendered Resonance after the Post-Yugoslav Wars." In *Gender in Armed Conflicts and in Post-War*, ed. Christine Eifler and Ruth Seifert, 219–43. Frankfurt: Peter Lang.

Hemment, Julie. 2007. *Empowering Women in Russia: Activism, Aid, and NGOs*. Bloomington: Indiana University Press.

———. 2012. "Redefining Need, Reconfiguring Expectations: The Rise of State-Run Youth Voluntarism Programs in Russia." *Anthropological Quarterly* 85 (2): 519–54.

Herzfeld, Michael. 1992. *The Social Production of Indifference*. Chicago: University of Chicago Press.

Hindess, Barry. 1996. "Liberalism, Socialism, Democracy: Variations on a Governmental Theme." In *Foucault and Political Reason: Liberalism, Neo-Liberalism and Rationalities of Government*, ed. Andrew Barry, Thomas Osborne, and Nikolas Rose, 65–80. Chicago: University of Chicago Press.

Hirt, Sonia. 2008a. "The Gates of Belgrade: Safety, Privacy and New Housing Patterns in the Post-Communist City." Working paper, National Council for Eurasian and East European Research, University of Washington, Seattle.

———. 2008b. "Landscapes of Postmodernity: Changes in the Built Fabric of Belgrade and Sofia since the End of Socialism." *Urban Geography* 29 (8): 785–810.

———. 2009. "City Profile: Belgrade, Serbia." *Cities* 26: 293–303.

Holloway, John. 2002. *Change the World Without Taking Power*. New York: Pluto Press.

Holmes, Douglas R. 2000. *Integral Europe: Fast-Capitalism, Multiculturalism, Neofascism.* Princeton, NJ: Princeton University Press.

Holston, James. 1989. *The Modernist City: An Anthropological Critique of Brasília.* Chicago: University of Chicago Press.

Honwana, Alcina, and Filip De Boeck. 2005. *Makers and Breakers: Children and Youth in Postcolonial Africa.* Oxford, UK: James Currey.

Hromadžić, Azra. 2011. "Bathroom Mixing: Youth Negotiate Democratization in Postconflict Bosnia and Herzegovina." *PoLAR: Political and Legal Anthropology Review* 34 (2): 268–89.

Hull, Matthew. 2003. "The File: Agency, Authority, and Autography in an Islamabad Bureaucracy." *Journal of Linguistic Anthropology* 23: 287–314.

———. 2010. "The Speech of Change: Technologies of Democracy from WWII America to Post-Colonial Delhi." *Journal of Linguistic Anthropology* 20 (2): 257–82.

Irvine, Judith. 1996. "Shadow Conversations: The Indeterminacy of Participant Roles." In *Natural Histories of Discourse*, ed. Michael Silverstein and Greg Urban, 131–59. Chicago: University of Chicago Press.

Irvine, Judith, and Susan Gal. 2000. "Language Ideology and Linguistic Differentiation." In *Regimes of Language*, ed. Paul V. Kroskrity, 35–84. Santa Fe, NM: School of American Research Press.

Jansen, Stef. 2001. "The Streets of Beograd. Urban Space and Protest Identities in Serbia." *Political Geography* 20: 35–55.

———. 2005. "Who's Afraid of White Socks? Towards a Critical Understanding of Post-Yugoslav Urban Self-Perceptions." *Ethnologia Balkanica* 9: 151–68.

Jeffrey, Craig. 2010. "Timepass: Youth, Class, and Time Among Unemployed Young Men in India." *American Ethnologist* 37 (3): 468–81.

Johnson-Hanks, Jennifer. 2002. "On the Limits of Life Stages in Ethnography: Toward a Theory of Vital Conjunctures." *American Anthropologist* 104 (3): 865–80.

Junge, Benjamin. 2012. "NGOs as Shadow Pseudopublics: Grassroots Community Leaders' Perceptions of Change and Continuity in Porto Alegre, Brazil." *American Ethnologist* 39 (2): 407–24.

Juris, Jeffrey. 2008. *Networking Futures: The Movements Against Corporate Globalization.* Durham, NC: Duke University Press.

———. 2012. "Reflections on Occupy Everywhere: Social Media, Public Space, and Emerging Logics of Aggregation." *American Ethnologist* 39 (2): 259–79.

Kalb, Don. 2009. "Conversations with a Polish Populist." *American Ethnologist* 36 (2): 207–23.

Kenney, Pedraic. 2002. *A Carnival of Revolution: Central Europe 1989.* Princeton, NJ: Princeton University Press.

Kideckel, David. 2008. *Getting by in Postsocialist Romania: Labor, the Body, and Working-Class Culture.* Bloomington: Indiana University Press.

Klein, Naomi. 2008. *Shock Doctrine.* New York: Metropolitan Books.

Kolind, Torsten. 2007. "In Search of 'Decent People': Resistance to the Ethnicization of Everyday Life Among the Muslims of Stolac." In *The New Bosnian Mosaic*, ed. Xavier Bougarel, Elissa Helms, and Ger Duijzings, 123–40. Burlington, VT: Ashgate.

Konrád, György. 1984. *Antipolitics*. New York: Harcourt, Brace, Jovanovich.

Konrád, György, and Iván Szelényi. 1979. *Intellectuals on the Road to Class Power*. New York: Harcourt Brace Jovanovich.

Koselleck, Reinhart. 2004. *Futures Past*. New York: Columbia University Press.

Kulick, Don. "Anger, Gender, Language Shift and the Politics of Revelation in a Papua New Guinean Village." In *Language Ideologies: Practice and Theory*, ed. Bambi Schieffelin, Kathryn A. Woolard, and Paul Kroskrity, 87–101. Oxford: Oxford University Press.

Kürti, László. 2002. *Youth and the State in Hungary*. London: Pluto Press.

Kuzio, Taras. 2006. "Civil Society, Youth, and Societal Mobilization in Democratic Revolutions." *Communist and Post-Communist Studies* 39: 365–86.

Kwon, Soo Ah. 2013. *Uncivil Youth: Race, Activism, and Affirmative Governmentality*. Durham, NC: Duke University Press.

Lažetić, Predrag, and Mihajlo Babin. 2009. "Financing a Disintegrated University in Serbia—An Institutional Case Study." In *Financing Higher Education in South-Eastern Europe: Albania, Croatia, Montenegro, Serbia, Slovenia*, ed. Martina Vukasović, 111–43. Belgrade: Center for Education Policy.

Lazić, Mladen. 1999. "Emergence of a Democratic Order in Serbia." In *Protest in Belgrade*, ed. Mladen Lazić, 1–30. Budapest: Central European University Press.

———. 2000. "The Adaptive Reconstruction of Elites." In *Elites after State Socialism*, ed. John Higley and Gyorgy Lengyel, 123–40. New York: Rowman and Littlefield.

Lee, Doreen. 2011. "Images of Youth: on the Iconography of History and Protest in Indonesia." *History and Anthropology* 22 (3): 307–36.

Lemon, Alaina. 1998. "'Your Eyes Are Green Like Dollars': Counterfeit Cash, National Substance, and Currency Apartheid in 1990s Russia." *Cultural Anthropology* 13 (1): 22–55.

———. 2009. "Sympathy for the Weary State: Cold War Chronotopes and Moscow Others." *Comparative Studies in Society and History* 51 (4): 832–64.

Leve, Lauren. 2001. "Between Jesse Helms and Ram Bahadur: Participation and Empowerment in Women's Literacy Programming in Nepal." *PoLAR: Political and Legal Anthropology Review* 24 (1): 108–28.

Longinović, Tomislav. 2011. *Vampire Nation: Violence as Cultural Imaginary*. Durham, NC: Duke University Press.

Low, Setha M., and Denise Lawrence-Zúñiga. 2003. Introduction to *The Anthropology of Space and Place: Locating Culture*, 1–48. Edited by Setha M. Low and Denise Lawrence-Zúñiga. Malden, MA: Blackwell.

Lukose, Ritty. 2009. *Liberalization's Children: Gender, Youth, and Consumer Citizenship in Globalizing India*. Durham, NC: Duke University Press.

Mains, Daniel. 2011. *Hope Is Cut: Youth, Unemployment, and the Future in Urban Ethiopia*. Philadelphia: Temple University Press.

Manning, Paul. 2007. "Rose Colored Glasses? Color Revolutions and Cartoon Chaos in Post-Socialist Georgia." *Cultural Anthropology* 22 (2): 171–213.

———. 2010. "The Semiotics of Brand." *Annual Review of Anthropology* 39: 33–49.

Markoff, John. 1999. "Where and When Was Democracy Invented?" *Comparative Studies in Society and History* 41: 660–90.

Marx, Karl. (1852) 1994. *The Eighteenth Brumaire of Louis Bonaparte*. New York: International Publishers.

———. (1932) 1998. *German Ideology*. New York: Prometheus Books.

Masco, Joseph. 2006. *The Nuclear Borderlands: The Manhattan Project in Post–Cold War New Mexico*. Princeton, NJ: Princeton University Press.

McAdam, Doug. 1988. *Freedom Summer*. New York: Oxford University Press.

McAdam, Doug, Sidney Tarrow, and Charles Tilly. 2001. *Dynamics of Contention*. Cambridge: Cambridge University Press.

Mead, George Herbert. 2002. *The Philosophy of the Present*. New York: Prometheus Books.

Mendel-Reyes, Meta. 1995. *Reclaiming Democracy: The Sixties in Politics and Memory*. New York: Routledge.

Miličević, Aleksandra. 2004. "Joining Serbia's Wars: Volunteers and Draft-Dodgers, 1991–1995." PhD diss., University of California, Los Angeles.

Mitchell, Don. 2002. *The Right to the City: Social Justice and the Fight for Public*. New York: Guilford Press.

Mitchell, Timothy. 2002. *Rule of Experts: Egypt, Techno-Politics, Modernity*. Berkeley: University of California Press.

Miyazaki, Hirokazu. 2004. *The Method of Hope*. Stanford, CA: Stanford University Press.

Mojić, Dušan. 2012. "Obrazovani i nezaposleni: Oblikovanje radnih biografija mladih" [Education and unemployment: Constructing the working biographies of youth]. In *Mladi—naša sadašnjost. Istraživanje socijalnih biografija mladih u Srbiji* [Youth: Our present—Research on the social biographies of youth], 111–26. Belgrade: Čigoja Štampa.

Mole, Noelle J. 2011. *Labor Disorders in Neoliberal Italy*. Bloomington: Indiana University Press.

Mudde, Cas. 2000. "In the Name of the Peasantry, the Proletariat and the People: Populisms in Eastern Europe." *East European Politics and Societies* 15: 33–53.

Muehlebach, Andrea. 2012. *The Moral Neoliberal: Welfare and Citizenship in Italy*. Chicago: University of Chicago Press.

Nadkarni, Maya. 2007. "The Master's Voice: Authenticity, Nostalgia, and the Refusal of Irony in Postsocialist Hungary." *Social Identities* 13 (5): 611–26.

———. 2010. "'But It's Ours': Nostalgia and the Politics of Cultural Identity in Postsocialist Hungary." In *Postcommunist Nostalgia*, ed. Maria Todorova and Zsuzsa Gille, 190–214. New York: Berghahn Books.

Naumović, Slobodan. 2006. "'Otpor!' kao postmoderni Faust: Društveni pokret novog tipa, tradicija prosvećenog reformizma i 'izborna revolucija' u Srbiji" ["Otpor!"—a postmodern Faust: New social movement, the tradition of enlightened reformism, and the electoral revolution in Serbia]. *Filozofija i društvo* 3 (31): 147–94.

Nugent, David. 2002. "Alternative Democracies: The Evolution of the Public Sphere in 20th Century Peru." *Political and Legal Anthropology Review* 25 (1): 151–63.

———. 2008. "Democracy Otherwise: Struggles over Popular Rule in the Northern Peruvian Andes." In *Democracy: Anthropological Approaches*, ed. Julia Paley, 21–62. Santa Fe, NM: School of American Research Press.

———. 2012. "Democracy, Temporalities of Capitalism, and Dilemmas of Inclusion in Occupy Movements." *American Ethnologist* 39 (2): 280–83.

Ost, David. 1990. *Solidarity and the Politics of Anti-Politics: Opposition and Reform in Poland since 1968*. Philadelphia: Temple University Press.

Oushakine, Sergei. 2009. *The Patriotism of Despair. Nation, War, and Loss in Russia*. Ithaca, NY: Cornell University Press.

Oxlund, Bjarke. 2010. "Responding to University Reform in South Africa: Student Activism at the University of Limpopo." *Social Anthropology/Anthropologie Sociale* 18 (1): 30–42.

Özyürek, Esra. 2006. *Nostalgia for the Modern: State Secularism and Everyday Politics in Turkey*. Durham, NC: Duke University Press.

Paley, Julia. 2001. *Marketing Democracy: Power and Social Movements in Post-Dictatorship Chile*. Berkeley: University of California Press.

———. 2002. "Toward an Anthropology of Democracy." *Annual Review of Anthropology* 31: 469–96.

———. 2008. *Democracy: Anthropological Approaches*. Santa Fe, NM: School of American Research Press.

Pampols, Carles Feixa, and Laura Porzio. 2005. "*Jipis, pijos, fiesteros*: Studies on Youth Cultures in Spain, 1960–2004." *Young* 13 (1): 89–114.

Pateman, Carole. 1970. *Participation and Democratic Theory*. Cambridge: Cambridge University Press.

Passerini, Luisa. 1997. "Youth as Metaphor for Social Change: Fascist Italy and America in the 1950s." In *A History of Young People*, ed. Giovanni Levi and Jean-Claude Schmitt, 281. Cambridge, MA: Harvard University Press.

Paz, Alejandro. 2009. "The Circulation of *Chisme* and Rumor." *Journal of Linguistic Anthropology* 19 (1): 117–43.

Peck, Jamie, and Adam Tickell. 2002. "Neoliberalizing Space." *Antipode* 34 (3): 380–404.

Peebles, Gustav. 2011. *The Euro and Its Rivals: Currency and the Construction of a Transnational City*. Bloomington: Indiana University Press.

Pervan, Ralph. 1978. *Tito and the Students: The University and the University Student in Self-Managing Yugoslavia*. Perth: University of Western Australia Press.

Pesman, Dale. 2000. *Russia and Soul*. Ithaca, NY: Cornell University Press.

Pitkin, Hannah. 1967. *The Concept of Representation*. Berkeley: University of California Press.

———. 2000. *The Attack of the Blob: Hannah Arendt's Concept of the Social*. Chicago: University of Chicago Press.

Popov, Nebojša. 1978. *Društveni sukobi—izazov sociologiji* [Social conflicts—the challenge to sociology]. Belgrade: Službeni Glasnik.

———. 2000. "The University in an Ideological Shell." In *The Road to War in Serbia*, ed. Nebojša Popov, 303–26. Budapest: Central European University Press.

Popović, Srđa. 2010. "Peti oktobar" [The Fifth of October]. *Peščanik*. http://www.pescanik.net/content/view/5716/89/.

Povinelli, Elizabeth. 2002. *The Cunning of Recognition: Indigenous Alterities and the Making of Australian Multiculturalism*. Durham, NC: Duke University Press.

———. 2009. "Beyond Good and Evil: Whither Liberal Sacrificial Love?" *Public Culture* 21 (1): 77–100.

Power, Nina. 2012. "Dangerous Subjects: UK Students and the Criminalization of Protest." *South Atlantic Quarterly* 111 (2): 412–20.

Razsa, Maple, and Andrej Kurnik. 2012. "The Occupy Movement in Žižek's Hometown: Direct Democracy and a Politics of Becoming." *American Ethnologist* 39 (2): 238–58.

Razsa, Maple, and Nicole Lindstrom. 2004. "Balkan Is Beautiful: Balkanism in the Political Discourse of Tuđman's Croatia." *East European Politics and Societies* 18 (2): 1–23.

Riles, Annelise. 2006. *Documents: Artifacts of Modern Knowledge*. Ann Arbor: University of Michigan Press.

———. 2011. *Collateral Knowledge: Legal Reasoning in the Financial Markets*. Chicago: University of Chicago Press.

Rofel, Lisa. 1999. *Other Modernities: Gendered Yearnings in China After Socialism*. Berkeley: University of California Press.

Rogers, Douglas. 2010. "Postsocialisms Unbound: Connections, Critiques, Comparisons." *Slavic Review* 69 (1): 1–15.

Rosenberg, Tina. 2011. "Revolution U—Otpor, CANVAS, Burma, and the Egypt Revolution." *Foreign Policy*, December 29. http://www.foreignpolicy.com/articles/2011/02/16/revolution_u.

Rusinow, Dennison. 1977. *The Yugoslav Experiment: 1948–1974*. Berkeley: University of California Press.

Sampson, Steven. 1996. "The Social Life of Projects: Importing Civil Society to Albania." In *Civil Society: Challenging Western Models*, ed. Cris Hann and Elizabeth Dunn, 121–42. New York: Routledge.

Sánchez Cedillo, Raul. 2012. "15M: Something Constituent This Way Comes." *South Atlantic Quarterly* 111 (3): 573–82.

Savić, Obrad, ed. 1997–98. *U odbranu univerziteta* [In defense of the university]. Nos. 3–4 1997/1-2/1998. Belgrade: Beogradski Krug.

Scott, David. 2004. *Conscripts of Modernity: The Tragedy of Colonial Enlightenment*. Durham, NC: Duke University Press.

Sewell, William. 1996. "Historical Events as Transformations of Structures: Inventing Revolution at the Bastille." *Theory and Society* 25 (6): 841–81.

Shankar, Shalini. 2008. *Desi Land: Teen Culture, Class, and Success in Silicon Valley*. Durham, NC: Duke University Press.

Sharp, Leslie. 2002. *The Sacrificed Generation: Youth, History, and the Colonized Mind in Madagascar*. Berkeley: University of California Press.

Shever, Elana. 2012. *Resources for Reform: Oil and Neoliberalism in Argentina*. Stanford, CA: Stanford University Press.

Shore, Cris. 2010. "Beyond the Multiversity: Neoliberalism and the Rise of the Schizophrenic University." *Social Anthropology* 18 (1): 15–29.

Shore, Cris, and Susan Wright. 2000. "Coercive Accountability: The Rise of Audit in Higher Education." In *Audit Cultures: Anthropological Studies in Ethics, Accountability, and the Academy*, ed. Marilyn Strathern, 57–89. London: Routledge.

Siegel, James. 1998. *A New Criminal Type in Jakarta*. Durham, NC: Duke University Press.

Silverstein, Michael. 1976. "Shifters, Linguistic Categories, and Cultural Description." In *Meaning in Anthropology*, ed. Keith H. Basso and Henry A. Selby, 11–56. Albuquerque: University of New Mexico Press.

Silverstein, Michael, and Greg Urban. 1996. "The Natural History of Discourse." In *Natural Histories of Discourse*, ed. Michael Silverstein and Greg Urban, 1–17. Chicago: University of Chicago Press.

Simić, Andrei. 1973. *The Peasant Urbanites: A Study of Rural-Urban Mobility in Serbia*. New York: Seminar Press.

Skocpol, Theda. 1979. *States and Social Revolutions: A Comparative Analysis of France, Russia, and China*. Cambridge: Cambridge University Press.

Snajder, Edward. 2008. *Nature Protests: The End of Ecology in Slovakia*. Seattle: University of Washington Press.

Song, Jesook. 2009. *South Korea in the Debt Crisis: The Creation of a Neoliberal Welfare Society*. Durham, NC: Duke University Press.

Spasić, Ivana. 2006. "ASFALT: The Construction of Urbanity in Everyday Discourse in Serbia." *Ethnologia Balkanica* 10: 211–28.

Spasić, Ivana, and Milan Subotić. 2001. *Revolucija i poredak: O dinamici promena u Srbiji*. Belgrade: Institut za Filozofiju.

Standing, Guy. 2011. *The Precariat: The New Dangerous Class*. London: Bloomsbury Academic.

Stojić, Atanasov Gordana. 2004. "Changes in the Labour Market—European Union and Serbia." *Philosophy, Sociology and Psychology* 3 (1): 17–31.

Strathern, Marilyn. 2000. "New Accountabilities." In *Audit Cultures: Anthropological Studies in Ethics, Accountability, and the Academy*, ed. Marilyn Strathern, 1–18. London: Routledge.

Stubbs, Paul. 2012. "Networks, Organizations, Movements: Narratives and Shapes of Three Waves of Activism in Croatia." *Polemos* 15 (2): 11–32.

Taylor, Karin. 2006. *Let's Twist Again: Youth and Leisure in Socialist Bulgaria*. Berlin: Verlag.

Tismaneanu, Vladimir. 2000. "Hypotheses on Populism: The Politics of Charismatic Protest." *East European Politics and Societies* 15: 10–17.

Todorova, Maria, and Zsuzsa Gille, eds. 2012. *Post-Communist Nostalgia*. New York: Berghahn Books.

Trouillot, Michel Rolph. 1995. *Silencing the Past*. Boston: Beacon Press.

———. 2003. *Global Transformations: Anthropology and the Modern World*. New York: St. Martin's Press.

Van de Port, Mattijs. 1998. *Gypsies, Wars and Other Instances of the Wild*. Amsterdam: Amsterdam University Press.

Varzi, Roxanne. 2006. *Warring Souls: Youth Media, and Martyrdom in Post-Revolution Iran*. Durham, NC: Duke University Press.

Verdery, Katherine. 1991. *National Ideology Under Socialism*. Berkeley: University of California Press.

———. 1996. *What Was Socialism and What Comes Next?* Princeton, NJ: Princeton University Press.

———. 2003. *The Vanishing Hectare.* Ithaca, NY: Cornell University Press.

Vladisavljević, Nebojša. 2008. *Milošević, the Fall of Communism, and Nationalist Mobilization.* New York: Palgrave Macmillan.

Von Kohl, Christine, and Wolfgang Libal. 1997. "Kosovo, the Gordian Knot of the Balkans." In *Kosovo: In the Heart of the Powder Keg*, ed. Robert Elsie, 3–104. Boulder, CO: East European Monographs.

Vujošević, Miodrag, and Zorica Nedović-Budić. 2006. "Planning and Societal Context: The Case of Belgrade, Serbia." In *The Urban Mosaic of Post-Socialist Europe: Space, Institutions, and Policy*, ed. Sasha Tsenkova and Zorica Nedović-Budić, 276–94. Heidelberg, Germany: Physica-Verlag.

Vujović, Sreten, and Mina Petrović. 2007. "Belgrade's Post-Socialist Urban Evolution: Reflections by the Actors in the Development Process." In *The Post-Socialist City: Urban Form and Space Transformations in Central and Eastern Europe after Socialism*, ed. K. Stanilov, 361–83. Dordrecht, The Netherlands: Springer Press.

Washburn, Jennifer. 2006. *University, Inc.: The Corporate Corruption of Higher Education.* New York: Basic Books.

Wedeen, Lisa. 2003. "Seeing Like a Citizen, Acting Like a State: Exemplary Events in Unified Yemen." *Comparative Studies in Society and History* 45 (4): 680–713.

———. 2008. *Peripheral Visions: Publics, Power, and Performance in Yemen.* Chicago: University of Chicago Press.

Wedel, Janine. 2001. *Collision and Collusion: The Strange Case of Western Aid to Eastern Europe.* New York: Palgrave Macmillan.

Willis, Paul. 1977. *Learning to Labor: How Working Class Kids Get Working Class Jobs.* New York: Columbia University Press.

Winegar, Jessica. 2006. *Creative Reckonings: The Politics of Art and Culture in Contemporary Egypt.* Stanford, CA: Stanford University Press.

Wohl, Robert. 1979. *The Generation of 1914.* Cambridge, MA: Harvard University Press.

Woodward, Susan. 1995. *Socialist Unemployment: The Political Economy of Yugoslavia, 1945–1990.* Princeton, NJ: Princeton University Press.

Woolard, Kathryn. 1998. "Language Ideology as Field of Inquiry." In *Language Ideologies: Practice and Theory*, ed. Bambi Schieffelin, Kathryn Woolard, and Paul Kroskrity, 3–50. New York: Oxford University Press.

Wright, Susan, and Annika Rabo. 2010. "Introduction: Anthropologies of University Reform." *Social Anthropology* 18 (1): 1–14.

Yeoman, Rory. 2006. "Urban Visions and Rural Utopias: Literature and the Building of a Nationalist Consensus in Croatia, 1924–1945." *Ethnologia Balkanica* 10: 109–40.

Yurchak, Alexei. 2003. "Soviet Hegemony of Form: Everything Was Forever Until It Was No More." *Comparative Studies in Society and History* 45 (3): 480–510.

———. 2006. *Everything Was Forever Until It Was No More: The Last Soviet Generation.* Princeton, NJ: Princeton University Press.

Zhang, Li. 2002. "Spatiality and Urban Citizenship in Late Socialist China." *Public Culture* 14 (2): 311–34.

Živković, Marko. 1998. "Jelly, Slush, and Red Mists: Poetics of Amorphous Substances in Serbian Jeremiads of the 1990s." *Anthropology and Humanism* 25 (2): 168–82.

——. 2011. *Serbian Dreambook: National Imaginary in the Time of Milošević*. Bloomington: Indiana University Press.

Consulted Newspaper Sources

Danas. 2003. "Nezadovoljni kašnjenjem kredita, stipendija i sredstava Studentskom centru studenti blokirali raskrsnicu" [Dissatisfied with late credit, stipends and resources for the Student Center, students blocked the intersection]. February 11.

Dnevnik. 2003. "Na uglu Stražilovske i bulevara Cara Lazara: Studenti i profesori danas blokiraju raskrsnicu" [On the corner of Stražilovska and Car Lazar Boulevard, students and professors blocked the intersection today]. February 10.

Dnevnik. 2003. "Studenti blokirali raskrsnicu Stražilovske i bulevara Cara Lazara: Performans za stipendije i plate" [Students block the intersection of Stražilovska and Car Lazar Boulevard: Performance for stipend and pay]. February 1.

Dnevnik (S.N.). 2003. "Pravo studenata je da protestuju" [The right of students is to protest]. February 11.

Glas Javnosti (N.C.). 2003. "Zbog neisplaćenih stipendija i kredita: Studenti blokirali raskrsnicu" [Students block the intersection because of unpaid stipends and credits]. February 11.

Index

Page numbers followed by "f" or "t" indicate material in figures or tables.